The Trial Narratives

The Trial Narratives

*Conflict, Power, and Identity
in the New Testament*

MATTHEW L. SKINNER

WJK WESTMINSTER
JOHN KNOX PRESS
LOUISVILLE · KENTUCKY

© 2010 Matthew L. Skinner

First edition
Published by Westminster John Knox Press
Louisville, Kentucky

10 11 12 13 14 15 16 17 18 19—10 9 8 7 6 5 4 3 2 1

Scripture quotations from the New Revised Standard Version of the Bible are copyright © 1989 by the Division of Christian Education of the National Council of the Churches of Christ in the U.S.A. and are used by permission.

Except as otherwise indicated, all translations of ancient texts are the author's.

Book design by Sharon Adams
Cover design by Mark Abrams
Cover art: He Qi, Pilate Washing His Hands

Library of Congress Cataloging-in-Publication Data

Skinner, Matthew L., 1968–
   The trial narratives : conflict, power, and identity in the New Testament / Matthew L. Skinner.
      p. cm.
   Includes bibliographical references and indexes.
   ISBN 978-0-664-23032-6 (alk. paper)
   1. Bible. N.T. Gospels and Acts—Criticism, interpretation, etc.   2. Bible. N.T. Gospels and Acts—Criticism, Narrative.   3. Trials in the Bible.   4. Jesus Christ—Trials, litigation, etc. I. Title.
   BS2548.S55 2010
   226'.066—dc22

                                                                                                2009028363

Contents

Preface

The Gospels and Acts include several scenes that describe formal and improvised judicial processes. Jesus, Paul, Stephen, and others find themselves brought before powerful individuals and groups who pass judgment on their claims and activities, often with deadly consequences. These scenes have captured my interest for some time, mainly because of their location at important junctures in the stories these books tell. Jesus' trial links his public ministry and his passion, beckoning us to consider both as related, each utterly significant for understanding the other. Stephen's trial results in widespread persecution of the Christian community in Jerusalem, terminating the almost utopian existence described in the early chapters of Acts. Paul's trial in Acts 21–28 brings a book that begins full of thrilling deeds to a prolonged and nearly understated end. Additional trials direct attention to the shape of the story Acts tells and the struggles that arise as the word of God travels into both familiar and new cultural contexts. A considerable part of my own attempts to understand the Gospel and Acts involves wrestling with their trial scenes.

I think of these scenes when in classrooms, the media, and churches I hear people state that there was nothing political about Jesus and his message, that some New Testament writings indifferently accede to Roman authority, or that certain books express a thoroughgoing resistance to empire. It seems to me that the narrative character of these scenes, as well as their functions within the broader narratives of the Gospels and Acts, reveal the inaccuracy of such sweeping claims. Instead, the New Testament narratives offer more nuanced reflections on how Jesus and his gospel "fit" within the sociopolitical landscape of the ancient world.

Many interpreters certainly have recognized the importance of these trial narratives and put various methods to work on them. They ask, historically, whether a given trial actually took place and what really happened. They focus on apologetic questions, wondering how the accounts of trials might have functioned for missionary-minded Christians trying to navigate ancient society. In a theological vein, each trial helps a biblical narrative convey a vision of God and God's ways in and on behalf of the world: in the Gospels, Jesus' trial says who he is; in Acts, Paul's legal circumstances say something about God and Paul's fidelity to God. This book travels among, between, and beside these avenues of inquiry as it poses its own related but distinct questions to the trial scenes.

Many people deserve my gratitude for the generosity, insights, and support that made this book possible. My idea for the project crystallized during research made possible by a professional-development grant from the Wabash Center for Teaching and Learning in Theology and Religion. Luther Seminary granted me a one-semester writing leave and later a one-year sabbatical, during which times I wrote the book. William F. Storrar and the Center of Theological Inquiry in Princeton generously and graciously welcomed me as a member in residence during my sabbatical in 2008–2009. Numerous colleagues in these and other venues offered helpful feedback all along the way, including a stimulating discussion of selections from the book during a colloquium at the Center of Theological Inquiry in spring 2009. The following people offered bibliographical suggestions that proved fruitful: João Biehl, Jaime Clark-Soles, Richard Pervo, Andrew Root, Carolyn Sharp, and Matthew Sleeman. Finally, Greg Carey, Jaime Clark-Soles, Brent Driggers, and Richard Hays read drafts of chapters and took the time to push me, appropriately, to be clearer.

Stephanie Egnotovich provided expert advice and steady encouragement as my editor until her untimely passing in April 2009. I will always associate this project with her as a personal reminder of her impressive talents and support. I thank David Dobson, Donald McKim, Daniel Braden, and their talented colleagues at Westminster John Knox Press for guiding my work to completion.

My gratitude extends, too, to Alexandra, Miranda, and Samuel, who kept their eyes eagerly peeled for tulips. Thank you, Cathy, for everything; I dedicate this book to you.

Abbreviations

AB	Anchor Bible
ABD	*The Anchor Bible Dictionary.* Edited by David Noel Freedman. 6 vols. New York: Doubleday, 1992
ABRL	Anchor Bible Reference Library
ACNT	Augsburg Commentary on the New Testament
AnBib	Analecta biblica
ANTC	Abingdon New Testament Commentaries
BBB	Bonner biblische Beiträge
BETL	Bibliotheca ephemeridum theologicarum lovaniensium
BibInt	*Biblical Interpretation*
BNTC	Black's New Testament Commentaries
BWANT	Beiträge zur Wissenschaft vom Alten und Neuen Testament
BZNW	Beihefte zur Zeitschrift für die neutestamentliche Wissenschaft
CBET	Contributions to Biblical Exegesis and Theology
CBQ	*Catholic Biblical Quarterly*
CSJH	Chicago Studies in the History of Judaism
DRev	*Downside Review*
GNS	Good News Studies
H	Heliodorus, *An Ethiopian Tale*
ICC	International Critical Commentary
Int	*Interpretation*
JBL	*Journal of Biblical Literature*
JRS	*Journal of Roman Studies*
JSNT	*Journal for the Study of the New Testament*

JSNTSup	Journal for the Study of the New Testament: Supplement Series
JSOTSup	Journal for the Study of the Old Testament: Supplement Series
JTS	*Journal of Theological Studies*
LCL	Loeb Classical Library. Cambridge: Harvard University Press
LXX	Septuagint
NET	New English Translation
NIB	*The New Interpreter's Bible.* 12 vols. Nashville: Abingdon Press, 1994–2004
NICNT	New International Commentary on the New Testament
NIV	New International Version
NovT	*Novum Testamentum*
NovTSup	Supplements to Novum Testamentum
NRSV	New Revised Standard Version
NTAbh	Neutestamentliche Abhandlungen
NTL	New Testament Library
NTS	*New Testament Studies*
OBT	Overtures to Biblical Theology
PG	Patrologia graeca. Edited by J.-P. Migne. 162 vols. Paris, 1857–1866
RSV	Revised Standard Version
SBLAB	Society of Biblical Literature Academica Biblica
SBLDS	Society of Biblical Literature Dissertation Series
SBLEJL	Society of Biblical Literature Early Judaism and Its Literature
SBLSP	Society of Biblical Literature Seminar Papers
SBLSymS	Society of Biblical Literature Symposium Series
SJ	Studia judaica
SNTSMS	Society for New Testament Studies Monograph Series
SP	Sacra pagina
SR	Studies in Religion
TDNT	*Theological Dictionary of the New Testament.* Edited by Gerhard Kittel and Gerhard Friedrich. Translated by Geoffrey William Bromiley. 10 vols. Grand Rapids: Wm. B. Eerdmans Publishing Co., 1964–1976
TS	*Theological Studies*
WBC	Word Biblical Commentary
WUNT	Wissenschaftliche Untersuchungen zum Neuen Testament
XE	Xenophon of Ephesus, *An Ephesian Tale*

1

Introduction

Not only are trials inherently dramatic, but they are something
more: they are tests of a society, and the special way those tests are
conducted can reveal a society's strengths and weaknesses.[1]

Courtroom proceedings tell us about ourselves, our world, and our shared
existence. The trials of Socrates, Jesus, Joan of Arc, Galileo, O. J. Simpson,
Timothy McVeigh, the Salem witch trials, the Scopes trial, the Nuremberg
trials—these occupy prominent places in cultural memories, not solely due to
the notoriety of either the defendants or their prosecutors, but also because of
what they reveal about societies and how those societies manage themselves.
They offer themselves as windows onto social conflicts, social processes, and
social identity. The same is true for any trial, involving any defendant.

Trials make for great theater. No wonder that, through the centuries and
across cultures, they appear in the pages of "high literature," pulp fiction,
and anything in between. Although literary critics debate the specifics of the
connection, they recognize a special affinity between courtrooms and literature. For one thing, every trial presumes a wider story, since its deliberations
examine events from the past and its verdicts aim to regulate the future. Trials
thus emerge from and influence the development of a history. Also, the dramatic nature of any trial—seen in its ways of employing dialogue, storytelling,
chronology, and multiple perspectives—can create a compelling experience
that allows audiences to participate vicariously while anticipating the range
of possible outcomes, with fears and hopes about punishment and vindication
hanging in the balance.

Trials, whether real or fictional, whether high profile or ordinary, create
a unique kind of social space, separated out of the everyday interactions of

society yet also deeply embedded within them. In trials members of a society reenact events, reconstruct narratives, or re-present ideas and debates concerning the validity of ideas, and then trials conclude with some sort of binding decision or verdict. The ramifications of a decision radiate beyond the boundaries of a courtroom, back into society. A verdict declares which version of the truth will prevail, or which actions will be permitted, and so influences a wider social system, even as the whole judicial process reflects the system's notion of itself and its defining values. As they review the claims people make and the deeds they commit, then render verdicts upon them, trials test a society, revealing and regulating a society's values, especially the values of those who hold power within or over it.

Judicial drama connects to the dramas of life, to the lived interactions of social existence through which people define themselves and connect with others. Trials, again both real and fictional, result from conflicts that inevitably arise in those interactions and from a society's commitment to address and resolve its conflicts. Decision is therefore part of most judicial events, for trials aim to impart judgments about what a conflict requires, even if they seldom pretend to end disagreement entirely or to reconcile opposing positions. Whether we view any given legal proceeding in a favorable or unfavorable light, or whether we understand it to reflect a quest for genuine justice or a systemic perpetuation of injustice, we usually expect a trial to issue a definitive statement concerning a person, idea, or set of actions that is under examination. Trials thus perform powerful roles for maintaining a social system's boundaries, promising to protect the acceptable from the unacceptable, to divide what is tolerable from what is threatening. They impose, endorse, or resist a set of values to support the interests of a wider social context, or at least the interests of those who control that context.

Things are no different with the trial scenes we encounter in the narrative books of the New Testament, the four Gospels and the Acts of the Apostles. These scenes are flush with drama and deeply significant for understanding the biblical stories about Jesus and his followers as well as the social conflicts and power struggles that these people's claims and actions repeatedly ignite. We gain a richer grasp of the trials' importance for making sense of the wider stories of Jesus and his followers when we attend to the dramatic texture of these scenes and to their capacity to comment on the sociopolitical realities of the ancient world and the Christian gospel's relationship to that world. By analyzing each trial in light of its place within a larger narrative, in light of the sociopolitical situation in which the trial is set, and in light of the action that occurs in the forensic drama, we discover that the trials do more than depict guiltless defendants faithfully facing the jurisdiction of presiding authorities. They also present the matter conversely: these defendants and the gospel message they represent issue their own claims or judgments upon those authorities and, by extension, upon the reigning values that those authorities represent and pursue. In their trial scenes, the Gospels and Acts provide windows onto Christianity's ambiguous and potentially precarious relationship to the sociopolitical structures that regulate its environments.

How do the judgments play out, and what do these windows reveal? In all of the New Testament's trial scenes, conflicts propel central characters into situations that require them to appear before recognized authorities to contend for themselves or for the beliefs they profess. The trials of Jesus before Jewish and Roman officials are probably best known among these, and the story of Jesus' prosecution comes to us in four expressions, as a prominent episode in each Gospel. However, since the four evangelists' accounts differ substantially, each Gospel offers a distinctive depiction of Jesus' encounters with the highest-ranking sociopolitical authorities of his time and place. Following the Gospels, the book of Acts includes numerous scenes in which Jesus' followers land under the judgment and discipline of those who hold positions of authority over public life. Acts does not preserve dispassionate records of these conflicts, for its trial scenes include implied commentary on what the conflicts mean: why Jesus' followers faced opposition, what risks their message may have posed to established sociopolitical values and institutions, and how their gospel found ways to inhabit the social structures into which it traveled.

In the trial scenes, powerful interests converge to hear the claims that Jesus and his followers make. Their presence is never unexpected, for the wider Gospel and Acts narratives note, in their own ways, that those claims do not sit comfortably with the prevailing sociopolitical authorities and their interests. The trials are venues for these officials to consider and judge, not just the defendants as individual moral agents, but also the gospel message that conflicts with the authorities' own political and religious assumptions. As these rulers of the sociopolitical landscape decide the defendants' fates, they simultaneously judge the values that the defendants profess and the general merits of their gospel message. They judge the gospel—whether it is true and whether their society can afford to abide it.

At the same time, and conversely, the narrative dynamics of these scenes depict the gospel—represented by the identities and arguments of the defendants who proclaim it—making claims upon or sometimes against the religious and political structures of the first-century world. These converse judgments occur in subtle forms. The Gospels and Acts tell their stories in ways that assume and mold certain perspectives in the perceptions of their audiences: these narratives express particular points of view about the world, events, and people that they describe. Sometimes the narratives nudge readers to encounter dissonant dimensions in the trials. For example, all the trial scenes of the New Testament, to varying degrees, exploit moments of dramatic irony, in which readers grasp the situation with more information than most characters in the story do. Consider, as examples, two passages that insist a trial is more than what some of its participants presume. First, John 19:10–11a makes a statement about the provisional nature of a Roman official's authority, as a brief exchange between Pontius Pilate and Jesus casts doubt on the governor's real power over Jesus' fate. Pilate, frustrated by his prisoner's refusal to speak, tries to coerce Jesus:

> **Pilate:** You won't speak to me? Don't you know that I have authority to release you, and authority to crucify you?
>
> **Jesus:** You would have had no authority over me, except for what was given to you from above [i.e., from God].[2]

Likewise, in Acts 4:27–28, a group of believers offers a prayer that states, perhaps paradoxically, that the will of God trumped or manipulated the wills of the authorities who condemned and executed Jesus. The prayer claims that Herod, Pontius Pilate, the Gentiles, and the peoples of Israel all came together against Jesus "to do whatever your [God's] hand and plan predetermined to happen" (see a similar statement in Acts 3:17–18).

The rest of John's Gospel and Acts provide more insight into these two statements: in a simple way each signals that the trials are scenes in which not all the parties involved enjoy access to all the relevant information, and claims about who really holds power are fundamentally disputed. If what Jesus says to Pilate is true, then the whole of his trial accumulates added layers of significance for readers, who see more than Pilate can concerning his authority to issue definitive claims about Jesus and end Jesus' influence among the people. This erodes Pilate's legitimacy in readers' eyes. Statements like these, and other less obvious details, indicate that authority over defendants and their fates is neither intrinsically nor exclusively vested in the prosecutors or magistrates, the ones who appear to hold all the power. The trials become occasions for ironically declaring and enacting the truth that things are not what they seem to the eyes of human authorities and structures; if a trial narrative can find ways to show that the power of the presiding officials is less than absolute, then it suggests that the gospel corresponds to a different way of construing power and understanding social existence. If the authorities' judgments, despite appearances, are not *really* able to express their unique power and enforce their religious and political values, then the trials come across less as obstacles or threats to the promulgation of the gospel, more as occasions for the gospel to advance and persevere over putative efforts to control or define it.

The trial scenes of the New Testament therefore do much more than attest to Jesus' and his followers' general success in attracting widespread notice, and to their general lack of success in convincing the world's rulers of the truth or acceptability of the gospel message (for most of the trials end with the defendant's death or the conflict unresolved). The testimony these characters give, the actions they perform, the responses they solicit, the treatment they receive, and even their mere presence before human authorities—all these result in subtle yet powerful demonstrations of the claims that the gospel makes on and about the world, its religious assumptions, and its expressions of power. These claims issue judgments, judgments challenging both the ways that human authorities use power and the supposition that they can exercise authority over the definition and dissemination of the gospel. These challenges put the influence or jurisdiction of the Jewish and Roman authorities at risk of being usurped or subverted by the power of the gospel and the God of whom it speaks. The trials in the Gospel and Acts, each in a distinctive way, evidence an uncomfortable relationship between the message of the gospel and the configurations of sociopolitical power that the gospel encounters. This book investigates the trial scenes to illuminate that relationship.

THE NEW TESTAMENT'S TRIAL NARRATIVES

It is easy to see that the Gospels and Acts contain numerous scenes in which characters find themselves subject to the judgments of human authorities. Less obvious is the rationale for designating a set of these scenes as *trials*. The New Testament writings do not describe the various accounts with consistent juridical vocabulary, and some of the scenes treated in this book lack the semblance of structure or procedure that might indicate a trial in a legally technical sense.[3] Almost every scene that might qualify as part of a trial follows its own procedural route and has its own particular purposes within the plot of a Gospel or Acts. Furthermore, some of the scenes (especially those in which Jesus is the defendant) exhibit more injustice than one might think possible in an acknowledged judicial proceeding. Others look more like a lynching (as with Stephen in Acts 6:7–8:1) or exercises in bullying by authorities bent on exercising control through intimidation (as with Peter, John, and others in Acts 4:1–22; 5:17–41). Moreover, not all of these scenes conclude with a formal resolution, judgment, or sentence. Several in Acts remain unfinished, only to be resumed later in the narrative under new circumstances. Others function as episodes in a larger juridical process, as informational hearings or interrogations (as with Paul in Acts 25:13–26:32, an event called an inquiry [ἀνάκρισις] in 25:26). As the discussion in the next chapter will reveal, however, these legal ambiguities are neither unique nor especially problematic; accounts of trials in other Greco-Roman literature also exhibit variations among their settings, procedural details, and legal or literary purposes. Trial scenes must be defined in general, functional terms, not solely according to specific procedural or formal criteria.

This book considers *trial scenes* to be narrative episodes in which accused persons give account of themselves or answer questions before recognized authorities who wield the power to issue rulings or declarations concerning the acceptability of the people and ideas being examined. The trial scenes in the New Testament, then, all include argumentation or exchange of perspectives among the participants, prompted by one or more accusations leveled against the defendant(s). In addition, trials differ from other occasions of public debate, because trials bring in governing authorities to issue definitive judgments concerning whether those under examination will be permitted to return to public arenas and resume their proclamation of the gospel.[4]

Given this understanding of what makes a trial scene, this book will investigate the following passages:

Jesus' trial: Mark 14:53–15:15; Matthew 26:57–27:26; Luke 22:66–23:25; John 18:12–19:16a.[5] These texts take readers from Jesus' initial hearing to the point where Pilate delivers him to crucifixion. Each Gospel's collection of separate but connected scenes advances that Gospel's plot by bridging and making sense of the relationship between Jesus' public ministry and his execution by the Roman state. This is about more than changing Jesus' legal status or transporting him from point A to point B, for by virtue of their location and function in each Gospel's plot, the trials bear the burden of integrating Jesus' ministry and death. They shed light on the theological questions of how Jesus' execution follows as a consequence of the kind of life he lives, and what his condemnation says about his message's relationship to the world's configurations and exercise of sociopolitical power.

Trials of various apostles before Jewish authorities in Jerusalem: Acts 4:1–22; 5:17–41. These two scenes present the first postascension instances of Jesus' followers facing local authorities. In the first, the ministry of Peter and John leads to their arrest. Then the highest-ranking Jewish authorities in Jerusalem interrogate, threaten, and ultimately release the prisoners. The second text describes the high priest and additional Jewish leaders putting Peter and other unnamed apostles into custody. After an angel delivers them from their confinement and sends them back to the Jerusalem temple, they experience rearrest, questioning from the Jewish leadership, and a punitive flogging before the authorities free them.

Stephen's trial: Acts 6:7–8:1. Stephen engages in a public ministry of signs, wonders, and wisdom so dynamic that it attracts the hostility of opponents who lay charges of blasphemy against him before the Jewish high priest and other members of his council. Stephen delivers a speech that concludes by indicting his accusers and judges. This so riles his audience that they stone him to death. Although clearly lacking the procedural discipline that one might expect from a legal process, this scene functions as a trial by depicting Stephen as defending himself against accusations and Jewish authorities supervising his martyrdom. Stephen's grisly slaying stands as one of the trial's de facto verdicts while also corroborating his charge that his hearers are recommitting the sin of persecuting God's prophets.

Trials of Paul, Silas, and their representatives before Roman authorities: Acts 16:16–40; 17:1–10a. In these two passages Paul and Silas (in Philippi) and then Jason and others (in Thessalonica) find themselves facing local officials after angry crowds accuse Paul and Silas of advocating anti-Roman activities and teachings. Although neither scene includes a detailed indictment from the accusers or any defense speech from the accused, in both cases the city magistrates issue judgments concerning the embattled believers. Although these texts offer only skeletal accounts, nevertheless both furnish enough activity to warrant consideration as trial scenes.

Paul's trial: Acts 21:27–28:28. Paul's trial constitutes the final fourth of the entire book of Acts. This large block of text begins with a crowd seizing Paul in the Jerusalem temple and ends with him under house arrest in Rome as he waits for the emperor to hear his case. The trial comprises a variety of scenes, seven in all, in which Paul must defend himself. These include two formal hearings before Roman provincial governors (Felix in 24:1–27 and Festus in 25:6–12), where members of Jerusalem's Jewish leadership contend for their charges against him. Paul also speaks before a Jewish crowd (at the Jerusalem temple in 21:27–22:22), before high-ranking authorities (a Roman tribune in 22:23–29; the high priest and his council in 22:30–23:11; King Agrippa, Bernice, plus additional elite figures in 25:13–26:32), and before other groups (the leading Jews of Rome in 28:17–28). Together, all of these scenes and the material that connects them recount "the trial of Paul."

THE APPROACH OF THIS BOOK

The New Testament's trial scenes tell us many things. Scholars have employed historical approaches in plumbing these passages to clarify details about the actual demise of Jesus, Paul, and others; about the nature of judicial procedures and legal realities in Roman provinces during the first century; and about the moral character of Pontius Pilate, Caiaphas, and additional political figures.[6] For other interpreters, the rhetorical aspects of the trials' dialogues and speeches yield evidence about these texts' possible sources, the purposes behind their composition, and their theological emphases.[7] Still others see the trial scenes as key pieces of the apologetic agendas that the Gospels and Acts pursue, and so they investigate how these texts might selectively intensify or mitigate the hostility, virtues, culpability, or innocence associated with various parties in the ancient context.[8] All of these avenues of inquiry have value, but none enjoys primary status as the foundational means of understanding the trials. Each approach is motivated, in part, by the interests and priorities of the interpreters who put it to use. Furthermore, these and additional methods of investigating the trial scenes regularly intersect and incorporate aspects of each other.

The analysis I undertake in this book is no different; it seeks answers to questions that I find compelling about these passages, and it is deeply indebted to the work of other scholars who have brought different and similar interpretive questions to the trial scenes. I do not pretend to offer a comprehensive analysis of all the ways in which the trials present themselves as meaningful passages. My aims are to complement other means of studying them by highlighting features sometimes overlooked and to demonstrate these features' relevance for a biblically informed understanding of the Christian message's capacity to engage the structures of human society.

The Narrative Character of the Trial Scenes

One distinctive feature of this book's approach is its focus on the narrative character of the trial scenes: it explores both the techniques used to narrate the juridical conflicts and the scenes' contributions to the shape and meaning of larger stories. Each trial comes not as a disinterested legal transcript or forensic treatise but as a narrative that makes selective use of action, dialogue, staging, symbolism, and other details. Careful examination of these narrative dimensions highlights the power dynamics at work in the trials. This kind of analysis discloses the subtle and often-overlooked dimensions of the gospel's challenges to the rulers who judge it in the trial scenes. Furthermore, the trial scenes do not exist in isolation; each comes situated in an overarching plot that molds perspectives on the trial's participants and their conflicts. A narrative analysis of these scenes and their depictions of conflict allows us to see them influencing the whole of a Gospel or Acts.

The New Testament books were written through the eyes of Christian faith: Christian convictions deeply influenced how stories about Jesus and his followers were remembered and disseminated via traditions and ultimately the biblical writings. This book's focus on the narrative dynamics of the trial scenes attends to the meaning that these stories might plausibly generate among their readers. This is neither a study of the historicity of the trial accounts ("What really happened?") nor an attempt to discern the evangelists' sources separately from their own editing and interpretation ("How did the biblical authors learn about it?"). Those kinds of projects are valuable, but I leave them to other scholars. At the same time, this focus on narrative and the perspectives it affords to audiences is hardly unconcerned about history, for it requires recognizing that the New Testament's historical context matters for understanding New Testament narratives. After all, these narratives emerge from and refer to particular historical conditions. We may not be able to reconstruct either these precise conditions or the complex perspectives of actual ancient readers. But we can familiarize ourselves with basic aspects of the political environment that the Gospels and Acts assume, allowing us to explore how the trial narratives might acknowledge, criticize, and manipulate those conditions. Toward this end, chapter 2 offers a general overview of ancient sociopolitical and literary conventions, conventions that would have been familiar to first- and second-century people who read or heard the Gospels and Acts as stories that shape Christian understandings of the gospel and its place in society.

The Trial Scenes and the Sociopolitical Environment

A second dimension of this study is to demonstrate the trial scenes' importance for understanding five of the New Testament books' outlooks on the relationship between the Christian gospel and the constructions of sociopolitical authority in the first-century Mediterranean world.[9] The New Testament offers a variety of perspectives on the imperial climate in which Christianity emerged, including this handful of relatively isolated yet notable passages: Jesus addresses the matter of paying taxes to Rome ("Give what is Caesar's back to Caesar"; Mark 12:13–17 and par.), Paul commends subjection to human governments ("The authorities that exist have been put in place by God"; Rom. 13:1–7; cf. 1 Pet. 2:11–17), and John of Patmos reports a vision that promises and celebrates Rome's final destruction ("Fallen, fallen is Babylon the great!" Rev. 18). While the trial scenes rarely deliver political statements in such bold language, they provide equally important vantage points for surveying the perspectives that the Gospels and Acts offer on the relationship among Jesus, his followers, and governing authorities.

The trial scenes comment on matters beyond the particular disputes that involve Jesus, Peter, Paul, and others. They also speak more broadly about the gospel negotiating its place in society. Part of this derives from the nature of trials. Trial scenes—not only in the New Testament but also in other ancient literature—unearth the interests and values that the characters in the trials represent; thus they frame contests over competing ideologies.[10] Moreover, the kinds of people who appear in the trials in the Gospels and Acts allow those passages to represent the wider sociopolitical landscape in distinctive ways, for the trial scenes provide opportunities for some of the most powerful members of ancient society to enter the stories, including Roman governors and Jewish high priests. On a few additional occasions Jesus and his followers interact with other social elites (see, e.g., Matt. 8:5–13; Mark 5:21–23; Acts 13:4–12; 28:7–8), yet the trials remain virtually correlative with the notion of the gospel making contact with the uppermost levels of sociopolitical power in Roman provincial society. When Jesus and others receive rulings from Roman officials, these verdicts speak authorized responses to the message of Jesus and his witnesses, assessments of the gospel's place in society. Trials thus usher the gospel into the presence of sociopolitical power; in this respect they provide a choice platform for considering theological perspectives on the gospel's relationship to that power and its exercise.

These ideological contests simultaneously accentuate and minimize the conflicts that envelop Jesus and his followers. The trials come as no surprise; the Gospels and Acts foreshadow most of them as culminations of political opposition or evil intentions. The encounters with authorities are perilous, as underscored when defendants typically stand alone against groups of powerful opponents. Furthermore, many of the accusers and judges who appear in these scenes come across as hostile or impetuous, as exemplified by the false witnesses produced to testify against Jesus and Stephen (Mark 14:56–59; Acts 6:13–14) and by the reprimands meted out upon Jesus and Paul (John 18:22; Acts 23:2). Corruption and injustice amplify the peril when opponents and magistrates show little interest in conducting impartial, open hearings. At the same time, these scenes defuse that sense of peril and vulnerability. The judgments that the narratives implicitly issue against the authorities and their exercise of power typically assert that each trial's verdict ultimately proves irrelevant or nonconstraining to the gospel's ability to be revealed or to persevere. Trials and their binding decisions do not hinder the gospel; they actually confirm it and regularly promise new arenas for its proclamation.

Many interpreters note sociopolitical conflict playing itself out in the New Testament's trial scenes, and they characterize this conflict in a myriad of ways. Owing to my desire to keep this book as accessible as possible and focused on the biblical texts in question, my approach speaks about society and power in generalized and not always deeply nuanced ways. By considering how these scenes depict the gospel and its human agents navigating networks of political authority and mechanisms of social control, this book poses a few angles of inquiry that probably would not have occurred to the earliest readers of the Gospels and Acts, who may not in the same way have drawn both separations and connections between institutions of social control and the power of God. I nevertheless consider these angles, in the process possibly blurring fine distinctions between ancient readers' perspectives and twenty-first-century readers' perspectives, because refusing to consider these angles risks confining the Bible to the status of a cultural artifact with little meaningful connection to our experiences as social beings. At the same time, I acknowledge that bringing the theological and sociopolitical perspectives of the Gospels and Acts into creative conversation with modern contexts is no simple task. My modest goal is to suggest that the outlooks of the New Testament's trial scenes still constructively and creatively inform present-day perceptions of the gospel's relationship to the exercise of authority in human society.

Theological Implications

There is, then, a distinctly theological dimension to this book: the approaches it adopts and the issues it pursues aim to illuminate the theological visions operating in the trial scenes. In speaking of *theological visions*, I do not limit the focus to the theological convictions that might have influenced the composition and redaction of these accounts nearly two millennia ago. Rather, I understand the theological visions of the Gospels and Acts to be connected primarily—both first and foremost—to the books' capacities to shape their readers' perspectives on the stories they tell, perspectives on the books' narrative representations of the way things are with human society and God.[11] Part of this involves considering what knowledge or prejudices ancient readers might have brought to their reading, but only approximations are possible here. Ultimately, our interpretation cannot be exclusively determined by speculation about the precise provenance of the individual New Testament writings. Furthermore, different ancient audiences would have encountered the trial scenes in varied ways, as do modern audiences. This hardly prevents these narratives from resonating effectively with human experience and exercising a capacity for shaping human identity and memory, in any time. If anything, it makes their ability to do so more impressive and wide-ranging.[12]

Around which issues might the trial scenes shape a reader's theological perspectives? Obviously Jesus' trial has deep significance for understanding the Gospels' christological claims, for the Gospels rely heavily on these scenes to establish who Jesus is and how he is known. Most of the trials in Acts are crucial pieces of that book's accounting of the fragile and nearly volatile relationship that emerged between the first-century church and certain sectors of Judaism, while some trials in Acts acknowledge Christians' increasing vulnerability to accusations of anti-Roman activity.[13] The trial scenes address these issues by keeping their theological claims intertwined with the opposition that Jesus and his followers face: Jesus manages to expose heavy-handed uses of power even as he becomes subject to them. Attempts to confine the proclamation of the gospel tend instead to catalyze it. It is not difficult to imagine that ancient Christian readers would have found these scenes capable of strengthening their resolve as they tried to make theological sense of their own relationship to governing authorities.

The theological visions of the trial scenes still provoke and inform an understanding of how believers might interpret and interact with the wider world, even as the particular world of temple officials and Roman governors has long since disappeared. Bible readers cannot assume facile equations between the Roman Empire and the imperialism of our contemporary world; nor should they accept the biblical narratives' depictions uncritically or without attention to these narratives' functions within their ancient contexts. Certainly many in today's world who read the New Testament as Scripture conduct their theological reflections within environments less acutely hazardous than those of the original audiences. Our reflections on the theological contribution of these books and their trial scenes require us to take account of the cultural assumptions operative in the narrated world and also those in the contexts from which we read.

The theological contours of this investigation inform my understanding of the audience that might benefit most from this book. I write for undergraduate and graduate students engaged in critical study of the New Testament and its ethical and theological claims, as well as for seminary or divinity-school graduates and Christian laypeople who seek a deeper understanding of the Gospels, Acts, and their theological contributions. Through the analysis of the four accounts of Jesus' trial, readers will better grasp the distinctiveness of each Gospel and the theological significance of the stories they tell. Through the analysis of the trials in Acts, readers will see how the idea of legal travails and bearing witness before authorities becomes a theological motif that shapes the sequel to the Gospel of Luke and interprets the experiences of Christians living approximately two to three generations after Jesus. All these scenes suggest that to be on trial was to stand in Jesus' legacy, to be sure, but they also verify that the gospel Jesus and his followers proclaim regularly challenges, confronts, and even sometimes manipulates the power structures that regulate human society. As we will see, the trials offer complex and not always uniform descriptions of a gospel that is neither completely amicable nor intrinsically hostile toward the sociopolitical structures of the first-century world. Those demanding simplistic theological platitudes or univocal prescriptions concerning these issues may be frustrated by the perspectives that present themselves through the various trial scenes.

2

Trials in Ancient Life and Literature

This chapter summarizes the sociopolitical and literary milieux of the New Testament trial narratives. Because the New Testament writings emerge from, presuppose, and once spoke to particular cultural contexts, our study of the trial scenes in the Gospels and Acts will be deeper and richer for what we know about those contexts. The chapter describes how contemporaries of the New Testament writings might have experienced or thought about trials, focusing particularly on the nature of judicial conflicts and the functions they performed in real life and in literature. Such an exercise will prevent us from imposing modern standards for litigation and justice upon our encounters with the biblical narratives and instead allow us to see how these narratives reflect the historical realities of jurisprudence and politics in the world Rome governed. The chapter also permits us to observe more going on in the New Testament's trial scenes than raw juridical deliberations over accusations and verdicts. Other ancient literature made use of trials to represent conflicts waged on a grander scale, sometimes offering implicit commentary on those contests. To the extent that the New Testament's trial scenes similarly frame conflict and comment on it, they reveal their potential to shape attitudes concerning the gospel's place within the sociopolitical currents of ancient society.

The chapter's scope must remain limited to an illustrative sketch rather than a comprehensive analysis. Nevertheless, an overview drawn in broad strokes still produces an informative image. Subsequent chapters will offer additional detail as they investigate individual trial scenes and deal with any particular literary and political assumptions at work in those narratives.

TRIALS AND ROMAN GOVERNANCE

All the New Testament's trial narratives, except for the last scene in Paul's final trial in Acts 28:17–28, which takes place in Rome, are set in provincial regions of the Roman Empire during the first century. By virtue of their historical setting, the trial scenes transport us into uncertain legal territory, for it is difficult to determine with much specificity whether these accounts accurately reflect conventional legal procedures from those times and places. Hardly any sources survive that can shed reliable light on the particularities of actual legal proceedings and the application of law in Judea and other Roman provinces during the first century. Those who study the judicial realities of this period must work from legal documents produced in later centuries, once imperial law had become more uniform and codified, and compare those texts with what is known about the political arrangements in the first century concerning the emperors' priorities for selecting and empowering provincial officials. From there, scholars are left to speculate in general terms about the nature of first-century provincial jurisdiction, despite all of its local particularities.[1] The conjectural and often circular aspects of this work mean that quests to discover established legal procedures prove misdirected or unfruitful.

An understanding of the New Testament's depictions of trials in their sociopolitical context therefore cannot confidently begin with a review of first-century judicial standards or legal codes; rather, the characteristics of imperial governance and provincial authority provide the context. The governors whom emperors installed to manage provinces, such as Judea, represented the emperor and accordingly possessed considerable authority as an extension of his own.[2] When 1 Peter 2:13–14 speaks of Roman officials ensuring "the punishment of those who do evil and the recognition of those who do good" specifically as agents of the "supreme ruler" (the emperor), it acknowledges governors as the face of imperial authority in the provinces. When Paul refuses a governor's attempt to transfer his trial to Jerusalem and says to him as they face each other in Caesarea, the seat of Roman power in Judea, "I am standing before the emperor's judgment seat, which is where I should be judged" (Acts 25:10), he acknowledges that the governor in Caesarea stands in for the emperor in Rome as "an outlet for the emperor's power," a representation of the emperor's interests and even the emperor himself.[3] As delegates of the emperor, governors possessed vast authority, extending to legal matters. Their authority permitted and encouraged them to deal with legal complaints and conduct judicial hearings as they saw fit. Although we cannot confidently say which, if any, juridical procedures a particular governor may or may not have usually followed, we can determine that local jurisdiction was his responsibility and its exercise was largely left to his discretion.

The Legal Authority of Provincial Governors

The Roman system of governance in the mid-first century appears to have had neither the inclination nor the resources to implement established, consistent legal procedures across the empire. Popular perceptions of the Roman emperors and their empire sometimes create an impression that imperial rule flowed from a strong centralized authority. Indeed, all the empire's authority resided in its head, the emperor, and emperors cultivated a strong, even charismatic imperial presence throughout the Mediterranean world via their officials, propaganda, statecraft, and religion.[4] But, at least until the empire grew older in subsequent centuries, the demands of day-to-day governance and jurisprudence, the vast expanse of Roman-controlled territory, and the lack of a sufficient number of legal functionaries made it impossible and perhaps inefficient to maintain a unified or centralized legal system. As a result the emperor charged local authorities to govern these regions on his behalf in ways that supported the goals of Roman society. The primary duties of these appointed officials were to collect taxes and to maintain order—duties aimed at keeping Rome strong and supplied, and keeping the people within the empire protected and pacified.[5] These responsibilities directly informed a governor's exercise of his judicial responsibilities by making social order a paramount value. As a leading scholar of Roman law puts it, "For the Romans 'crime' meant actions which threatened social well-being and stability; the repression of crime aimed to protect society more than its individual members, who were traditionally expected to be responsible for their own safety."[6] The foundational question beneath a governor's ruling in criminal cases, then, was not necessarily "Has this person broken a law?" (although that could be a relevant, secondary question). The inquiry was more along the lines of "Has this person done anything that endangers social welfare or threatens Roman values?" A governor's criteria for answering such a question could certainly vary depending on the circumstances.[7]

Legal judgments stemmed from more than governors' political whims; matters of law and privilege played some role. To preserve social stability and promote imperial well-being, provincial governors during the first century—including those we meet in the New Testament, namely Pilate, Felix, and Festus—possessed what the Romans called *imperium*: power to command and authority for governance and criminal jurisdiction.[8] It allowed them to control every aspect of a trial: presenting evidence, hearing arguments, delivering verdicts, and issuing sentences.[9] Certain legal foundations—rooted in the emperor's authority, in older Roman law codes, and in legal principles derived from local practices—often gave governors general guidance in weighing civil and criminal justice.[10] Yet when it came to deciding guilt and punishment, imperium granted them great discretion over how they would exercise their responsibilities, allowing them in most cases to render decisions with a mixture of justice and political expediency, even to impose severe penalties if those might serve particular ends. While a limited number of society's elite members could appeal a governor's judgments in certain cases, to most people governors gave the final word on an issue, a prerogative that some governors did not hesitate to exploit to great and terrifying effect.[11]

This is not to say that the system was necessarily corrupt or that governors and their agents possessed carte blanche to act as tyrants. The mechanisms of provincial governance and the goals it pursued meshed quite neatly with certain Roman social values. For one thing, the governor's work often had to benefit a province's local elites, in that these people's position of dominance over the rest of society was assured by Roman legal, social, and economic policies.[12] As a result, society's elites and Roman citizens, provided they stayed in the empire's good graces, enjoyed prerogatives. All this usually encouraged a symbiotic connection between protecting the interests of society's elites and advancing the priorities of the state.

The structures of Roman-ruled society depended upon a hierarchy of rank, and the realities of social ranks were reinforced through virtually every public activity, especially in urban centers. The clothes people wore, where they sat at public events, the systems by which food was distributed to a needy population—these and other public displays communicated social status and upheld the privileges and disadvantages pertaining to it. As two classical scholars explain, "Putting everyone in his proper place was a visual affirmation of the dominance of the imperial social structure, and one calculated to impress the bulk of the population of the empire."[13] These displays and practices varied from place to place and would look much different in a very pro-Roman society such as Philippi's than they would in a generally less receptive environment such as Jerusalem's. Nevertheless, the point speaks to the empire's interest in preserving social systems that kept social and economic privileges in the hands of an aristocratic elite.

Trials could hardly be exempt from this hierarchical structure; jurisdiction also discriminated according to the social class and public status of the accused and accuser, as well as according to the consequences a verdict might pose for public life.[14] The operations of a trial reflected the inequities and status distinctions that were part and parcel of Roman governance and society.[15] Proceedings and verdicts showcased differences in power (understood in terms of a person's perceived value in society and a person's ability to influence a community's social or economic well-being) among the parties involved, culminating in the magistrate's determining the credibility of all parties and making rulings that related their status to questions of the common (imperial) good.

Common laborers typically had little chance in legal disputes against wealthy citizens, and punishments levied upon those from the lower classes would be much more severe than those given to elites.[16] "To the Romans the source of legal privilege was *dignitas* (*honor*, prestige). *Dignitas* was derived from political position or influence, style of life (character, moral values, education, etc.), and wealth."[17] *Dignitas* ensured that the uppermost strata of Roman society could expect to see their benefits preserved. In some instances bribery through cash and favors might guarantee this.[18] Trials, therefore, were not fair fights in which all parties could expect equal treatment under the law or from those charged to maintain order.

Justice and fair treatment were not automatically out of reach in all cases, but a governor had many factors to consider. Because trials bore such close connections to the state's cultural and political priorities, they provided opportunities for preserving and consolidating the power of imperial officers and their allies. This is hardly something unique to Roman society. Nor does it mean that everyone chafed at all these inequities and bemoaned them as "unfair," although some people, some who espoused other social values, certainly resisted them. In any case, such conditions were part of life, resulting from the social structures and privileges that made Roman society possible and durable in the first place.[19]

The Provincial Governor and the Local Aristocracy

Because some of the New Testament's trial scenes include no Roman officials, and in others local Jewish leaders prosecute cases before Roman governors, the relationship between provincial Roman authorities and members of the local aristocracy deserves additional attention. Although legal authority over all but the most high-stakes cases resided in provincial governors, this responsibility stretched them thin and required them to delegate authority. On this system of local delegation, as Aelius Aristides wrote in the second century CE, "There is no need of garrisons holding acropolises, but the most important and powerful people in each place guard their countries for you [Romans]."[20] The limited supply of Roman officials also required governors to elicit cooperation from local people of high status to ensure social stability and the ongoing collection of maximum revenue. Furthermore, members of a province's local aristocracy could create serious problems for governors who did not adequately tend to their political and economic interests.[21]

Local bodies, such as γερουσίαι (councils) in eastern parts of the empire, therefore played occasional roles in provincial governance.[22] These roles were usually advisory or for mediating between imperial authority and a segment of the local population, and their specifics varied from place to place and time to time. Nevertheless, such bodies could exert influence in civic and moral affairs. Therefore, governors could look to community groups to assist with mediating disputes, resolving minor civil conflicts, and eliminating threats to the system.[23]

This general description squares well with the particular evidence concerning first-century Judea, the setting for most of the New Testament's trial scenes. Once Emperor Augustus designated Judea a province in 6 CE, placing its administration under Rome's direct oversight, the empire began a process of identifying and empowering local Judean elites who could support the authority and administration of the Roman governor. Rome chose the Jewish high priests and their associates for this role, vesting the top levels of the Jerusalem priesthood (the high priest along with those called "chief priests" in many translations of the New Testament) with local political authority under the auspices of the governor. Elevating the priests and their well-placed associates (including many Sadducees and "elders" [πρεσβύτεροι]) in this way allowed the Romans to maintain a sense of cultural continuity in Judea, showing their acceptance of the Judeans' religious identity and allowing Jews to keep the Jerusalem temple central in their religious practice and cultural identity. Within a short time, these priests, their families, the Sadducees, and other associates increased in economic and social importance to the point where they constituted a genuine aristocracy, separated from the vast majority of the Judean population in terms of wealth and prestige.[24] Their historic connection to the temple and its ongoing cultic functions nevertheless kept them well-positioned and influential in the social, religious, and political consciousness of many sectors of Palestinian Jewish society during the time Jesus lived.

The political alliance between high-ranking Jews in Jerusalem and the Roman governor of Judea matters deeply for most of the New Testament trial scenes, those in which representatives of both groups appear. Despite their religious differences, the governor and the high priest share much common sociopolitical ground. Any governor who wanted to maintain order in Jerusalem and preserve his political career would do well to consider the high priest's interests in matters related to the maintenance of social stability and could expect loyalty in return. Those in the ancient world who heard about trials in Jerusalem would have been cognizant of this alliance. The judicial maneuvering we see in the New Testament's trial scenes emerges in part from the high priest's and governor's shared recognition of the need for political cooperation. As one interpreter notes, concerning Jesus' trial:

> Hence when the Jerusalem elite hands Jesus over to Pilate around the year 30 C.E. it would be incorrect to imagine that the scene is playing off "religious" personnel with limited interests and power against

political personnel, or Jews against Romans. These are inappropriate categories for a hierarchical system that essentially allied the small Roman and local Jerusalem elite against the rest of the population. This system does not have checks and balances, burdens of proof, and a sense of public accountability. Instead, there are aristocratic alliances, "legal privilege," and bias against those of lower status.[25]

One should therefore avoid the all-too-familiar practice of dividing the New Testament's trials too neatly between those involving "Roman concerns" and those involving "Jewish concerns." When provincial governors and high priests appear, more is at stake than matters of ethnicity and religion. In terms of class and power, and the impetus to preserve the prerogatives that come with them, these parties sometimes occupy similar or complementary territory.

At the same time, the situation was complex, and at least two points deserve nuance. First, the partnership between the priestly aristocracy in Roman Judea and the Roman powers was one of enforced cooperation, not equal standing. The Romans retained the power to install and dismiss the Jewish high priest. They even kept guard over the vestments the high priest wore for certain festivals and observances—no small reminder of where final authority resided.[26] Further, the high priest's judicial powers appear to have been limited so that they were essentially on par with those of village leaders charged with arbitrating simple disputes.[27] The Jewish aristocracy did not try defendants on Rome's behalf. The Jerusalem sanhedrin (from συνέδριον, meaning "council"), which figures prominently in the trials of Jesus and various apostles in Acts, had no formal judicial authority in Rome's eyes. The high priest could convene associates from the Jerusalem religious and social elite, who could advise him and help to legitimate and consolidate his political power among the Jewish population.[28]

Second, the partnership was often acrimonious. Although Roman political strategy elevated the status of these Jewish elites among the local population, evidence suggests that for the most part the Roman authorities throughout the first century persisted in regarding them with suspicion and perhaps disdain, never fully welcoming them into all the privileges that elite status could grant in wider Roman society.[29] As for the aristocracy, their willingness to collaborate with the Romans does not necessarily imply affinity with Rome. They were hardly pro-Roman in an ideological sense. Theirs was a partnership of political expediency and mutual benefit, one not without its tensions.

We will revisit these conditions when we investigate Jesus' trial in the Gospels and Paul's final trial in Acts 21–28, where high-ranking Jerusalem Jews' concerns over Jesus' and Paul's claims dominate the contests. Our interpretation of those scenes must attend to how the biblical narratives themselves assume and address the sociopolitical realities we have surveyed.

TRIALS, POWER, AND THE ROMAN EMPIRE

The discussion to this point has described the basic channels of authority that operated in the New Testament context, adding depth to our understanding of the political structures and assumptions that surround the trial scenes. This information shows that judicial events, those involving either the Roman provincial governors or the local elites whose interests and responsibilities intersected with theirs, were integral parts of the larger sociopolitical terrain. Probably the legal life of any society lies embedded within its dominant social and political values, at least to a degree. But this rapid overview of first-century Roman provincial society adds particularity to such a claim, revealing that the accounts of Jesus' trial and his followers' trials locate all their participants within a complicated set of relationships and priorities, all within a social structure designed to help officials exercise and fortify their power, for the stability of the empire and its identity. The trial scenes in the New Testament therefore inform us not only of the defendants' relationship to matters of law, deviance, and falsehood; these scenes also provide insights into the significance that the defendants' deeds, beliefs, and assertions pose for the maintenance of social well-being and the ongoing political health of the Roman Empire. The question of "guilt" extends beyond definitions of infractions and transgressions of specific legislation. It touches on questions of defendants' acceptability and who they will be in that society.

Every society has its networks of power that advocate values and influence its people's understanding of who they are and how they can or cannot express themselves. Scholars who study empires shed additional light on these dynamics by offering analyses of the ingrained means by which political and economic interests reinforce those who govern such societies.[30] For some who study the New Testament and the emergence of Christianity in the Roman world, theoretical models of agrarian societies dominated by an aristocracy comprising a small percentage of the total population have offered a general framework for mapping the social context.[31] More particularized scholarship—on specific matters such as Roman militarism, the emergence and importance of emperor worship, taxation policies, and Roman social orders—contends that the Roman Empire's dominance was experienced pervasively within the social contexts from which Christianity emerged and into which it grew. In many ways, the material presented in the previous section supports such an understanding.

Sociological models about empires are helpful insofar as they provide stark reminders of the social stratifications that preserved inequities in power and influence between the Roman imperial elite and the vast majority of the empire's population. The theoretical underpinnings of these models suggest that Rome went to great effort to display and preserve power by fostering an imperial identity—political, social, economic, and religious, all integrated— that pervaded the culture. At the same time, however, we cannot assume that these models equate extensive imperial sociopolitical dominance with absolute constraint of individuals. The inequities of power built into this society did not leave the lower classes entirely unable to influence their part of it or to exercise resistance. As sociologist Anthony Giddens contends, power relations—even those in which a preponderance of the power resides in one of the parties—always include a degree of reciprocity:

> We should not conceive of the structures of domination built into social institutions as in some way grinding out "docile bodies" who behave like the automata suggested by objectivist social science. . . . But all forms of dependence offer some resources whereby those who are subordinate can influence the activities of their superiors.[32]

This means that individuals and groups, depending upon the means of leverage at their disposal in a given context, can find ways to influence a social system, even if only slightly, merely by virtue of their being part of that system. Peasants can withhold crops. Workers can alter the pace of their efforts. Prisoners can resist or refuse to cooperate. Dissenters can speak. At the same time, if people can resist, they can also reinforce. Certainly both action and nonaction within a social system have power to confirm or contest a status quo.

Sometimes the influence of relatively powerless people—whether rendered powerless by their social class or their circumstances as accused or imprisoned persons—is subtle, or subtly communicated. This prompts us to look carefully for signs of influence and criticism at work among the narrative accounts of trials in the New Testament. Even as the trials, according to their place in a societal design that placed judicial authority in the hands of the sociopolitical elite, might manifest an overwhelmingly one-sided sense of sociopolitical control, they do not entirely exclude opportunities for defendants to be heard. In fact, by providing defendants unique access to powerful people, trials can actually provide additional resources that defendants might employ for leveraging a social system or advocating for alternative ways of construing it. With that unique social access, defendants possess the potential to exercise power in response to—or over against—the sociopolitical structure, either through dissent, noncooperation, creative manipulation, or appeals to a different social or religious logic. Even if the authorities conducting a trial cannot themselves detect a defendant's influence in these ways, readers of a trial narrative can.

Models and general proposals about the exercise and preservation of sociopolitical power set the stage for our study by directing us to certain social realities. However, they remain prefatory and approximate, for they ultimately cannot reveal the attitudes of individuals within those realities. We must recognize that attitudes toward the empire certainly varied from person to person, and they surely varied among the earliest readers of the Gospels and Acts. For example, although the cultural and religious divides between Rome and the Jewish people during the first century fueled continual tensions that occasionally flared up around different issues, certainly not every Judean Jew experienced all aspects of Roman rule as oppressive, especially prior to the onset of the Jewish-Roman War in 66 CE.[33] Christians' attitudes were probably similar, for it is not clear that Christians in that area at that time understood themselves as appreciably distinct from other Judean Jews of comparable social standing. Also, more widely throughout the empire, Christians later in the first century and into the early second century generally did not encounter sustained, systemic persecution from Rome.[34] Nevertheless, it appears that the Gospels' early audiences anticipated or were familiar with judicial contests and persecution from governing authorities (Mark 13:9–11; Matt. 10:17–20; 24:9; Luke 12:11–12; 21:12–15; cf. John 15:20; Rev. 2:10). Certainly differences of opinion toward Roman rule existed among Christians; perhaps some held to a range of opinions that expressed themselves across a continuum that included both acceptance and outright rejection.[35] When we consider that the writing of the Gospels and Acts postdates the war of 66–70 while these books narrate events set in the years 30–60, the potential for encountering ambiguous attitudes toward Roman power in their narratives increases all the more.

These qualifications relate to our study because they allow us to recognize that some ancient readers could have been encouraged or emboldened when trial scenes criticize aspects of the first-century sociopolitical system, while other readers could have been shocked and challenged by the same criticisms. This does not deny the suggestion that the trial scenes offered potent resources for early Christian readers trying to make theological sense of their efforts to negotiate this sociopolitical terrain in their own lives. These scenes describe their world and help them see their place and the gospel's place in it. The purpose of this study is not to treat ambiguity and ambivalence around these issues as problems to be solved or subtleties to be aggrandized. Rather, it is to explain, appreciate, and reflect further on these things, where we find them, in the New Testament's trial scenes.

TRIALS IN GRECO-ROMAN LITERATURE

Our attention turns next to the functions of trial scenes in ancient literature. How might stories of trials contribute to the narratives in which they are situated? What ideas might they signify? What experiences might they generate among their audiences?

Tales of courtroom drama appear in literature throughout the ages, revealing their capacity for exciting readers and prompting reflection on justice, social values, rhetoric, and meaning. Whether we are talking about the trial of Antigone in Sophocles' fifth-century BCE drama of the same name or the trial of Tom Robinson in Harper Lee's 1960 novel, *To Kill a Mockingbird*, stories of sympathetic figures facing legal jeopardy can "heighten critical awareness of the legal system as a whole" and often function "as vehicles for discussions of larger social issues rather than rehashings of judicial procedure."[36] Ancient historians and rhetors recognized the importance of courtroom events for promoting, criticizing, and testing social values, as seen in the writings of Cicero, Livy, Plato, Tacitus, and many others. In some parts of the ancient world, forensic venues were viewed as arenas for social struggle and self-definition as members of distinguished social strata used courts and judicial rhetoric to negotiate their relationship to their wider society.[37]

Even without speculating on precisely which literary works or genres might have been familiar to the writers and earliest readers of the New Testament narratives, we may still reasonably assume that literature from that period permits us to glimpse assumptions that those people might have held about trials and judicial conflict. If literature contributes to the cultural undercurrents that inform people's understanding of themselves and their social networks, then the perspectives of other ancient writings influence our understanding of the rhetorical potential of the biblical texts. Other ancient narratives relied on trial scenes to make their points, to stage contests over ideas, and to explore questions of self-definition. By noting how they accomplish these tasks, we can arrive at a clearer sense of what ancient readers might have expected from or associated with accounts of legal showdowns. We will also be better able to identify similar dynamics operating in the New Testament's trial narratives.

Greek Novels

Our exploration of the ancient literary milieu, which must remain a representative rather than an exhaustive undertaking, begins with fiction.[38] To compare New Testament narratives with ancient novels need not commit us to assigning all these works to the same literary genre. Rather, fictional accounts prove quite informative for one of the main purposes of our study: to understand how the trial scenes in the Gospels and Acts contribute to these books as meaningful narratives, to understand these scenes' significance within the whole of their wider stories.

Of the unknown number of novels written in Greek during or very near the first three centuries CE, complete versions of five remain extant: Chariton's *Chaereas and Callirhoe*, Xenophon of Ephesus's *An Ephesian Tale*, Longus's *Daphnis and Chloe*, Achilles Tatius's *Leucippe and Clitophon*, and Heliodorus's *An Ethiopian Tale*. These books contain a total of thirteen trial scenes, each one distinctive but all sharing a common structure.[39] These trials, taken together, suggest the existence of a conventional, recognizable type-scene: a literary form in which scenes adhere to and maneuver around fixed, conventional patterns.[40] In an analysis of these scenes, classicist Saundra Schwartz recites many of their familiar elements: "Weeping defendants, vengeful accusers, overblown speeches, and cheering mobs clutter the novelistic courtroom. The fickleness of the jury, the clemency (or antagonism) of the judge, the last-minute introduction of crucial evidence, the injustice of false accusation, the pain of imprisonment and torture: all are aspects of the trial scene in the Greek novels."[41] Almost all of these same details or some variations on them appear in the trial scenes in the New Testament, further beckoning us to consider literary resonances between those scenes and the trials in the novels.

With the possible exception of Chariton's novel, the five almost certainly postdate the New Testament writings. The differences they exhibit in details of genre, provenance, and dating further militate against any suggestion that the New Testament narratives and Greek novels exhibit dependence on each other or share so much in common that we should overlook their differences. When it comes to the trial scenes in these novels, we find a notable difference in the nature of charges brought against defendants. Heroes in the novels defend themselves and others against accusations of sensationalistic crimes such as adultery, abduction, and murder. While those crimes matter deeply for questions of public order and security, they remain different from what appears in the Gospels and Acts: accusations of blasphemy, apostasy, disturbing the peace, and sedition, offenses that threaten to dismantle social stability in distinctive ways. Trials prompted by all these issues pose deeply detrimental consequences for defendants' positions in society, but the issues remain slightly different between the novels and the biblical writings.

Another difference lies in the dramatic focus of the trials. For the most part, the novels reflect an interest in entertainment through the occasional pageantry and dramatic tension that come out in spectacular details and romantic plots revolving around separated lovers who must endure all sorts of adventures and battle seemingly insurmountable obstacles before they can be reunited. The Gospels and Acts, although they include their share of entertaining elements, focus on quite different kinds of drama and use their drama to promote different ends. Trial scenes in the novels function as romantic spectacles; trials in the New Testament are theological spectacles. In them, central theological claims—claims about God, the authority of God's representatives, and the message they bear—are put on display for official review, provoking the question of whether God will be rejected or thwarted by the officials' judgments.[42]

The novels nevertheless help identify the ways in which contemporaries of the New Testament writings may have understood a trial's ability to frame specific conflicts and present the verdicts on those conflicts for an audience's scrutiny and entertainment. We might begin with the question: What makes a trial so special? How are these kinds of scenes especially effective in making a narrative meaningful? Schwartz's investigation of trials in the Greek novels asks similar questions, stimulated for her by a climactic scene in Heliodorus's novel. There the story's heroine, Charicleia, proves before the Ethiopian king, Hydaspes, her lost but true identity as his very own daughter and thereby at the last minute saves herself from being made a human sacrifice. Any novelists worth their salt would surely stage such a monumental point in the plot as a moment of high drama, and Heliodorus does not disappoint. Yet strikingly, Heliodorus has this revelation of mistaken identity come out through a trial scene. Charicleia demands to be heard in a formal "lawsuit and trial" (δίκη καὶ κρίσις) before the Ethiopian Gymnosophists who have the authority to hear cases (H 10.10.1). In the course of the trial, she presents arguments that demonstrate her true identity. Schwartz inquires, then, why a novelist possessing complete freedom over the construction of a story might have seen it as appropriate or effective to set such a scene specifically as a trial.[43] What can trials do for a narrative?

At a basic level, trials provide and intensify melodrama. Courtrooms serve as appropriate venues for unveiling truth and for putting matters that pertain to social well-being to the test. Moreover, trial scenes include a participatory element, for they draw readers in as courtroom observers who also await an outcome or verdict, nearly urging readers to react to claims made in the trials and their outcomes. The novels exploit this potential for experiential drama by avoiding the technicalities of legal detail, preferring instead to compress the courtroom contests into descriptions of courtroom rhetoric while keeping the final verdict in doubt as long as possible, heightening the moment of decision that legal deliberations promise. "Legal realia function as a backdrop to the moment when something extraordinary will be exhibited for all to see. The reader is expected to share the same reactions as the trial's fictional spectators: . . . to gaze with pity, wonder, astonishment, and delight."[44] The ability to elicit such reactions takes precedence over legal verisimilitude or attention to forensic procedures. Not only the courtroom setting makes for an engaging trial scene; so too does a skillful use of courtroom rhetoric, intrigue, and even indeterminate verdicts or delayed judgments. These same features appear also in the New Testament's trial scenes. Although they accomplish it in different ways, around different topics, and toward different ends, the trials in the Greek novels and the New Testament all make their readers watch, hope, and wait.

A deeper look at the Greek novels helps us see that trial scenes manage drama through their techniques of staging legal conflict. Trial type-scenes do not limit themselves to a single function; they can perform a number of duties in a narrative. In the novels, trials provide readers with multiple layers of exposure to accusations, contested ideas, and judgments. Trials reveal, often subtly and artfully, much about the characters involved in them and the significance that the alleged crimes have for questions of justice and the integrity of a social system. To illustrate how they do this, we will build from three of Schwartz's observations, taking them as starting points for considering the potential narrative functions of trials. This will provide guideposts that prove instructive for our exploration of the New Testament's trial scenes in the chapters that follow.

A first observation is that trials in the Greek novels do not usually conclude in easy, decisive resolutions. Schwartz notes that circumstances frequently stymie the judicial processes or, through the introduction of new evidence or insoluble dilemmas, stretch them so as to extend the conflicts as long as possible.[45] Sometimes supernatural forces cause the complications by disrupting the proceedings or altering the outcomes, such as when the unjustly condemned hero in *An Ephesian Tale*, Habrocomes, hangs on a cross overlooking the Nile and prays to the god of Egypt for vindication. In response a strong wind blows him into the river, and he survives despite the dangers of the fall, the water, the ropes that had bound him, and wild animals (4.2.4–6).[46] Through the ordeal, divine and natural forces attest his blamelessness. In effect, Habrocomes' deliverance restarts his trial because the authorities seize him again, assuming that he has escaped his execution, and so he must ask for divine intervention to save him once more, next from being burned alive. At last, the ruling prefect interprets all these developments as evidence of Habrocomes' innocence (XE 4.2.7–10). The god's testimony on his behalf is apparent only to those with insight, and it demands that Habrocomes' trial remain unresolved until justice can be done.

Schwartz sees delays and subversions of efficient, expected legal processes as serving two literary functions: first, a simple intensification of dramatic suspense; second, an opportunity for a narrative to draw attention to opposing arguments concerning the value of a specific issue or what would be truly just. Both functions matter for our study, but the second is the more important, and is achieved more subtly. Trials certainly heighten narrative suspense, but so do many other kinds of scenes and plot twists. The format of a trial creates occasions particularly suitable for storytellers to pit contested ideas against each other and allow audiences to consider multiple dimensions of the contest while rewards or punishments hang in the balance. In addition, the ideas or commitments that reside at the heart of a trial's conflict often hover over the proceedings. Since, as Schwartz rightly claims, "the formula of the trial scene is ideally suited to the illumination of opposing social values," trial scenes in the novels involve issues that "were important to the novelists and their reading public."[47] In the novels, these issues typically center around sexual morality and its relevance for the maintenance of social stability. In their own vein, the New Testament trial scenes allow readers to consider contrasting arguments about theological issues—not abstracted, disembodied theological principles but theological claims declared and disputed within a particular social context, assessed in light of the effects they might have on that system, by the people who wield authority over the system.

Many trials in the New Testament resist quick and decisive resolution because the issues under deliberation are not easily resolved, because conflicting political pressures stall the deliberations, or because God intervenes in implied or explicit ways. The Greek novels help us see that these developments maximize dramatic suspense and underscore the sociopolitical import of the claims at the heart of the trial. The verdicts that the trials produce about the fates of the defendants stem only in part from defendants' deeds or an assessment of their "guilt." The trials also issue judgments about people's claims to represent or obey God. The trials provide insight into how other characters—powerful characters representing certain prerogatives—understand the Christian message to matter for society. The deliberations among human beings and occasional statements from God recognize the gospel's potential to influence the wider culture, its values, and its structures.

Second, trial scenes provide felicitous environments for dramatic irony, easily lending themselves to situations in which characters lack information known to other characters or readers. Such irony almost has to exist when a narrative supplies readers with the truth about accused people and their alleged crimes or identities before it presents a trial, which is the case in the Greek novels and the New Testament. But trial scenes can employ dramatic irony to great effect by allowing that irony to persist and even to leverage a trial's outcome, such as when characters prove themselves unable to grasp information that readers see clearly, or when they remain blind to the fact that the truth is the complete opposite of what they think it is. For example, returning to the story of Habrocomes in *An Ephesian Tale*, the authorities interpret his postcrucifixion emergence from the river as an escape attempt, compounding their assessment of him as a lawbreaker. The irony lies in their not knowing what readers have been shown, that he was miraculously delivered from his crucifixion in response to his prayer. The authorities who for a time remain unaware of Habrocomes' acquittal by miracle appear at risk of becoming tragic figures in their ignorance of the truth.

Dramatic irony has powerful effects. True, it can fuel suspense, and in a trial scene it may intensify "the pathos of the wrongly accused defendant" and make the eventual vindication all the more exciting.[48] But irony's payoff extends beyond a reader's quickened pulse, especially when the scene is a hostile courtroom. Irony provides commentary. This comes out in trial narratives because judicial decisions normally depend upon a clear accounting of pertinent facts and a reasonably informed basis of judgment. When authoritative figures prove themselves ignorant of or resistant to what other courtroom participants and eavesdroppers know, they do more than contribute to a tense or pitiable mood. They call into question their own authority or credentials to judge the matter at hand. Irony thus criticizes their capacity to discern and therefore denigrates their qualifications to regulate social well-being and offer judgments on truth or justice. In the case of Habrocomes, the Egyptian authorities show themselves to be ignorant of both justice and the will of their god, thereby calling judgment upon themselves.

When it comes to the New Testament's trial scenes, which also make heavy use of dramatic irony, the irony delivers theological statements. For one thing, when the trials ironically affirm truths about the identity or teachings of Jesus and his followers, they characterize the nature of those truths as contested. When irony serves as the vehicle for providing such a characterization, it lends those truths an aspect of alterity, presenting them to readers not merely as truths disputed by other people but especially as truths somehow displaced from them. A character's ironic inability to recognize the theological claims affirmed by a narrative implies that character's inability to comprehend the ways of God in the world. "Biblical ironists," including those authors who depict truth as veiled, misunderstood, and multifaceted in their narrative techniques and use of trial scenes, "dramatize what is at stake in encountering the word of God, offering an alluring invitation to insiders and enacting a polemics against those who do not understand, those who are not positioned rightly."[49] We will see this time and again in the New Testament's trials.

Third, trial scenes direct readers' attention outward, away from the boundaries of the scene. Although trials are crucibles for contesting truth and values, these scenes also invite readers to experience such contests distinctly in relation to the rest of a narrative. They prompt readers to examine how or where else a story addresses questions of a defendant's guilt or innocence. In her analysis of ancient novels, Schwartz maintains: "It is necessary to distinguish between the verdict and the end. The verdict is the vote which occurs subsequent to the speeches in the trial. The end, on the other hand, is what ultimately happens to the characters in the framework of the larger narrative."[50] For Schwartz, this means inquiring into how novelists might have understood the general, theoretical relationships between judicial processes and society's ability to pursue justice. From Heliodorus's *An Ethiopian Tale*, the Athenian trials of Cnemon and his father Aristippus give an example. As a result of these two trials, full of twists and turns, both men find themselves wrongly convicted and exiled on account of other characters' machinations. The trials are occasions of injustice that the narrative later rectifies when poetic justice, manifested in acts of revenge and high adventure, overcomes the plotters and their accomplices. Cnemon's story concludes with him free to return to Athens, where he can seek a pardon for his father.[51] What the trials do to these two men, events later in the story undo, thereby holding the trials and their decisions up for scrutiny throughout the plot.

Relating a trial's verdict and a story's "end" is also crucial for interpreting the New Testament's trial narratives, for these scenes come to us and make sense as means of hearing and understanding a broader story. As subsequent chapters will demonstrate, the trial scenes mean more as components of larger narratives than they do alone, for each depends on the rest of a story to make it significant, and its significance extends backward and forward into the wider plot. The whole story comments on a trial—its causes, its issues, its outcomes—and the trial scene comments on the story. For example, Jesus' crucifixion as "king of the Jews," recalling language distinctive to the charges against him in his trial scenes, connects his trial to his execution. The end of the story, his resurrection, forces readers to move backward and consider what that event says about his condemnation and the meaning of his trial. The resurrection does not merely negate the trial; it also answers back to it, reopening it and reconfiguring its outcome to call for a new judgment.

Other Literature

Greek novels are valuable to consider in some detail because their use of courtroom drama demonstrates that trial type-scenes can be flexible, appearing in a variety of forms and well-suited for effecting a variety of literary functions. Trials in other literature express additional ideas, such as implicit and explicit criticism of judicial and political power. The trial scenes in the five Greek novels do not make this move; when injustices manifest themselves in those trials, the narrative typically blames individual characters and not the legal system or the government behind it.[52] Other ancient literature, however, makes effective use of trials' ability to frame contests over power by using a forensic environment to lodge criticisms that comment on how power is properly exercised, who really wields power, and who subverts justice.

The short story of Susanna, which probably originated during or near the second century BCE and eventually circulated in multiple Greek manuscripts of the book of Daniel, offers an example of a trial scene that dramatically unmasks those who abuse power and defy God. Two Jewish elders responsible for judging legal matters try to force Susanna into having sex with them, threatening to accuse her of adultery if she refuses. Choosing not to sin against God, she resists the men, is brought to trial before all the elders, and is condemned to death on the basis of her two antagonists' false testimony. After the sentencing, she calls out to God, who hears and inspires the bystander Daniel to criticize the hasty trial and expose the two elders' lies, leading to their conviction and death.

When Susanna prays to God, a number of roles in the forensic drama suddenly shift: Daniel becomes prosecutor, and the two elders transition from accusers to defendants. Susanna herself appears as a person virtually powerless before a court, yet one who nevertheless survives an unjust legal process because of her righteousness and God's commitment to vindicating her. Despite her relative powerlessness, Susanna exhibits a moral strength that exposes and upends the powerful people who try to control a legal proceeding to serve their own corrupt interests.[53] The trial scene concentrates and heightens the critique of those who prove themselves disobedient to God through their misuse of power (Sus. 5, 52–53, 57) even as the trial itself becomes the means for exposing and punishing that disobedience. The theological recognition of the story is much like the outcome of legal difficulties Daniel faces in stories involving Kings Nebuchadnezzar and Darius (Dan. 3, 6): all those assembled "blessed the God who saves those who hope in him" (Sus. 60).[54] The trial of Susanna thereby also issues a judgment concerning God's character, affirming God's commitment to justice and to vindicating the righteous. The book of Susanna assumes that readers will be positively disposed toward the story's protagonists and positive ending. This likely lends a reassuring effect to its theological dimensions: the story's criticisms of power aim just as much at confirming God's faithfulness in the face of a corrupt system as they do at denouncing that system.

Trials serve as venues for the critique of power also in the writings known as the *Acts of the Pagan Martyrs*.[55] This is a collection of manuscripts that likely originated as protocols or official minutes of legal appeals and defenses delivered by actual members of the Greek community in Alexandria before the courts of Roman emperors during the first and second centuries CE. The manuscripts' authors reworked the judicial records to support the cause of these Greeks, who in the hearings protest the oppression they experience by lashing out against Roman authority and sometimes against the Jewish community in Alexandria. The texts include pointed exchanges, hostile caricatures of Roman officials, strong emotional responses from assembled crowds, and the Greeks' bold contempt for death and punishment. The writings are propagandistic, crafted by people interested in preserving memories of their heroes' sufferings and assigning blame for that suffering to imperial policies.[56] Almost certainly no direct historical or literary connections exist between the *Acts of the Pagan Martyrs* and the New Testament writings. The point of introducing these documents is to observe that they reflect a persecuted group's attempt to engage in polemic by using literary accounts of trials as a mode of resistance. Given the sheer fact that trials usually place powerful people in the same room with defendants and those defendants' claims, trials by their nature demand that defendants at least be acknowledged and heard. This dynamic allows, at least in the eyes of readers sympathetic to the defendants' causes, opportunity for those claims to be legitimated, even if that legitimation in their eyes must come from a hostile judge and from heroes' martyrdom. In such a trial, the defendants' bold persistence demonstrates their commitment to what they say and denies that judgments against them possess inherent validity. By giving voice to the defendants' protestations, these writings perpetuate a witness against the official verdicts of their trials and against the authority that rendered those verdicts.

Other currents in Greco-Roman literature suggest that trials furnish occasions to reflect on justice and how it may be exercised or perverted when defendants face the judgment of societies and their guardians. The trial of Socrates before the Athenian jurors, remembered most notably in his defense speech offered by Plato in the *Apology*, generated a tremendous legacy in its ability to express sociopolitical and ideological critique by stoking pathos for an unjustly condemned defendant. Later Greek and Latin authors viewed other popular teachers who were overwhelmed by Roman power and legal processes against the backdrop of Socrates' trial and execution.[57] By juxtaposing the irresistible power of Rome against the wisdom, self-control, and virtues of ostensibly overwhelmed defendants, judicial settings and themes could voice resistance, rebuke, and vindication.

CONCLUSIONS

The information presented in this chapter alerts us to the kinds of theatrical and agonistic dynamics we might find at work in the New Testament's trial scenes. These passages contribute to the Gospels and Acts more than profiles in judicial courage or narrative protestations of protagonists' innocence. We need to attend to more than the words spoken in each trial and listen carefully to what these scenes communicate as literary and social dramas. This chapter, then, goes beyond providing background material that supplements our study of the trial scenes. It also points our focus forward to be open to what these scenes might be capable of addressing, to consider how they might communicate. Based on our investigation into the ancient sociopolitical and literary milieux, the dynamics we can expect to find through a careful examination of a trial scene's narrative and political dimensions include the following:

- *The legal authority and sociopolitical priorities of provincial governors.* Governors represented imperial interests by preserving Roman values concerning sociopolitical well-being. They provided the last word on legal matters in the provinces and were empowered to dispatch their legal responsibilities largely at their own discretion.
- *The relationship between Roman imperial authority and the high priests of Jerusalem.* Although the relationship between the two parties was often deeply strained, the Jewish aristocracy in Jerusalem and the Roman provincial authorities needed one another to survive. Their political interests frequently intersected.
- *The capacity for trials to intensify drama and set opposing values against each other.* By nature, trials are contests over power and ideas. Practices and deliberations in a judicial context reflect a society's values even as they work to preserve or alter those values.
- *The presence of dramatic irony and ironic relationships in literary depictions of trials.* When characters do not share the same access to the truth or when a narrative depicts a transformation of the roles people play in a forensic drama, a trial scene can offer commentary on the topics being deliberated and the people deliberating them.
- *The relationship between the assertions made during a trial scene and the claims of a wider narrative.* Because trial scenes sit within a larger story, they lead readers to consider how developments elsewhere in a plot might confirm or question the judgments issued in a trial.
- *The capacity for trials to criticize or minimize the power of recognized authorities.* Because trials require an authoritative voice to issue a judgment, a voice that represents or shapes a wider culture, a trial's means of criticizing or calling into question that authority can extend more broadly. Trials provide venues for sociopolitical commentary. This commentary and readers' responses to it depend upon the narrative's and the readers' dispositions toward the issues and characters involved in a trial scene.

3

Jesus on Trial in the Gospel according to Mark

The accounts of Jesus' trial in the Synoptic Gospels are some of the most variable scenes among all the material that these three books share in common: Mark, Matthew, and Luke present the story with significant variation in its details. This variation urges us to consider each narrative on its own, comparing and contrasting the three as we proceed.

Interpreters regularly note the Markan trial's importance for this Gospel's understanding of Christology and discipleship. The trial employs theological themes that reach across the entire narrative and provides the singular moment in which Jesus unabashedly declares himself to be the Christ, the Son of God.[1] Through its focus on the trial scenes' contributions to Mark's narrative whole, our investigation will assume and confirm this theological significance. Furthermore, we will see that Mark's trial scenes, by setting the topic of Jesus' messianic identity specifically in relation to issues of power, invite us to consider the sociopolitical dimensions of Jesus' authority and the gospel he proclaims.

OVERVIEW OF THE TRIAL SCENES

Jesus' trial in Mark consists of at least two distinct proceedings that result in his being taken away to his execution. The first (14:53–65) occurs at night, immediately after a crowd dispatched by the Jewish aristocracy in Jerusalem arrests him at Gethsemane. The narrative reveals neither the size nor the exact makeup of this posse; they are probably security personnel or loyal servants. At least one of them is the high priest's slave. They deliver Jesus to their superiors—the high priest, chief priests, elders, and scribes—who assemble to

33

gather testimony against him.[2] Simultaneously, Peter denies any association with Jesus (14:66–72). Peter's interrogation and testimony, narrated immediately following Jesus' first proceeding, provides a foil, for Peter preserves himself by denying Jesus, precisely as Jesus condemns himself by affirming his identity.[3] These verses underscore the fact that no one in or around the trial defends Jesus or tries to thwart his downfall. The second trial scene (15:1b–15) occurs after morning has dawned, when members of the Jewish leadership convey Jesus to the Roman provincial governor, who interrogates him and considers his fate while dialoguing with a crowd.

Mark presents the first scene, Jesus before the Jerusalem council, as a travesty of justice, virtually a show trial meant to justify a predetermined verdict (v. 55a).[4] Many people deliver untrue and inconsistent testimonies, including variations on the technically false yet ironic assertion that Jesus pledged to destroy the temple and build another in three days. The high priest then questions Jesus directly, demanding that he make sense of the accusations against him. When Jesus remains speechless, the high priest asks, "Are you the Christ, the Son of the Blessed One?" Jesus replies, "I am, and you will see the Son of Man sitting at the right hand of the Power and coming with the clouds of heaven." The high priest immediately interprets this as blasphemy, tearing his own clothing in response to the offense, and everyone on the council agrees, condemning Jesus and calling for his death. The scene concludes with Jesus spat upon, blindfolded, and beaten.

After the first proceeding and the account of Peter's denial, Mark mentions that the chief priests, elders, scribes, and "whole council" caucus together early in the morning (15:1a). The narrative offers no additional details, declining to divulge what they discuss or whether Jesus is even present. The ambiguous expression συμβούλιον ποιήσαντες in 15:1a hardly indicates a formal hearing. Since the previous night's proceeding concluded with "all" the members of the gathered council condemning Jesus, it is unlikely that the morning meeting includes any kind of juridical activity, such as interrogation of the accused, testimony of witnesses, or rendering of a sentence. This short statement provides a literary connector, transitioning from night to day and making clear that those who actively conspired against Jesus and condemned him are the same ones who also "give him over" (παραδίδωμι) to Pilate, just as Jesus previously declared that these officials would deliver him to Gentile authority (10:33). The briefly narrated events of 15:1a suggest something like an ad hoc strategy session, allowing the rushed authorities to determine how to succeed when they bring Jesus to Pilate.

Jesus' appearance before the governor begins with Pilate asking him if he is "the king of the Jews." Jesus' supposed kingship is obviously the imperial representative's chief concern and something he will repeatedly use as a sarcastic barb to antagonize Jesus and the other Jews who are present. Jesus answers Pilate enigmatically, "So *you* say" (σὺ λέγεις). When the chief priests hurl more accusations, Jesus remains silent. Pilate asks an assembled crowd whether they want him to release Jesus in accordance with his custom of freeing a prisoner at Passover. The chief priests rouse the crowd, which calls for the release of a prisoner named Barabbas and the crucifixion of Jesus. Commenting on Pilate's desire to satisfy the crowd, the scene concludes with Pilate sending Jesus to crucifixion.

THE TRIAL WITHIN A WIDER PLOT

Persistent conflict with Jewish authorities gives rise to Jesus' trial. Throughout the narrative Mark directs attention to this conflict. Groups of Jewish adversaries begin plotting against Jesus as early as 3:6, but it is members of the Jerusalem priestly elite who finally seize and prosecute him after he arrives in the city and teaches incendiary things in and about the temple.[5] Jesus' criticism of the temple operations in 11:17 prompts the chief priests and scribes to plot against him because they recognize the seriousness of the prophetic accusation he levels against them as the temple's managers, using an expression from Jeremiah 7:11, "*You* have made it [the temple, God's house] a 'den of robbers.'"[6] A subsequent parable reiterates Jesus' rebuke of the aristocracy that desires to eliminate him (12:1–12). Jesus' criticisms of the temple and its leadership are intertwined, as are the Jerusalem aristocracy's political and religious interests.

Jesus' perspective on the temple and its functions touches the core of the conflict between him and the Jerusalem priestly aristocracy. The temple represents many things, corresponding to the varied political interests and religious values the high priest and his associates surely aim to protect when Jesus arrives in Jerusalem. It represents particular understandings of God and obedience to the Torah, as well as a vision of Israel's divinely granted exceptionalism. It also represents the cultural and religious foundations of the Jewish aristocracy's sociopolitical power, foundations that provide a cultural continuity upon which Rome capitalized by granting limited authority to that aristocracy. By rebuking the temple operations and prophesying its destruction, Jesus criticizes elements of dominant streams in Palestinian Judaism.[7] However, combating the threats he represents proves a delicate matter for the aristocracy that feels the sting of his criticisms, given his popularity and the political volatility that accompanies Passover celebrations (see 14:1–2).

Yet Mark indicates that this conflict in Jerusalem serves only as the trial's trigger point. Other scenes set the stage for the trial, priming readers' expectations for it and their understanding of its causes. Although Jesus never talks about his *trial* in particular, before reaching Jerusalem he repeatedly fore-tells his arrest, sufferings, death, and resurrection (8:31; 9:31; 10:32b–34).[8] Through this, and through Jesus' determined refusal to quit the activities that attract opposition (his qualified preference to avoid the "cup" of suffering, articulated in 14:36, notwithstanding), Mark preconditions readers to regard Jesus' passion, including the trial that sets it in motion, as certain to happen. The narrative depicts at least two sides of this certainty: it is *inevitable* (the expected consequence for someone who teaches and lives as Jesus does, as the proclaimer of God's reign), and it is *required* (the purposeful end for the Son of God, somehow part of a meaningful plan).[9] Both the inevitable and requi-site dimensions of Jesus' demise create a subtext for his trial.

First, how does Mark's narrative situate Jesus' passion as the inevitable outcome of his public ministry? The nature of his ministry easily provokes serious concern and opposition. The Gospel's frequent references to Jesus' authority describe a high-stakes contest between him and some of his Jewish contemporaries. It begins with the first detailed scene of Jesus' public minis-try, which contrasts his authority with the formally credentialed scribes' lack of it (1:21–28), and persists through his activity in Jerusalem, which keeps attention on the scandal that his claims to authority as a preacher, healer, exorcist, and interpreter cause for many among the most powerful Jews in Jerusalem (11:12–12:44).[10] Recognized religious leaders interpret Jesus' deeds and statements as blasphemous (2:1–12; 3:22–30); they attribute the source of his authority to satanic power and fail to recognize God's rule being enacted through Jesus' ministry. Jesus, for his part, expresses little interest in establishing rapprochement with these people.[11] The ongoing controversies over the source of Jesus' authority keep the question of his identity (Who is he?) subordinate to the question of his authorization (Who has authorized or empowered him to teach and heal effectively?).[12] Assertions and suggestions that Jesus operates as God's appointed agent deeply offend and criticize his opponents, who come across as unable to see how he and his teachings can possibly align with their deeply held theological convictions.

Questions about the source of Jesus' authority connect to Mark's dra-matic depiction of Jesus engaged in a struggle between opposing kingdoms (see 3:22–30). No wonder the gospel Jesus proclaims attracts opposition from those whose abuse of power it criticizes and whose values it assails.[13] The account of John the Baptizer's execution (6:17–29) suggests that those who hold power will not leave unpunished those who level prophetic chal-lenges against them. In this macabre morality drama, Herod Antipas comes across as irresponsible with power and recklessly ignorant of the depths of his wife's animosity toward John. Later, in 9:11–13, Jesus elliptically recalls John's death. He claims that Elijah "has come" in John, the one preparing the

Christ's way, yet "they did to him all that they wanted." The identity of this "they" is unspecific, since the immediate context mentions scribes, yet the reference to John's death points to Herod and his household. The ambiguous, impersonalized "they" therefore has Jesus speak in generalities, folding John's tragic end into the larger tradition (of which the prophet Elijah is a part) of God's representatives' meeting active opposition from those who wield socio-political authority for self-preservation. Herod and his household thus function as types, brief illustrations of what happens when God's representatives, such as John, encounter human authorities who either are bent on destroying them (as Herodias in 6:19) or show no compunction in sacrificing justice to save face and protect themselves (as Herod in 6:26).[14]

Furthermore, at a crucial point in Mark where Jesus interprets his death, he describes his own example as antithetical to the tactics that Gentile authorities value for coercing and controlling others to maintain their dominance and prerogatives (10:42–45).[15] They specialize in overpowering (κατακυριεύω) and tyrannizing (κατεξουσιάζω) others, descriptions of power that Jesus' adversaries will starkly exemplify during his trial. His parable about murderous tenants in a vineyard (12:1–12) portrays the chief priests, scribes, and elders in Jerusalem (11:27) as greedy, willing to use violence to protect their privileges, and by their ignorance actually disdainful toward God. When readers arrive at Mark's trial scenes, then, they recognize that the narrative has suggested no possibility of an easy, peaceful resolution to conflict. In the trial, Jesus and his claims face opposition that a ministry like his inevitably provokes from powerful figures unwilling to yield established assumptions. An important aspect of the trial scenes is their ability to address the nature of that opposition, for the trial provides venues that showcase it, venues in which the opposition's authority enjoys virtually free rein to act as it will.

Second, how does Mark situate Jesus' passion as the required outcome of his ministry? Mark suggests that God has a role in initiating Jesus' passion, infusing the drama with a sense of necessity in that Jesus' fate somehow results from divine intentions; yet this Gospel shows no interest in delineating God's specific purpose. Readers search the narrative in vain to discover the precise nature, motive, and function of God's involvement in human affairs. Mark describes the causes of Jesus' death in an almost paradoxical manner; people and God both play their parts.[16] But facile notions of divine "causality" do not apply, because Mark never goes as far as saying that God ordains all the decisions and details that result in Jesus' death, only that Jesus enters his final hours of life as one willing to experience what God *desires* for him (14:36). He goes into those hours delivered (or left) by God. Mark characterizes God as willingly allowing humanity to do as it wishes with Jesus. Although Jesus speaks knowingly and accurately about his fate (14:8, 17–31, 41–42), and his crucifixion unfolds with resonances to biblical texts (including Pss. 22:1, 7, 18; 69:21; Amos 8:9; see also Mark 14:49b), the narrative places primary emphasis on the claim that God initiates these events by delivering Jesus into the machinations of human power.

Mark signals this deliverance through two key terms that describe Jesus' being handed over and experiencing abandonment. The first is Mark's preferred term for describing Jesus' transfers through many people's control on his way from arrest to the cross, παραδίδωμι, which means to give over. Depending on the wider context, the specific "giving over" could be an arrest, betrayal, or surrender. Familiar in the legal literature of the wider Greek-speaking world, the word saturates the story of Jesus' passion, serving itself as a concise, one-word summary of all that happens from arrest to death. It describes Judas's betrayal, delivering Jesus into custody of the Jerusalem authorities (3:19; 14:10, 11, 18, 21, 41, 42, 44). It indicates these authorities' sending him in bonds to Pilate (15:1, 10). It is Pilate's final action, dispatching Jesus to the soldiers who execute him (15:15). But, before all these moments of "giving over" transpire, Jesus predicts in 9:31 that he will be given over to the power of people, placed into their "hands." With this statement he announces that God sets the passion in motion by relinquishing Jesus to the authority and will of his society.

The syntax of 9:31 ("The Son of Man is to be given over into people's hands") provides only subtle hints that God initiates the "giving over."[17] The passive voice of παραδίδοται (see also 10:33) may communicate divine agency, but a passive verb hardly makes that case by itself.[18] A stronger piece of evidence from 9:31 is the mention of *people's* hands (χεῖρας ἀνθρώπων), which could indicate through contrast that a nonhuman will deliver Jesus over to human authority.[19] There are several other instances where Mark places ἄνθρωποι (as humanity in a collective sense) as explicitly or implicitly opposite to God (7:7, 8, 21; 8:33; 10:27; 11:30), suggesting a similar contrast also at work in 9:31.

The most convincing reason for concluding that God initially hands Jesus over to the will of human beings comes from considering 9:31 in light of Jesus' final words in Mark, which include our second key term. As he dies on the cross, in anguish Jesus cites the beginning of Psalm 22 (Ps 21:2 LXX), "My God, my God, why have you forsaken me?" (15:34). With these words he bemoans the fact that God has abandoned (ἐγκαταλείπω) him. The lament betrays more than Jesus merely *experiencing* a sense of desolation or isolation at death. It serves as his theological interpretation of all that has taken place since his arrest, all that has befallen him since the point at which Jesus is relinquished into "sinners' hands" (14:41).[20] Between Gethsemane and death, it is the only thing he says that directly comments (cf. 14:49) on God's connections to his current circumstances, and it laments God's absence from the entire situation.[21] The words ἐγκαταλείπω in 15:34 and παραδίδωμι in 9:31 connect to each other through their complementary semantics of withdrawal and relinquishment. The two verbs appear paired in other writings in ways indicating that abandoning (ἐγκαταλείπω) expresses itself or results in acts of giving over (παραδίδωμι).[22] Jesus' cry of dereliction from the cross therefore recapitulates his statement in 9:31: God gives him over to be vulnerable to the hands of mortals, and Jesus experiences this as God's abandonment. God surrenders Jesus to the designs of others, not merely through some existential and wrenching divine absence from Golgotha, but through the events of the passion in toto, through everything that human authority inflicts upon Jesus.

Jesus therefore goes to his trial as one left to the powers and devices of human society, just as his followers left him alone to face those forces when they deserted him at Gethsemane. Before reaching Jerusalem, Jesus exercises divinely authorized mastery over unclean spirits, illness, disability, natural elements, death, and scarcity. In Jerusalem, he defeats those who challenge his authority, leaving credentialed opponents and onlookers defensive, amazed, shamed, impressed, and silent (12:12, 17, 27, 28, 34). But the trial and crucifixion occur in an entirely different kind of atmosphere. The verb παραδίδωμι does not suggest God capriciously betrays or punishes. It indicates that Jesus' trial will be part of a process in which human authority is permitted to do whatever it wants with him (recall 9:13), the required consequence of God's withdrawal of the authority that has empowered and perhaps preserved God's "beloved Son" (see 1:11; 9:7; 12:6) throughout his ministry. The trial thus becomes a kind of proving ground for human authority, an exhibition of its power and interests vis-à-vis the one whom God has commissioned.[23]

Mark's readers therefore encounter Jesus' trial as a certain consequence of the persistent conflict between Jesus and specific human authorities. The passivity that Jesus displays throughout his prosecution and his subsequent procession to Golgotha—noted by some in his infrequent speech and the small number of times that he is the grammatical subject of an action—comes across, therefore, hardly as resigned endurance or sullen disdain.[24] It complements the narrative's presentation of Jesus' transition from subject to object, just as the verbs παραδίδωμι and ἐγκαταλείπω keep attention on Jesus and what happens *to* him throughout the passion. Mark's point is not that Jesus' nature or confidence changes when God gives him over to human beings, but that he now has become subjected to the human constellations of sociopolitical authority. Vulnerable before the system, he must now confront and endure its authority without the protective benefits he once enjoyed from his divinely granted authority and mysterious identity. In precisely this environment, he states his boldest, plainest claims to his identity as God's anointed one.

THE TRIAL

Scene 1: Jesus before the High Priest
and His Council (14:53–65)

As soon as the arresting party delivers Jesus to the high priest and his associates, Mark reveals that these people do not intend to probe questions of truth but to substantiate accusations that will bring down Jesus. At the same time, the narration imbues the short trial scene with confusion and desperation as the authorities find themselves unable to uncover or produce consistent testimony that can substantiate their desired verdict. Exacerbating the chaos and injustice, much of the episode transgresses rules for Jewish legal procedures described in later rabbinic literature.[25] If we can assume that at least similar juridical standards were valued during Jesus' day, then Mark depicts a trial utterly out of order, a raw abuse of power. Even if no such standards existed then, it remains that Mark describes a judicial farce. Whatever the source of such details, whether they are historical or derived from theological or polemical motives, they characterize the trial as a political conspiracy and the tactics of the high priest and his associates as just as oppressive as those regularly employed by "those recognized as rulers among the Gentiles" (10:42).

   The only testimony against Jesus that Mark quotes focuses on him as a threat to the temple and as one claiming the ability to replace it with something altogether new and superior. Some state that Jesus said, "I will destroy this sanctuary that is made with hands, and in three days I will build another not made with hands" (14:58). The narrator identifies this as false testimony presented inconsistently. Technically speaking, then, Jesus cannot be guilty of having made this provocative statement about his own power over the temple. Readers know that his earlier words in 13:2 do not make the same claim. The false testimony nevertheless produces irony. Mark's earliest audiences, who read and heard this Gospel as the Jerusalem temple lay in ruins as a result of the Jewish-Roman War of 66–70 CE, would have seen truth in the false witnesses' statement, for Christians took Jesus' death and resurrection as establishing a new locus of God's presence.[26] In the trial narrative, when the false charge sticks, echoed by passersby who taunt Jesus as he dies in 15:29, the irony deepens and the alternative meaning it acquires in view of Jesus' crucifixion and resurrection becomes reaffirmed. From the Jewish authorities' perspective, when Jesus minimizes the theological significance of the temple he questions its ability to express God's design for God's people. He therefore threatens the sociopolitical advantages they derive in part from the temple's centrality in Jewish self-definition.[27] The temple symbolically connects the Roman-granted practical sociopolitical authority of the Jewish aristocracy with their religious responsibilities as God's priests and priestly advocates. They hold their offices to the extent that, and in order that, they discern and protect the ways of God *and* satisfy Roman interests in the province.

Frustration prompts the high priest to speak in 14:60: he essentially calls on Jesus to provide his own testimony so that it might be used against him. Jesus does not respond, refusing to give his opponents words that will rescue their sorry case.[28] At last the priest articulates the issue directly. His climactic question—"Are you the Christ, the Son of the Blessed One?"—may seem discordant, since the question of Jesus' identity as a supposed "Christ" or "Son of God" has not been an explicit ground of controversy between him and the Jewish authorities, even though there have been questions about the basis of his authority and confusion about who he is. But the high priest has not swerved off topic. His question actually connects to the possibility that Jesus has made astonishing claims about his supremacy over the temple (note the "again" in v. 61b), for some Jews at that time expected that the coming Christ would build a new, eschatological temple.[29] By associating "the Christ" with the notion of another temple, the high priest's question makes explicit what the false testimony of 14:58 implies about Jesus' identity and authority. If Jesus replies affirmatively, he claims a supreme authority from God that would utterly transform much of what the current temple represents as the locus of God's presence among God's people. Again, not only does this go against the chief priests' theological commitments; it also stands to lessen the authority that the high priest and his associates derive from their administration of the temple and its significance for Judean society. In their perspective, such a claim represents an assault on everything that is in place.

Jesus' answer in 14:62 marks the only point in this Gospel where he openly assents to the names "Christ" and "Son of God." His simple "I am" (ἐγώ εἰμι) makes a bald statement that parallels the high priest's unambiguous "Are you?" (σὺ εἶ;) from the previous verse. While Jesus' words echo other times he refers to himself (6:50; 13:6), the narrative does not consider them an abbreviation of the divine name revealed to Moses in Exodus 3:14 (ἐγώ εἰμι ὁ ὤν in the LXX). The "I am" affirms his identity, then he immediately gives more information than the high priest requested, unpacking the nature of his messiahship with a declaration that combines phrases from Psalm 110:1 (seated ἐκ δεξιῶν of God [109:1 LXX]) and Daniel 7:13 (the son of man coming with τῶν νεφελῶν τοῦ οὐρανοῦ). Jesus asserts God-given authority, speaking of an enthronement made apparent when the divine reign comes to its consummation and promising an ultimate, undeniable expression and exercise of that authority. The trial thus becomes the occasion for the definitive christological statement, a declaration of Jesus' royal identity as one anointed by God and enthroned with God, but also a qualification of that kingship as something not yet fully manifested.[30] Jesus is the Christ, but the full measure of his royal authority remains to be displayed and understood. He says, "I am" God's Anointed, standing here before the council now, and at a future time "you [plural] will see" the fullness of my authority.[31]

Jesus' testimony does not threaten a violent comeuppance but promises that the leadership's failure to perceive that God is the source of his message and ministry will one day be overcome. Inasmuch as his words reiterate what he told his followers in 13:26–27, they indicate his future vindication and also the emergence of God's reign. To the council he insists that what they see in the trial is not entirely what they get. His "You will see" also prompts readers to view the trial in light of the ends of the larger story. His statement is not escapist or "otherworldly." Jesus avers that the future manifestation of his kingship will be both undeniable and certain to render other expressions of authority and devotion obsolete. His testimony insists that the human powers' verdicts against him will not be the end of the trial; they merely demonstrate these people's efforts to protect themselves from him at any cost.

The high priest's declaration that Jesus commits blasphemy raises questions that are complicated by limited knowledge of what constituted such an offense in Jesus' context. Because Jesus does not pronounce God's name, punctuated by his careful use of the circumlocution "the Power," it remains most reasonable to conclude that no blasphemy occurs and that the high priest fudges the technical definition to justify the outcome he desires for the trial. Some scholars nevertheless insist that a broader understanding of blasphemy was operative during Jesus' day, broad enough to include Jesus' appropriation of Psalm 110:1 and Daniel 7:13, which ascribes to him an authority that belongs uniquely to God.[32] Such technicalities aside, what matters for this investigation is that the council seizes precisely this moment, the point of Jesus' definitive christological confession, to declare him deserving of death. The condemnation flows solely from Jesus' own words. He claims an authority that constitutes blasphemy only if it is untrue, as his opponents surely take it to be. His words are thus equally self-definitive and self-incriminating, turning the trial into the moment in which the leadership sanctions the uniting of his confession and condemnation. His confession incriminates him. In Mark's view, no falsehood exists at this point in the trial, precisely because the authorities condemn Jesus on the basis of who he reveals himself to be.

To be sure, Jesus' encounter with the high priest has great christological relevance, and the juridical context formalizes the offense this Christology causes. Just as previously people acclaimed Jesus' teaching as new (1:27) and he spoke of a radical, volatile discontinuity between old and new (2:22), his opponents judge his claims to authority to be utterly incompatible with established and familiar theological convictions. But the nature and mode of the christological revelation—as testimony delivered and condemned in a trial setting—indicate that this scene also possesses great sociopolitical relevance. The christological statement occurs not before crowds but before the high priest and his associates, not in an open venue such as a synagogue or the temple but in a surreptitious trial conducted in space controlled by the aristocracy. They certainly have religious reasons for opposing him and the theological implications of all he says about himself and the glory of God. But those weighty interests also stand yoked with the unique sociopolitical benefits that they possess and that appear imperiled as well by Jesus' popularity and his vision of a new religious order. The sociopolitical authority they enjoy, employed under the aegis of Roman authority, is not all that matters to them in this scene, but it is hardly absent. It actually equips them with their most effective tools for preserving and protecting their whole range of interests: a blasphemy condemnation and an alliance with the Roman governor.

The testimony Jesus gives before the council, which promises the future authentication of his claims, can receive no substantiation beyond Jesus' own insistence. The trial comes down to his vision of God's authority and purposes against the leadership's vision. The narrative will offer later events as verifications of Jesus' claims: the crucifixion depicts an ironic enthronement of a king; the tearing of the temple curtain in 15:38 recalls this trial scene; the resurrection implies God's vindication of Jesus. But in the unique space of the trial, which finally admits testimony only from Jesus to render a decision, only his words and the judgments of those present matter. By acting decisively against him, the leadership ironically confirms Jesus' identity, exactly as they confirm the depiction of power that his identity criticizes (see 10:42–45). In this way the Markan trial offers a definitive moment that declares Jesus' gospel right and exposes the priestly aristocracy as unable to grasp the truth about him.[33]

Scene 2: Jesus before Pontius Pilate (15:1b–15)

Through the centuries countless exegetes have described Pilate in this scene as little more than a pawn of the Jewish leadership and crowd. Such an interpretation, however, does not adequately take account of the contours of Mark's narrative (the drama of the judicial event) and the sociopolitical realities (the power that Pilate holds and the interests he represents), which together suggest that Pilate controls the proceeding. As the analysis of Pilate's behavior will show, throughout the scene he operates as anything but a neutral arbiter. As for the sociopolitical realities, the Jewish leadership that opposes Jesus remains dependent upon Roman authority. This scene brings Jesus into a higher echelon of sociopolitical authority and peril, as illustrated by the contrast of extremes created when he appears before the emperor's representative as one virtually powerless, still bound and likely disfigured from the beatings he suffered in the first scene.

As the forensic drama unfolds, the priests and crowd also find themselves subject to Pilate's power and engaged in a contest with him. The high priest and his associates stand to gain by delivering up a subject who claims authority as a rival king. Their vigilance in identifying such a person may demonstrate their loyalty to the governor, and Pilate's clear condemnation of Jesus may reduce their chances of facing a backlash from Jesus' supporters (recall 11:18, 32; 12:12, 37; 14:1–2). Pilate is hardly unaware of these dynamics motivating the priests, for he even detects "envy" (15:10) among them. He therefore uses the trial to exploit his advantages. As we will see, by holding Jesus up for special contempt, he sends a message to any who would contest Roman power. Simultaneously he cements that power by acting out his dominance over the priestly aristocracy and their supporters among the Jewish population.[34]

Pilate's consistent interest in Jesus as "the king of the Jews" catches readers' attention since the title "king" has not yet appeared in this Gospel in connection to Jesus, even though royal imagery adorned Jesus' arrival in Jerusalem in 11:1–10.[35] The shift in language, brought about when Pilate uses the term without elaboration in 15:2, confirms what one would expect in this political context, that he and the priests have previously communicated about Jesus or even planned aspects of the prosecution in concert.[36] Clearly the high priest's council has seized upon the royal, governing foundations of both the title "Christ" and the image of Jesus at God's right hand and thus presented Jesus to Pilate as one with pretensions to royal authority. From a Roman perspective, even an ostensible king implied resistance to the empire. Accordingly, Rome regularly crushed people who took such a title for themselves.[37] The implications of Jesus' being a king bring great concern to the official vested with imperium.

His opening question to Jesus therefore does not desire to parse the connotations of Jewish expectations for an "anointed one" but seizes directly upon the pretensions to supreme authority that the high priest recognized in the previous scene. The political context of undisputed Roman rule makes the substance of the question serious, while the narrative context of deep disconnect between kingship and Jesus' present appearance makes the question an expression of amused disbelief. Pilate's emphatic σύ—"Are *you* the king of the Jews?"—adds to these contexts a gentle grammatical flourish that signals his contempt for such a ridiculous figure. Jesus' retort mirrors the same syntax and contempt: "So *you* say" (σὺ λέγεις). Within the confines of the narrative, the answer provides Pilate neither a confirmation nor a denial. A plain "Yes" or "I am" from Jesus here could swiftly end the trial. Instead, Jesus' circumvention serves the ironic tenor of the entire trial, and it allows Pilate more time on the narrative stage to connect Jesus to the royal title in a way that demands the wider crowd's participation. For Mark's readers, however, the answer transcends its apparent ambiguity by underscoring the authentic testimony imbedded in Pilate's dismissive question. Readers also observe that these are Jesus' final words spoken to human beings (cf. 15:34) and that he will die with the same title inscribed above him: "The King of the Jews" (15:26).

Just as a Galilean Jew stripped of nearly every vestige of honor strikes Pilate as an absurd candidate for a king, Pilate appears to him as an absurd candidate to determine what kingship for the Jewish people—particularly Jesus' conception of that kingship—should look like. With his σὺ λέγεις, Jesus insinuates that Pilate cannot possibly adjudicate or understand the nature of the authority that has been given to him as the Christ, for that authority manifests itself in a manner totally contrary to how Pilate understands the rights and exercise of power (recall Mark 10:42).[38] Jesus' silence in the trial from this point forward further sets him apart from the power arrayed against him, which will do to him whatever it pleases to protect itself and its interests. His silence reaffirms that he will not act to deliver himself, for this is the nature of his present kingship. Such a posture suggests neither frustrated resignation nor obedience to a call to suffer.[39] It distances Jesus from Pilate and his authority, just as the manifestation of Jesus' full authority as God's anointed one remains in the future.

Jesus embodies an unfamiliar kind of kingship; when the scene shifts in 15:6, Pilate embodies the familiar tyrannical behavior that Jesus criticized in 10:42. The developments introduced by the prospect of a prisoner release and the crowd's arrival on the scene are unforeseen.[40] Although Jesus fades to the background in 15:6–14, these verses shape the forensic drama in critical ways and matter for the judgments issued against him. Pilate's sustained reference to Jesus as "the king of the Jews" resonates with spite and derision both for Jesus and for the people for whom such a pathetic figure might claim to be king. In verse 10 the narrator reveals that Pilate recognizes "envy" (φθόνος) behind the prosecution. This does not mean that he finds the whole issue inconsequential, for envy neither equals jealousy nor implies pettiness. The term indicates a contest over honor and social standing, suggesting that Pilate perceives that the priests see Jesus as a legitimate threat to their honor and the source of the privileges that ensure that honor. Jesus' offense is not merely personal but also political. While such an offense compels Pilate to take Jesus seriously, he may also find the envy amusing; for since competition over honor in ancient society occurred among social peers, the envy might allow him to view the peasant Jesus and the Jewish aristocracy with a common disdain.[41] Pilate explores the possibility of granting the customary amnesty by offering to release this pathetic challenger while using the offer to embarrass the aristocracy and remind them of their place in the imperial pecking order.

Immediately, however, it becomes clear that this crowd does not support Jesus. When the crowd acts in league with the Jewish authorities, it offers a sharp contrast to the crowds that protected Jesus from these same people in Mark 11–12. The contrast suggests that these people have been handpicked for the occasion. The narrator does not explain why the chief priests would prompt them to ask for Barabbas instead of another; presumably the release of a man closely associated with deadly insurrectionists would not ingratiate the priests to Pilate. Perhaps the aristocracy knows that Barabbas and those imprisoned with him enjoy significant support among the wider population, which would reinforce the aristocracy's standing among the people. In any case, the desire to release someone associated with a violent rebellion betrays a desire for that brand of power by force over Jesus' model of service.

With his question to the crowd in 15:12, Pilate puts them on trial, reaffirming that the scene is about more than merely weighing Jesus and his claims.[42] The question does not cast Pilate as tractable. He neither abdicates responsibility nor seeks advice from his subjects but shrewdly tests the crowd's loyalty so that he might quell any support for Jesus and reassert Roman dominance. Those who would openly support a supposed king in this setting risk condemning themselves, as Peter's episode in the high priest's courtyard demonstrates, and so by interrogating the crowd Pilate strong-arms them into denouncing the one who would claim to be their king. Because the crowd has chosen and insists upon Barabbas, he makes them own the confession of Jesus' kingship by calling them to endorse the consequences that follow such a claim. By asking "What will I do with the king of the Jews?" (v. 12), Pilate compels the crowd to voice its support of, or at least acknowledge, what Roman authority demands when faced with a purported king.[43] The high priest and his supporters who deliver Jesus to Pilate must therefore also witness and perhaps participate in the disavowing of the idea that there can be a king of the Jewish people. The demonstration of loyalty that Pilate elicits does not aim to spread blame as much as it underscores the seriousness of the charges against Jesus. Jesus' mere possession of the title "king of the Jews" threatens to implicate all of them as subversive to Roman authority unless they thoroughly denounce him and with him any Jewish aspirations to a king of their own in the face of Roman rule.

At a climactic moment in 15:13, everyone acknowledges that rival kings receive death. But the crowd, sensing the magnitude of the situation and Jesus' potential for offense, calls for a particular kind of death: crucifixion, a means of execution whose use and symbolism meant "to emphasize the victim's final and irrevocable rejection from the civic and international community."[44] Through crucifixion, Jesus is not merely excised from society; he also becomes terminally (and thus, in a sense, perpetually) at society's mercy. Such a death defines his relationship to the society that crucifies him as one made publicly exposed, vulnerable, and censured.[45] At the same time, crucifixion makes a declaration of Pilate's sovereignty, as an extension of the emperor's. The final verdict, first voiced by the crowd then made effective through Pilate's act, becomes inscribed upon Jesus as the permanent consequence of God's relinquishing him to the designs of human authority.

The prospect of Barabbas's release allows the trial to define further the nature of Jesus' royal identity. The juxtaposition of the two men comes across starkly in the name "Barabbas" (from the Aramaic for "son of the father") and in Jesus' identity as God's beloved Son. As the scene gradually allows Barabbas and Jesus to emerge as options for release, their ironic pairing "suggests that there is something ideationally comparable about them": the brief description of Barabbas in 15:7 suggests that Pilate and the crowd consider the two would-be seditionists in light of their sociopolitical impact.[46] But the narrative fractures the parallel in verse 14, making the irony explicit when Pilate introduces the matter of "what evil" Jesus might have done. Up to this point in the scene, nothing has suggested that Pilate does not regard Jesus' claims as a present danger; releasing him would indeed be *amnesty*. Even if Jesus does not cut an imposing figure, his claims and defiance pose symbolically meaningful threats of their own. By focusing on Jesus' activity, Pilate strikes a contrast with Barabbas, whom the narrator has associated with known murderers and rebels. Pilate, perhaps unwittingly, admits that Jesus may not pose the same caliber of threat as Barabbas and his ilk, at least at this moment in time, although he never intimates that he desires to release "the king of the Jews." Pilate's question responds to the severity of crucifixion, whether Jesus' offense warrants that particular mode of execution. He acknowledges the lack of "evil" in Jesus' behavior, yet the incited crowd renews the call for crucifixion, thereby enjoining Pilate to do what everyone knows he must do as agent of imperial authority.

The crowd gives no direct answer to Pilate's final question but only restates the call to crucify Jesus. This may impute some responsibility for Jesus' death to this particular crowd, but more emphatic is how it shows that Pilate's judicial posturing has finally created a monster of a scene.[47] At the end, this becomes a trial in which questions of guilt, innocence, or deserved punishment become rendered totally irrelevant in face of the insistent and widening desire to cast out Jesus. A similar thing occurred when John was in Herod Antipas's custody in 6:17–29, although there the ruler boxed himself into a position where he could not prevent the execution, at least not without sacrificing his high standing. Here Pilate retains control. When the narrator says in 15:15 that Pilate wished "to satisfy the crowd," this does not suggest capitulation on his part. The expression carries the sense of "indulge."[48] Pilate allows the crowd to heed their envious priests and have their Barabbas, as gifts granted by their powerful governor. Their cries against Jesus affirm the folly of positioning oneself against Roman authority. He has heard them disown their king, and so he scourges him in their presence and sends him to crucifixion.

The last-minute emergence of a contradistinction between Jesus and Barabbas around Pilate's question of "what evil" Jesus might have done helps the trial accomplish at least three things for Mark's portrait of Jesus and his kingship. First, by attributing a sense of harmlessness to Jesus, it reaffirms his earlier statement to the high priest that his royal status is not fully recognizable now. Second, it contrasts the way of the gospel with Barabbas and his associates' methods for social change. Third, it reconfirms that the whole of Jesus' trial pulses with injustice and irony; what began as the show trial of a man not guilty of the accusations originally brought against him ends with the condemnation of a man whose self-spoken messianic claims have been misunderstood but nevertheless ironically authenticated and rejected by those in power. When Jesus is handed over to the authority of human beings, they exploit every available resource to crush him and cast him out, and in the process they try to reinforce their basis of authority by rejecting his theological claims as incredible, unwanted, and incongruous with the way things are. He has no place in such a system.

CONCLUSIONS

Jesus' encounters with the high priest's council and the provincial governor address the question of his offense and the warrant for his crucifixion. In this way they contribute to Mark's understanding of Christology and the meaning of Jesus' death. But our reading of the trial scenes in light of their wider narrative context and sociopolitical milieu suggests that they also portray Jesus in direct confrontation with expressions of power antithetical to what his gospel exemplifies. Mark asserts that Jesus and his message are certain to elicit opposition from others; *through the trial* this opposition becomes a constitutive piece of Jesus' identity as the Christ. Just as such opposition informs Markan Christology through the trial, it likewise informs the narrative depiction of Jesus and his gospel's relationship to human societies' ways of exercising power. Several aspects of our exploration illuminate these matters.

Narrative Coherence

In a long and otherwise forgettable footnote from an essay on the Gospels' portrayal of Christ, over a century ago theologian Martin Kähler wrote, "To state the matter somewhat provocatively, one could call the Gospels passion narratives with extended introductions."[49] Kähler's point was to emphasize, correctly, that the Gospels do not pretend to offer comprehensive accounts of Jesus' life and ministry. But sometimes interpreters wrench Kähler's words from their context and make them assert that what precedes the story of Jesus' condemnation and death is substantively and theologically ancillary to the passion itself. Any trial assumes and only makes sense within a wider narrative. Jesus' trial in Mark prompts readers to consider it in light of the context and evidence presented previously in the Gospel narrative; such material is not mere introduction, for it deeply shapes readers' understanding of what occurs in the trial. Likewise, the trial gives substance to previous statements about the dominion exercised "among the Gentiles."

In particular, Jesus' trial leads readers to consider the opposition to Jesus in light of previous controversies concerning his authority and his previous declaration about the abuses of political power. The wider narrative not only allows Jesus to point to his passion through his predictions; it also asserts that the trial comes specifically as a consequence of his ministry. Likewise, Mark presents readers with privileged testimony that supports and gives definition to the christological claims that the trial makes. The trial, for all its concentration on christological revelation, actually picks up on the christological foundations that pervade the narrative and provoke opposition to Jesus. For all that the trial sets in motion in terms of lethal action against the Christ, its force and theological logic depend upon a whole antecedent story about a person whose authority was in dispute and whose gospel called for a way of service that flew in the face of his contemporaries' notions of power and greatness.

The Irony in and of the Trial

Many have noted the irony in Mark's story of the trial and crucifixion. Mark's is an ironic Christology, especially to the extent that it ascribes royal authority to Jesus through the trial. The trial scenes employ dramatic irony to great and serious effect, as New Testament scholar Donald Juel summarizes:

> For a variety of reasons Jesus is judged to be religiously and politically dangerous by the recognized religious and political leaders, and he is condemned to death. The reader knows, however, that the situation will be reversed: Jesus will be vindicated and his judges judged. There is a tension between appearance and reality inherent in the events as the author perceives them.[50]

Irony stamps the Christology as inscrutable, made stark when members of the council blindfold Jesus (14:65) while they remain unable to glimpse the truth about him. Irony also makes for a Christology that is fundamentally contested, introduced as such in the trial and confirmed when Jesus dies as "the king of the Jews." The disclosure of Jesus' identity as the Christ remains inextricably bound to a context in which he is made vulnerable to the will of human authority. Juel's language about judging perhaps acknowledges this sense of *contestedness*, for a trial stages a contest and demands dispute. In such a setting, people must declare allegiances and contend for their understanding of the truth. Mirroring the trial proper, Peter refuses to acknowledge Jesus; the priests side with the physical temple over Jesus as the builder of a new one; Pilate enforces Rome's prerogatives and elicits support and submission from a Jewish crowd. These declarations certainly paint Jesus' opponents as liable to judgment, a liability made all the more acute by the injustice of the trial as a mechanism of political expediency.[51] More important, the contested Christology works symbiotically with the judgments that the trial implicitly issues against Jesus' opponents, as both reassert the radical discontinuity between Jesus' confession of kingship now, as the accused, and his future role as the bearer of God's undeniable authority.[52]

The Politics of the Trial

The naked contrasts in power and the contested Christology cause the trial to accentuate the political nature of the story and identity of Jesus. Prior to this point in the narrative, most of the christological queries and disclosures occur in private or remain relatively confined. Trials define and impact their wider societies; likewise, Jesus' trial makes his christological assertions a social matter. The trial serves as a venue for the governing authorities, the "hands" that Jesus referred to in 9:31, to conduct their business and weigh his claims so as to reach a binding decision. The trial offers a microcosm of the human power to which God gives Jesus over, and it becomes an arena for rulers to overwhelm and tyrannize others for their own benefit, specifically in response to Jesus' statements about his unique authority. Perhaps the narrative expresses this exercise of power most grimly when Pilate presses the crowd to acknowledge that Jesus' purported identity as their king demands that they renounce him and endorse his execution. Even if the crowd or the priests suppose that they are acting in God's service when they seek to eliminate Jesus, Pilate's question to them demands that they achieve that goal through a clear expression of their subservience to Rome.

In the trial, as well as the ensuing crucifixion, Mark shows the ways of human power described in 10:42 exhibiting themselves at the same time that Jesus declares his messianic identity and promises a future revealing of the fullness of that identity. The juxtaposition provides nuance to the Gospel's depiction of human power. The trial goes beyond setting opposing visions against one another: it is not simply that the authorities oppose Jesus and the identity he claims for himself, nor is it merely that the future vindication of Jesus' authority stands in opposition to the political machinery that crushes him in the present. Instead, Jesus' identity and corresponding authority acquire some of their offense and reveal themselves as threatening precisely in their inevitable ability to *expose* other forms of authority as oppressive and willing to use their resources to resist God's purposes. Mark proclaims a Christ and a gospel that collide head-on with human constellations of sociopolitical power, provoking and exposing their abuses as the story of Jesus Christ holds out hope for a different order to come. This does not mean that the Christian gospel, according to Mark, presents itself as anarchic or insubordinate. Nor does Mark give much attention to triumphalistic visions of human governments withering in advance of the fullness of God's rule through Christ becoming established. In the trial Mark paints a stark portrait of sociopolitical power to prescribe wariness to readers by vividly characterizing that power as ruthlessly defensive and bent on self-preservation when faced with the disclosure of Jesus Christ and the claims he makes. The trial shows up the failings of the Roman Pilate and the Jewish high-priestly aristocracy in particular, yet it offers little that might suggest there is anything unique about the systems those ancient figures represent. The Gospel's characterization and criticism apply widely.

4

Jesus on Trial in the Gospel according to Matthew

More than any other Gospel, Matthew's story of Jesus' trial declares severe judgment on those who participate in the events—not merely for acting against Jesus, but also for doing so in ways that neglect the truth and lead others to reject him. Some of these participants enjoy privileged access to the truth about Jesus, yet they do all they can to shield themselves from it. The priestly aristocracy and the Roman governor use the proceedings to reshape public perception of Jesus and to deflect their responsibility for his death. The trial reveals the devious and manipulative ways in which the authorities use their power to achieve their own ends and to defend themselves from Jesus and his message.

OVERVIEW OF THE TRIAL SCENES

The events constituting the two trial scenes in Matthew are nearly the same as those in Mark. Both Gospels also portray Jesus as essentially objectified and nonparticipatory in his trial, and they offer only slight variations in the words he speaks. Substantial differences emerge, however, in Matthew's additional details and their unique way of narrating the forensic drama; these elements lend distinctive significance to Matthew's story of Jesus and his conflicts with human authorities. The character of the Matthean trial shows itself clearly when we compare Matthew and Mark, and so this chapter assumes familiarity with the preceding chapter and the content of Mark's trial scenes.

The first scene in Matthew (26:57–68; 27:1), like the arrest that precedes it, bears great resemblance to Mark's account. Matthew adds specificity by identifying the high priest as Caiaphas and the setting as his house. Matthew follows Mark in setting Peter's denial as a concurrent event, even magnifying the dramatic parallel by mentioning Peter's oath in 26:72 (cf. 26:63).

Distinctive aspects of Matthew's account then emerge. The shocking mention of unscrupulous attempts to produce "false testimony" (26:59) that can serve Caiaphas, the chief priests, the scribes, and the elders' desire to put Jesus to death confirms that these people do not intend to uncover or debate truth; they hope to eliminate someone they have already judged as dangerous.[1] This depiction of the aristocracy resonates with their behavior elsewhere in Matthew's final chapters: they rebuff Judas's repentance (27:3–10), ask Pilate to place guards at Jesus' tomb (27:62–66), and bribe those guards after the resurrection (28:11–15). They refuse to let Judas's remorse, the possibility of Jesus' resurrection, or the guards' explanation of the empty tomb influence their settled opinion. In Matthew's trial, the aristocracy's inability to manufacture a contrived case against Jesus nevertheless cannot prevent *valid* testimony from finally emerging: two witnesses report something Jesus said about destroying and rebuilding the temple.[2] When Jesus responds with silence, Caiaphas calls on him to answer with God as his witness and asks whether he is "the Christ, the Son of God." Jesus replies, "So *you* said" (σὺ εἶπας) and declares his future vindication. Caiaphas and the council call this blasphemy and judge him worthy of death. Then the jurists become thugs, beating him as they use the name "Christ" to taunt him. The narrator, having paused to tell of Peter's threefold denial, returns to the trial scene in 27:1 with the statement that the representatives of the Jerusalem aristocracy determined how best to "put to death" their prisoner, closing the scene by repeating a word that introduced it in 26:59: θανατόω.[3]

Between trial scenes Judas, contrite and aware of Jesus' condemnation, visits the chief priests and elders. His earnest confession acknowledges that Jesus is "guiltless" (27:4), but the others display cold indifference. This brief encounter contributes to the trial scenes in at least two ways. First, it furthers Matthew's depiction of the Jerusalem leadership as unresponsive to the truth and morally bankrupt. Judas's repentance exposes their own sin as his coconspirators (see 26:14–15), but they reply, "What's that to us? *You* see to it" (27:3–4). While they neglect the weightier matter of justice (cf. 23:23), they hypocritically concern themselves with the legal use of "blood money," a bounty they themselves paid Judas. Their encounter with Judas provides a devastating portrait of what it means to "strain a gnat but swallow a camel," to borrow words from Jesus' criticism of scribes and Pharisees in 23:24. Second, Judas embodies a counterpoint to Pilate in the subsequent scene, for the sinful disciple contritely acknowledges his responsibility while the powerful governor deftly deflects his own.[4]

Matthew's second trial scene (27:11–26) begins much like Mark's, as Pilate and Jesus trade contemptuous words to confirm Jesus' identity as "king of the

Jews." When Pilate turns to ask a crowd about releasing a prisoner, he offers a choice between two men named Jesus: a "notorious" Jesus Barabbas and the Jesus "who is called Christ." Suddenly the governor's wife sends him word about a dream she had concerning Jesus and cautions him about entangling himself with "that just man." When the Jewish aristocracy persuades the crowd to ask for Barabbas and call for Jesus' death, pushing the crowd close to the point of unrest, Pilate washes his hands to protest his innocence in the matter and echoes the priests' words to Judas in 27:4 when he tells them, "*You* [plural] see to it." The crowd declares its role, placing Jesus' "blood" upon themselves, and Pilate delivers him for crucifixion.

THE QUESTION OF GUILT AND THE JEWISH PARTICIPANTS IN THE TRIAL

As the history of their interpretation indicates, the trial scenes in all the Gospels are among the most challenging and controversial biblical texts that can be consulted for making sense of Christianity's gradual separation from Judaism and for articulating a biblical understanding of ongoing relationships between Christians and Jews. Matthew's Gospel makes the matter particularly acute. Several unique dimensions of its trial scenes and their surrounding context (such as Jesus' parables of judgment in Matt. 24–25, Judas's attempted repentance, and the Jewish crowd's stunning statement in 27:25 about placing Jesus' "blood" upon themselves and their children; cf. also 27:62–66; 28:11–15) perpetuate this Gospel's acid polemic against certain elements within the Jewish context known to its earliest readers.

The limited scope of the current study prevents us from exploring in detail Matthew's polemical bent, as well as the ways Christian interpreters duplicate and distort it when they use the trial scenes to justify theologies and politics of violence toward Jewish people. Some of the ugliest appropriations of these scenes exhibit a preoccupation with assigning "guilt" in the trials and extrapolate theologies of exclusion and condemnation from said guilt. My analysis of the trial in light of its narrative dynamics and sociopolitical milieu will conclude that Matthew places great, but not exclusive, blame at the feet of Caiaphas and his aristocratic associates, especially in their ability to influence the crowd like a blind person leading another into a pit (see 15:14).[5] It hardly follows, however, that these leaders represent all Jewish people of any time and place.[6] If they represent anyone or anything beyond themselves, it is irresponsible and imperceptive religious leadership, generally understood, a brand of leadership that the author of Matthew probably sees duplicated in his own historical context. We cannot and should not interpret away Matthew's offense or dismiss it as superficial. At the same time, I think it is worth emphasizing that the interpretation I offer, especially concerning the narrative's depiction of powerful people spreading and evading responsibility, would better serve Christians' future understanding of these texts. Such an interpretation does not, however, deny the existence and pervasiveness of the Matthean polemic itself or the hazards it always presents.

THE TRIAL WITHIN A WIDER PLOT

Matthew sets the stage for Jesus' trial in ways similar to Mark, situating it as the result of intensifying conflict between Jesus and certain Jewish authorities and as anticipated through Jesus' multiple predictions of his passion. Resistance to Jesus crystallizes early in the story (12:14), for some insist that he is a satanic agent (9:34; 12:24). The opposition becomes more resolute once he comes to Jerusalem, criticizes the use of the temple by its leadership, and teaches (21:12–17, 33–46; 26:1–5). Through the fray, Jesus' mode of service exposes and offers a radical contrast to the tyrannical practices of powerful Gentiles (20:25–28; cf. Mark 10:42–45). Matthew accentuates the conflict between Jesus and Jewish authorities, partly through Jesus' withering criticism of scribes and Pharisees as hypocritical and exploitative (see 23:1–36).[7] Again akin to Mark, Matthew presents Jesus' passion as the inevitable and required outcome of his teachings and ministry, and the narrative suggests that God gives Jesus over to the will of human authority (see παραδίδωμι in 17:22; cf. Mark 9:31), relinquishing him to a vulnerability punctuated when the crucified Jesus laments his abandonment (see ἐγκαταλείπω in 27:46; cf. Mark 15:34).

Matthew prepares for and narrates the passion narrative with a strong sense of the events' resonance with the Scriptures. Jesus' words at his arrest, in 26:53–54, speak of fulfilled Scriptures, even as they reaffirm that God is permitting human authority to do as it pleases with God's Son (cf. 17:12). In addition to Matthew's biblical echoes and general statements of fulfilled Scriptures that have parallels in Mark's passion, this Gospel describes a field bought with Judas's blood money as a fulfillment of specific prophecies (27:3–10). Furthermore, additional derision from the chief priests and others at the cross (27:43) draws another connection with Psalm 22 (v. 8). Finally, the foreboding comment that Peter comes close "to see the end" (26:58) hints that Matthew regards the trial as bringing things to completion (cf. τὸ τέλος in 10:22; 24:6, 13–14).

Concerns about the sociopolitical significance of Jesus and his ministry span Matthew's narrative. Interest in Jesus as "king of the Jews" emerges soon after his birth, when the magi's arrival and their use of that title strike fear in Herod the Great and "all Jerusalem" (2:1–4). When Pilate in the second trial scene applies the same title to Jesus and uses it interchangeably with "the Christ," readers recall the narrator making the same terminological connection when describing King Herod's plots (2:2, 4). Herod prefigures Pilate in his concern about a rival king known as the Christ.[8] Herod's fear and murderous rampage establish Jesus as no small threat to his political stability, and so Pilate's language at the beginning of his trial scene makes readers suspect that the Roman governor can be no more tolerant of Jesus. In addition, and again unique to Matthew, twice Jesus explicitly foretells that he will die by crucifixion, a manner of death that marks its victims as enemies of the Roman state (20:19; 26:2).

As with Mark, Matthew's trial is vital for bringing Christology into clearer view. When comparing these two narratives, however, Matthew does not make the trial such a singular moment of christological revelation. The scenes involving Herod in Matthew 2 also direct attention to Jesus' identity as the Christ. Other verses have Jesus elaborating on this identity (11:2–6; 16:13–20; 23:10). That material takes a measure of christological suspense away from the Matthean trial. Yet, as we will now see, several distinctive aspects of the trial serve Matthew's depiction of who Jesus the Christ is and what he means for the society in which he makes himself known.

THE TRIAL

Scene 1: Jesus before the High Priest and His Council (26:57–68, 27:1)

Matthew's scene in Caiaphas's home looks as much a parody of justice as Mark's first trial scene, perhaps even more so in light of the leadership's underhanded attempt to secure "false testimony." Nevertheless, truth comes out when the topic turns to Jesus' attitude toward the Jerusalem temple, which the narrative presents in 26:61 as a statement Jesus previously made, presumably off the narrative's stage.[9] His claim, "I can destroy God's temple and build it in three days," is shocking, although it delivers less a threat than the one in Mark 14:58 and does not insinuate that a different kind of temple will follow. In comparison to the Markan trial:

> Jesus' hostile attitude to the temple is softened from his *intent* to destroy to his *power* to do so; a reverential tone is introduced; the contrast between this temple and another is removed. Matthew's consecutive, legally and theologically connected narrative eliminates Jesus' opposition to the temple but only shows his power in it. This

accords with Matthew's previous version of temple sayings (12:1–8; 21:10–17) which makes them serve christological ends.[10]

Jesus thus claims authority over the temple. The institution providing the visual and cultic representation of the Jerusalem aristocracy's religious and political authority serves as a symbol of Jesus' superior authority and a locus of his self-revelation.

When Caiaphas appears frustrated over Jesus' refusal to elaborate, he asks directly whether he is the Christ, the Son of God. The question carries significant force, for he calls upon "the living God" to bear witness to Jesus' remarks. The verb ἐξορκίζω in 26:63, in its syntactical context (κατὰ τοῦ θεοῦ), does not mean that Caiaphas orders Jesus to reply to the council "under oath," as if Jesus must swear upon a higher authority. Rather, the high priest himself brings the interrogation before God, for the oath language calls for Jesus' answer to be made in God's hearing, perhaps so God might bear witness to the answer's truth. Caiaphas means to set the stakes high, suggesting that God demands that Jesus acknowledge his true identity.[11] Caiaphas knows that the question of who Jesus is, in light of the authority he claims vis-à-vis the temple, impinges directly on God's own self and authority. The question lays a trap; it makes it doubtful that Jesus could give any kind of a positive answer that would not be considered blasphemous in this setting.

Caiaphas's question matters for understanding the first part of Jesus' reply, "So *you* said." These words lack the unambiguous clarity of Jesus' "I am" in Mark 14:62, but the wider context of Matthew's Gospel leaves no doubt that they give a positive response.[12] Jesus spoke the same words in 26:25 to identify Judas as his betrayer. They allow Jesus, with a derisive edge, not only to say "Yes" but to do so with reciprocal force that puts Caiaphas's question and its oath language back to the high priest. With his ἐξορκίζω expression, Caiaphas has essentially said that God requires Jesus to declare the truth. Jesus' answer does not evade that responsibility. His point is not to resist swearing a formal oath, as if revisiting his teaching in 5:33–37. He turns Caiaphas's just-spoken adjuration back upon him, as if Jesus is stunned by the high priest's incredulity wrapped in pious talk about "the living God." God requires the truth from Caiaphas, and Jesus implies that God has already borne the witness Caiaphas needs to grasp the truth. Indeed, others in Matthew have correctly interpreted the evidence (see 9:8; 14:33; cf. 21:23–27). Theologian Rowan Williams accurately describes the force of Jesus' answer:

> It may remind us of Jesus' response to the sons of Zebedee when they ask for places of honour in the kingdom. "Do you know what you are asking?" he says on that occasion (Matthew 20:22; Mark 10:38). Or it may call to mind the exchange with the religious leaders over

the authority of Jesus and John the Baptist (Matthew 21:23–27; Mark 11:27–33): how *do* you know where to recognize divine authority? Jesus' answer to the High Priest at his trial has a twofold force: you *know* how to look at the world, you already have the categories to make sense of it; but you use these categories as if you had *no understanding* of what they might truly mean.[13]

Jesus accuses Caiaphas of failing to comprehend the ways of the living God, of missing all the ways that Jesus' teaching and ministry have demonstrated his divine authorization. Jesus' words expose a tragic irony: Caiaphas should know the truth. Because he does not, or he resists it, he has forfeited the religious authority and responsibilities attached to his office as a leader of the Jewish people.[14]

As in Mark, Jesus refers to Psalm 110:1 and Daniel 7:13 to elaborate on his identity as God's anointed.[15] The full manifestation and vindication of the authority God gives to him remains to come, although he declares that the whole council "will see" it in time.[16] Jesus will sit at God's right, in contrast both to the high priest's current position, standing to interrogate Jesus (26:62), and to Pilate in the next scene, sitting on an elevated platform (βῆμα) while Jesus stands before him (27:11, 19).[17] Jesus' words speak the truth in the trial, truth about himself, the temple, his future, and God's authority. They further criticize Jerusalem's current leadership, those who lead the temple and God's people. These words earn him a death verdict, later confirmed with allusion to a formal judgment in 27:1, which Judas in 27:4 perceives as certain condemnation. In 26:67–68 the council acts out its judgment and its rejection of Jesus and his claims through vivid displays of degradation, violence, and mockery. They will bring him, bound, to the governor to have him executed.

Scene 2: Jesus before Pontius Pilate (27:11–26)

The previous chapter argued that Mark does not portray Pilate as a pawn of the assembled Jewish leadership and crowd. Attention to sociopolitical realities and the contours of Matthew's narrative leads to similar conclusions for this scene. But Matthew's account of Jesus before Pilate takes readers along a different path, one in which the responsibility for Jesus' condemnation—and thus the power that engineers Jesus' execution—becomes obfuscated. Furthermore, this Gospel assigns significant responsibility to the Jewish aristocracy, and the expense of doing so is to make Pilate's power and involvement less prominent. Despite the ambiguity the narrative lends to Pilate and his role, Pilate's deeds and rhetoric provide the trial's decisive hinge, insofar as they finally bring about Jesus' crucifixion as a spectacle of Roman sovereignty.

At the same time, Pilate's prevarication while conducting the trial shows him both guilty of an unwillingness to do what is right and capable of a cunning ability to use his power to avoid openly acknowledging his role.

We must not overlook the action of 27:11–14 and the gravity of a Roman governor dealing with a prisoner delivered to him by the Jewish aristocracy and associated with the title "king of the Jews." Those details establish Pilate's interest in this judicial affair. But since these verses virtually duplicate the brief exchange between Jesus and Pilate described in Mark 15:2–5 and discussed in the previous chapter, we will direct our attention here toward more distinctive components of the Matthean scene.

A unique detail that underscores Pilate's interest in Jesus is the narrator's frequent references to him by his office: "the governor." This resonates with Jesus' warning to the Twelve in 10:17–18, that they will be handed over to councils (συνέδρια) and brought before governors (ἡγεμόνες) and kings. Standing before the province's top political official, Jesus becomes his followers' forerunner and exemplar. More specific to this scene, the repetition of "the governor" keeps Pilate's office and the imperium attached to it in view, reminding readers that Pilate is the face of Roman authority, an authority hardly prone to trifle with rival claims of kingship.[18]

The decision between Jesus and Barabbas dominates this trial scene, requiring twelve verses to bring it from beginning to resolution (27:15–26). With the verb θέλω (vv. 15, 17, 21) the narrator and Pilate present the matter as a choice the gathered crowd must make between two men; also, the rhetoric throughout these verses presents the two prisoners in a balanced way as alternatives.[19] With their differences downplayed, Matthew has them emerge more as parallel figures than as opposites. Yet their fates will be opposite, for the release of Barabbas back into society will have an obverse consequence: Jesus' banishment from society through crucifixion (vv. 20–22, 26).

The prisoners' names reinforce the idea of a choice between similar alternatives, for both are called "Jesus."[20] Furthermore, the lack of specificity about Jesus Barabbas's wrongdoing does not permit readers to make definitive moral judgments about him; Matthew offers only that he is a "notorious prisoner." "Notorious" (ἐπίσημος; v. 16) does not necessarily imply "reprehensible," but it does indicate Barabbas is locally renowned, popular like "Jesus who is called Christ." In any case, Pilate shows no hesitation in offering Barabbas as an option. Since both are Pilate's prisoners, the governor considers neither man inconsequential to Roman interests. Each represents some kind of threat or danger. Yet, by offering them as options for his customary gesture of amnesty, Pilate cannot consider the release of either one capable of creating too severe a political liability for him and the empire. The situation actually allows him to maneuver to exploit the "envy" (v. 18) he sees motivating the aristocracy, as he does in Mark. Pilate can toy with the prisoners' popularity to reassert his authority and assess the breadth of that popularity.

By framing the release of a prisoner as a balanced choice between one Jesus or the other, this part of the trial accomplishes at least two things. First, in a christological vein, it widens the population of people who send Jesus to death as a *rejected* Christ. Not only do authority figures cast him out; so too no one from the company of his followers or the wider populace comes forward to defend Jesus—except, ironically enough, Pilate's wife. The crowd's choice against Jesus looks less shocking, however, when Matthew says that the religious leadership persuades (πείθω; v. 20) them to make that choice. Second, the choosing has a political dimension. The drama that develops through a choice presented for the people's consideration provides political cover for Pilate and the Jerusalem aristocracy, as will be seen in their efforts to deflect responsibility throughout the deliberations that follow. Governor and aristocracy alike create triangular dynamics in the trial, using the crowd against Jesus to reduce the public visibility of their interests and the responsibility that they themselves assume on account of the power they possess.

Beginning in 27:17, Pilate interrogates the crowd, using language similar to that already examined in Mark's account. Pilate cannot be trying to encourage the crowd to request Barabbas's release, for verse 18 indicates that he responds to or is motivated by the aristocracy's envy. When he asks his initial question, the context makes any answer potentially dangerous, for Pilate has done nothing to suggest that he prefers releasing one Jesus over the other (cf. Pilate's more leading question in Mark 15:9). Without surprise, then, the narrator relays no response from the crowd. Who would venture one in this context? Only after the aristocracy convinces the crowd in verse 20 do they state a preference for Barabbas, after Pilate repeats the question (v. 21).[21] In aligning themselves with the chief priests and their aristocratic allies, at least they stand in privileged company and perhaps on safer ground.

Something else occurs between Pilate's questions in verses 17 and 21: a message from his wife reaches him. While the Jerusalem aristocracy influences the crowd on the basis of its own envy, the governor's unnamed wife tries to influence him on the basis of the truth revealed to her in a dream. Dreams served as reliable methods of revelation in 1:20–25; 2:12–15, 19–23. Matthew gives no reason to doubt the authenticity of what she learns about Jesus. Still, her dream communicates more than a confirmation that Jesus is just, since dreams in the ancient world often had relevance for announcing or confirming social, political, and religious developments and transitions, a fact whose ominousness may not have been lost upon either Pilate or Matthew's original audience.[22] Her identification of Jesus as "just" or "righteous" (δίκαιος; v. 19) speaks truth in a trial determined to remove Jesus from society no matter what. Readers know that Jesus is just, and when Pilate's wife refers to him as such, not only does it set him apart from his opponents who seek his death; it also breaks open a contrast between him and Barabbas.[23] It seems, however, that her warning makes no immediate influence upon Pilate, for in restating his question to the crowd, he creates the impression that his strategy remains unchanged. Yet the message he receives increases his liability for what he does with the truth, whether or not he recognizes it as truth. His wife's message exposes both his ignorance and his refusal to do what is right. His responsibility as an imperial official demands one thing; her dream demands another.

In 27:22, Pilate replies to the crowd's declaration for Barabbas, "Then what will I do with Jesus who is called Christ?" It is not an expression of dismay or genuine puzzlement. The narrative does not depict him as cornered. With the authority he possesses as governor, he could release both prisoners, should he actually consider Jesus just and harmless. The crowd has yet to call for Jesus' destruction, so at this point Pilate cannot be afraid of inciting popular unrest if he follows his wife's advice and releases him. So he does not *want* Jesus to go free. His question, then, as in Mark 15:12, compels the crowd to acknowledge what Rome must do to a rival, to "the Christ," to one claiming authority as a king. The crowd knows how to answer, having been persuaded by the priests and elders. Possibly they think of themselves as acting in fidelity to God in their desire to have Jesus punished as a blasphemer, assuming that was their leaders' line of persuasion. Depending upon the size and precise makeup of the crowd, however, that persuasion could have been difficult, perhaps requiring the aristocracy to make deals, threats, or both. In any case, the crowd has been enticed (misled, in Matthew's perspective) to its position as the safest ground to occupy in this context.

Then, in Matthew 27:23, Pilate asks about the "evil" Jesus has done, again paralleling Mark's account (Mark 15:14). This has an effect similar to what was discussed in the previous chapter, widening a distinction between Jesus Christ and Jesus Barabbas. It appears that the people's call for crucifixion—as opposed to a less severe or poignant mode of execution—gets Pilate's attention. Moreover, given his knowledge of the aristocracy's envy toward Jesus, this final question to the crowd explores whether they will continue to side with the priests. But Pilate quickly learns that he cannot take advantage of any opportunities for influencing this crowd in a way that would frustrate or embarrass the aristocracy, for in verse 24 he perceives that he is "gaining nothing" (οὐδὲν ὠφελέω) or, as the NIV puts it, "getting nowhere."[24] This does not mean that Pilate is powerless in this situation, that he disapproves of crucifixion, or that he is hamstrung by the will of a mob that will not obey him. Rather, he can make no inroad toward driving a wedge between the crowd and those who have influenced them. He cannot leverage the situation to maximize any further the aristocracy's dependence on him. The crowd's growing unrest emphasizes the success and responsibility of the priestly authorities; that emphasis begins to move Pilate's responsibility toward the background, a development his next maneuver tries to exploit.

By washing his hands, Pilate declares his own innocence. He does not declare Jesus innocent but takes advantage of the crowd's growing hostility by making them part of the means by which Jesus is condemned, symbolically yet hypocritically handing over his role as judge. A sickening irony permeates the gesture. First, to the extent that the hand washing recalls a procedure from Deuteronomy 21:1–9, prescribed to protect a city from the bloodguilt issuing from an unsolved murder, Pilate "employs a ritual that was used to prevent any further calamity from coming upon *the land of Israel* to profess his own innocence and in so doing insinuates that the execution of Jesus is nothing less than murder."[25] The biblical connection to the ritual is understandable within Matthew's symbolic world, but the identity of the hand washer and the trial context make Pilate's gesture as offensive as ironic. Second, by using language also found in Matthew 27:4, when Judas grieved over Jesus' guiltlessness and the priests and elders cynically told him, "*You* see to it," Pilate's hypocrisy appears just as odious as the priests'. The forensic drama and the power inherent in the governor's office situate him as being far from innocent or ignorant. By his hand washing he brazenly tries to shape the public judicial transcript so as to deny his ultimate responsibility. From Matthew's perspective, this makes the deed all the more despicable and highlights the abuses and machinations behind Jesus' condemnation. The act further exposes the trial as political theater. The governor's attempt to disavow responsibility only redounds to his blame.[26]

The crowd responds in one voice, "His blood be on us and on our children" (27:25), bringing the scene to a climax with their acknowledging their involvement in Jesus' condemnation. Neither the semantics of this notorious verse nor the dramatic circumstances in which the crowd speaks indicates that the people summon a curse that sanctions evil to afflict them and their descendants.[27] Nor does Matthew's identification of the crowd as πᾶς ὁ λαός (v. 25) indicate that this group represents the whole people of Israel or Jews of every place and time.[28] Such presumptions have contributed to the most sinister parts of this passage's interpretive history. The crowd claims a role, a prominent one, in Jesus' prosecution. The role is to choose Jesus' destruction; it is the same role that that the priests and Pilate have been trying to deflect and conceal for themselves. The people who assume this role of judges and sentencers in verse 25 are not a larger, abstracted group but the people present on the narrative stage, members of the population of Jerusalem under the persuasive influence of their chief priests and elders. Their statement is shocking because it expresses deep assurance that Jesus is a dangerous man. This assurance reveals how thoroughly the aristocracy has persuaded them. Their opposition to Jesus has become just as thoroughgoing as the aristocracy's. They have become as their leaders are. To side with those rulers is to side against Jesus. Finally, the crowd's statement also suggests that merely to witness this farce of a trial is to share complicity in its outcome; thus the statement can, as an expression of Matthew's theology of Jesus' condemnation, extend as well to the Gospel's readers.

Having successfully sloughed off the appearance of judicial responsibility, at least in the public theatrics of the trial, in verse 26 Pilate sloughs off Jesus himself when he provides the formal impetus for the crucifixion, presenting him to the Roman soldiers who will execute him. But first, by flogging Jesus in full view of everyone at the trial, the governor reminds them of his authority. The syntax of verse 26 can indicate that Pilate himself performs the flogging; this makes for quite a display of public effrontery from someone who just publicly professed his innocence regarding Jesus' fate.[29]

CONCLUSIONS

The Wider Narrative and an Ironic Christology

The similarities shared by the Markan and Matthean trial scenes lead to several similar conclusions. First, Matthew's trial also directs attention to the whole of the Gospel narrative. This means that the judicial contest extends beyond questions of true testimony and guilt or innocence; it pits different kinds of authority in opposition to each other, bringing to a head conflicts that fill the Gospel. Jesus embodies a kind of authority that he has already demonstrated but that remains foreign to those steeped in antithetical practices of coercion and domination (20:25–28; cf. 5:3–12, 43–47; 7:12). The judicial setting and drama indicate that Jesus' identity has a way of exposing such manifestations of power, by bringing them upon himself. In addition, the trial's wider narrative context prompts readers to consider the verdict against Jesus in light of the Gospel's end, as the resurrected Jesus commissions his disciples to continue his ministry (28:16–20). The resurrection and assertions Jesus makes about the future minimize the ultimate power of the human authority that crushes Jesus.[30] That power may oppose Jesus and his ministry; but instead of stopping him, it brings his nature and the implications of his gospel into brighter light. Such power enjoys only provisional status; its days are numbered.

Second, the trial in Matthew pulses with dramatic irony and ironic relation-ships and so constructs a fundamentally contested Christology like Mark's, yet one given a more tragic character through the actions of people who should know better: Caiaphas's calling Jesus to account "before the living God," the priests and elders' indifferent response to Judas's repentance, Pilate's non-responsiveness to his wife's dream, the governor's hand washing, and the crowd's choosing to deny Jesus' authority as God's anointed and approve his crucifixion.[31] The ironies extend Matthew's criticism of the officials and interests that orchestrate Jesus' death even as they define the nature of Jesus' identity as the Christ. Without diminishing the ironies' force or denying their christological importance for Matthew, one wonders what they indicate about the political dynamics of the trial. Does irony characterize the aristocracy, crowd, and governor as weak, idiotic, and impervious? Or do their mistaken assessments and political subterfuge point to more at work? Matthew's trial narrative indicates the latter. The irony exposes the trial as a theatrical display of hidden roles and displaced responsibility. It is a drama of political evasion, coercion, and denial.

The Politics of Evasion

Matthew's depiction of the governing authorities is frightening for the clever depravity they display, a depravity that Jesus and his gospel expose and call to account. Readers gain insight into the ways these authorities operate against Jesus as various characters' roles shift in the forensic drama. With the aid of his associates, Caiaphas, functioning essentially as judge and prosecutor, predisposes the testimony given in both trial scenes when he seeks false wit-nesses and persuades the crowd that appears before Pilate. Pilate speaks like a defendant when he declares his innocence regarding Jesus' condemnation and sentencing. Through his hand washing he tries to symbolically transfer a judge's authority. His wife enters privileged testimony on Jesus' behalf. The crowd, whose supposed purpose was to request the release of one prisoner, ends up welcoming its role in condemning another.

On the narrative level, these changes in the judicial roles reflect the mag-nitude of the aristocracy's and governor's power; the chief priests exercise great influence over the crowd, and Pilate's vast authority allows him to conduct the trial and shape the public perception of his involvement as he sees fit. To readers, however, these shifts reflect the injustice of the trial and pass judgment on the negligence of the priests and governor who have been given knowledge to understand Jesus differently. Caiaphas ironically comes across as a high priest who actively opposes God, and Pilate as cynically reti-cent to openly acknowledge his own responsibility. The widespread denial of responsibility stems from more than convenience or judicial laziness; it also comes as catalyzed by the crowd's vulnerability to the persuasive power of the priestly aristocracy. When the people finally choose against Jesus, the authorities can then gain political advantage from the situation.[32] Pilate can fulfill his imperial obligation and retreat in the process. A conspiracy of evasion thus pervades the scene, in which those with the most authority put it to use by denying or veiling their power. The ability to manipulate the proceedings in such a way actually derives from the authorities' power and influence, and so they manufacture their desired outcome while reaping the benefit of disclaiming their own responsibility.

The conspiracy of evasion brings the crowd to demand the Christ's death and accept a role in condemning him to capital punishment at the hands of Rome; that conspiracy characterizes the governing authorities as able to manipulate public perceptions and the acceptance of ideas. Their rejection of Jesus is not merely a legal or religious act; they make it a social one, hypocritically yet ironically packaged as society's decision. By observing the crowd, Matthew's readers learn that playing in the authorities' games leads to being compelled to share in their interests and responsibility.

Those dynamics underscore Pilate's political shrewdness. Matthew does not exonerate Pilate or portray him as overmatched. The authority vested in provincial governors should make us suspicious of interpretations suggesting that Jesus' trial reduces Pilate to a powerless puppet, or that Pilate abnegates his judicial authority to others. The governor recognizes the danger that Jesus represents, and he accomplishes what Roman authority requires. At the same time, Matthew introduces a measure of ambiguity into Pilate's characterization, primarily through his wife's dream, which gives him incentive to find a different way of ending the trial. Pilate's refusal to heed his wife ascribes a moral weakness to him. He cannot see beyond his own perspective on the situation. He is trapped in his role and responsibilities as the imperial representative. Matthew thus indicates that Jesus and his gospel expose constellations of human sociopolitical power but cannot always deliver people from them.

As the conspiracy of evasion obscures Pilate's responsibility, the narrative accentuates the role of the priestly aristocracy. The whole span of Matthew's passion narrative keeps Caiaphas and his chief priests in view, from 26:3 to 28:15. As we have seen, Matthew consistently portrays this group's behavior as shameful and ruthless, and their ability to influence the crowd's choice is overwhelming. The aristocracy brings the crowd to the center of the trial, in the process allowing the Roman governor to hide at the edges.[33] In the end, this is not a denial of Pilate's judicial authority, but the means by which his ruse succeeds. The governor and the priests find relative political security along the edges, where they manipulate the action. When the crowd willingly plays a part to bring about the shedding of Jesus' blood, the statement is shocking—not only because a crowd has been whipped up to declare such a thing about Jesus, but also because their doing so reifies Matthew's portrait of their leaders' insidious ability to influence and even transform the people. The trial's judgment against that leadership, like the rest of this Gospel's judgment, is devastating.

5

Jesus on Trial in the Gospel according to Luke

Jesus quickly fades into the background during his trial in Luke's Gospel, as conflict emerges between Roman officials and Jewish authorities, joined eventually by the people of Jerusalem. What begins as an apparent railroading of Jesus toward his execution morphs into a contest of competing wills as all the participants except Jesus try to discredit and humiliate one another on the way toward securing their desired outcome. Jesus' trial in Luke may last longer than those in Mark and Matthew, but a protracted trial does not necessarily mean a thorough or a just trial. When the trial has concluded and the narrative offers retrospective comments on it, readers see a political drama wherein matters of truth and justice are overwhelmed by the will of those who reject Jesus and by the will of a governor who aims to exploit Jesus for political advantage. They also see a theological drama wherein God's will accomplishes itself through the course of human misperception and political maneuvering. In the strange coexistence of these dramas, Luke's trial scenes assert that God's plan of salvation manages to actualize itself within the apparatuses and tensions of the first-century sociopolitical environment.

OVERVIEW OF THE TRIAL SCENES

Luke's trial scenes describe events quite different from those in the Markan and Matthean trials; Luke also includes peculiar and incredible happenings.[1] Unlike Mark and Matthew, Luke reports no witnesses and no mention of the temple when Jesus appears before the Jewish leadership. Also unique to Luke are the dialogue between Jesus and the Jewish authorities, the accusations that those authorities make before Pilate, Jesus' appearance before Herod Antipas, and Pilate's ambiguous final verdict. As for the trial's more curious aspects, Pilate appears ready to dismiss the accusations after asking Jesus only one question (23:3–4), and the Jewish crowd and leaders demand Barabbas's release with no apparent justification (23:18), for the narrative says nothing about a customary prisoner release.[2] Perhaps most shocking, Pilate desires to release Jesus, but the assembled crowd thwarts him. The Lukan narrative, including material from the book of Acts that comments on Jesus' trial, acknowledges the shocking aspects of the trial and provokes many questions in response. Could Pilate be so lenient, a maladroit defender of Roman interests? Why do the people suddenly turn against Jesus and demand Barabbas? What is the nature of the political struggle in the trial, and what is its significance for viewing the trial as a theological drama? Grappling with these and other questions, biblical interpreters have suspected that there is more than a simple judicial decision occurring here, that Luke insinuates a deeper layer to who or what is really "on trial."[3] In the end, Jesus' trial provides a vehicle for his rejection and execution. Luke provokes readers to consider how that vehicle operates, and who makes it operate.

The trial transpires over four scenes. Initiating the action, the chief priests, elders, and high-ranking temple guards arrest Jesus at the Mount of Olives (22:47–54a). These chief priests will appear in all four scenes, always accompanied by other members of the Jewish leadership in Jerusalem, making them the primary but not exclusive face of Jesus' opposition.[4]

Before the trial Luke relates Peter's threefold denial in 22:54b–62, thereby setting that scene apart in narration and time. Although Peter disowns Jesus at night before the trial commences in the morning, Luke retains a juxtaposition through the two men's proximity, for Jesus can see his disciple from the high priest's residence (v. 61). That glimpse recalls his statement about Satan's intention to "sift" Peter and the others "like wheat" (22:31–32).[5] Peter's denials thus focus attention on Satan's role in Jesus' passion, a role we will revisit shortly.

Also during the night before the trial, those detaining Jesus beat and deride him. As they do so, they mock his reputation as a prophet by commanding him to identify his assailants while he remains blindfolded and vulnerable. The violence thus directs attention to Jesus' identity as a prophet, another facet of Luke's Gospel that we will discuss later.

The first trial scene (22:66–71) occurs before the high priest's council.[6] None of Luke's trial scenes singles out the high priest, but his slave's presence at Jesus' arrest (22:50) and the decision to detain Jesus at his house (22:54a) implicates him and suggests that he is among the rest of the chief priests in this and the following scenes (see Acts 5:27–28). The opening scene moves quickly, for nothing indicates that anything is said beyond the reported dialogue. No one seeks or gives false testimony. No one talks apart from the council members, who speak in a single voice, and Jesus. They tell him to declare whether he is the Christ, but he replies that they will neither believe him nor reply to his questions (Luke 22:67–68). He adds, "From now on the Son of Man will be seated at the right hand of the power of God." They respond by asking whether he therefore is the Son of God, and he states, "*You* say that *I* am." This affirmation is all they need to hear (vv. 69–71). The scene concludes with neither a formal condemnation nor the hatching of a plan to secure Jesus' demise. The council immediately ushers him to Pilate.

Those Jewish authorities open the second scene (23:1–7) by laying before Pilate accusations that Jesus corrupts their nation (ἔθνος), forbids them to pay taxes to the emperor, and claims to be "Christ, a king." Pilate asks about the final charge; he and Jesus trade the same contemptuous words found in Mark and Matthew: "Are *you* the king of the Jews?" "So *you* say" (σὺ λέγεις). Suddenly, despite the seriousness of the charges and the brevity of the inter-rogation, Pilate tells the priests and their associates that he finds no cause to substantiate their accusations. They redouble their indictment by calling Jesus an agitator who has been inciting "the people" (ὁ λαός) from Galilee to Jerusalem. The mention of Galilee prompts Pilate to send Jesus to Herod Agrippa, the appointed ruler of Galilee, who happens to be in Jerusalem. The scene includes no mention of either Jesus' remaining silent or Pilate's amaze-ment at such behavior.

Jesus does not speak again during his trial. To Herod he says nothing, even though the ruler asks him a considerable number of questions while the chief priests and scribes fervently hurl accusations. Finally, Herod and his soldiers mock and abuse Jesus before returning him to Pilate. This scene (23:8–12) has the strange outcome of reconciling Herod and Pilate, who had previously been enemies.

In the fourth scene (23:13–25) Pilate assembles the chief priests, other unidentified Jewish "rulers," and "the people" (ὁ λαός) to hear his decision about Jesus. This is the first appearance of nonelite characters, except for Jesus and soldiers, in the Lukan trial scenes, yet the narrative leaves readers uninformed about how many people are present and how they have been gath-ered. Pilate finds no basis, and reports that Herod also found none, behind the capital accusations against Jesus. The governor announces his intention to whip Jesus and send him on his way. The entire assembly—priests, lead-ers, and people—protests in unison, calling for Jesus' death and the release of Barabbas, a man in Roman custody for insurrection and murder. Although Pilate desires to release Jesus and insists that he will do so, the crowd repeat-edly calls for Jesus' crucifixion. At last the crowd's voice overpowers Pilate so that he decides "to grant their request." He releases Barabbas and submits Jesus "to their will."

THE TRIAL WITHIN A WIDER PLOT

Luke describes the conflict involving Jesus and anticipates his passion in ways similar to Mark and Matthew, but does so with its particular accents. New Testament scholar Donald Senior suggests five categories that summarize the narrative context in which Luke sets Jesus' passion.[7] Taking these categories as a foundation upon which to build allows us to consider the breadth and depth of relevant dimensions of Luke's plot.

First, Jesus preaches and embodies a message about the establishment of God's justice. Second, conducting such a ministry requires Jesus to transgress boundaries that governed the social and religious lives of his contemporaries. Readers see these two related categories at work throughout the Gospel when Jesus faces off against recognized religious leaders who resist his activity because for them it stirs up controversies about the demands of Jewish law and religious practice.[8] Jesus' words to these people are sometimes severe (see Luke 11:37–52). Once he enters Jerusalem and criticizes the priestly leadership for their misuse of the temple (19:45–48; cf. Mark 11:15–19; Matt. 21:12–17), a final showdown appears certain. At the same time, the Gospel also declares that Jesus' ministry of justice envisions a wide and long-lasting reach, for Luke 1 narratively locates it in the foundational claims of the angel Gabriel, Mary, and Zechariah. There Luke roots this image of justice in the powerful and explicitly political activity of God, who will give David's throne to Jesus, brings the mighty down from their thrones, saves Israel from its enemies, and will give light and peace to those in darkness and death (1:32, 52, 71, 78–79).

With the exception of that unique material in Luke 1, the core of Luke's emphases on Jesus' message resembles the Gospels of Mark and Matthew, especially the portrayal of the Jerusalem aristocracy's offense at him and their determination to do away with him. Yet Luke relates this familiar story of conflict while maintaining important differentiation between the Jewish leaders in Jerusalem and the Jewish people there. Although Jesus does not enjoy unanimous support from the general population during his ministry (see 4:28–30; 11:14–16), once he arrives in Jerusalem the narrative is careful to set the acceptance he receives from "the people" (ὁ λαός) in juxtaposition to the antagonism directed against him by the temple-based Jewish authorities (e.g., 19:47–48).[9] Jesus' popularity among the people keeps him safe (e.g., 20:19), and the aristocracy tries to goad him into discrediting himself in the people's presence (20:26).[10] When Jesus goes to trial, then, readers have little reason to suspect that the λαός, collectively representing the population and identity of Jerusalem in a general sense, will side with the Jerusalem aristocracy against him.[11] When "the people" do so in the final trial scene, subsequently confirmed when statements in the book of Acts fault them for Jesus' death

(2:22–23; 3:12–15; 4:27), it therefore comes as a shock. The contours of this surprise will prove quite relevant for our investigation of the trial.

Third, Luke casts Jesus' journey to Jerusalem as an occasion for another of God's prophets to suffer persecution.[12] Luke–Acts describes Jesus as a prophetic figure (Luke 4:24; 7:16; 11:49–51; 24:19; Acts 3:22–23). The pivotal statement of Jesus' setting his face to journey to Jerusalem (Luke 9:51) recalls the prophet Ezekiel's oracles against groups and cities (e.g., Ezek. 21:2). A number of passages interpret Jesus' death as the rejection of a prophet (Luke 13:33–34; 17:25; Acts 7:52). According to his words in Luke 19:42–44, Jesus dies in Jerusalem because the city fails to perceive that he brings peace and embodies God's benevolent oversight (ἐπισκοπή; cf. 1:68, 78–79). When Jesus delivers this prophecy, it makes readers wonder just how his rejection will come about, particularly since "the people" will support him once he enters Jerusalem. The prophecy suggests that lack of recognition and ignorance play a part (cf. 13:34). Indeed, the trial resumes this theme, for those involved in the case against Jesus display a thorough inability to comprehend his true identity and significance.

Fourth, Luke connects Jesus' demise to Satan's opposition. When Satan enters Judas (22:3), readers suspect that Satan finds the choice "opportunity" (καιρός) that he earlier anticipated after testing Jesus in the wilderness (4:13). Satan's implied presence means that an "authority" other than Jesus' operates during the trial and the rest of the passion. Jesus confirms this when he tells those who arrest him that now, in contrast to the times when he taught in the temple, "this is your hour, and the authority of darkness!" (22:53). The narrative does not dwell on perplexing issues concerning Satan's agency—how Satan influences events, and how he may operate according to or contrary to God's will. Yet Satan's acknowledged role in the passion means that Jesus' trial unfolds on multiple levels. In the trial, Jesus faces some who are determined to annihilate him and others who try to exploit him as political currency, but their evil is not entirely the sum of their choices and actions. A hidden drama involving God and Satan also transpires. This relates to the fifth point.

Fifth, Luke places special emphasis on the certainty of Jesus' rejection and death. As in Mark and Matthew, Jesus' predictions of his passion (Luke 9:22, 44; 17:25; 18:31–33; cf. 24:7) and occasional scriptural echoes lay a foundation for this even before Jesus' arrest.[13] For example, Luke includes a quotation from Isaiah 53:12, when Jesus says he must be "counted among the lawless" (22:37).[14] A significant amount of postresurrection passages retrospectively make even stronger statements about the necessity of the passion. Some see it in accordance with Scriptures (Luke 24:25–27, 44–47; Acts 3:18–24; 13:27–29; 17:2–3; 26:22–23; cf. Luke 18:31). Others describe it as planned or foreknown by God (Acts 2:22–24; 4:24–28). These passages usually introduce the issue of

Jesus' certain death and resurrection while they assign culpability to people or declare their ignorance. Jesus' passion, carried out through all sorts of human decisions and actions, somehow fulfills a divine design, just as, in his prayer at the Mount of Olives, Jesus acknowledges that his Father's "will" (θέλημα) will be accomplished (Luke 22:42).[15] For Luke, this design is ineluctably bound up with human deeds. The certainty of Jesus' condemnation does not mean that people operate with impunity during the trial, or that the drama's satanic undercurrents prove inconsequential.

Finally, we must observe that in his trial, Jesus faces two leaders who are the subjects of serious conversations earlier in the Gospel: Pilate and Herod Antipas. The Roman governor's name appears in 3:1, and 20:20 acknowledges his political authority over the Jerusalem scribes and chief priests. In addition, the cryptic yet grisly reference in 13:1 to Pilate's mingling Galileans' blood with their sacrifices resonates with his reputation for brutality.[16] These references characterize him as someone capable of doing great harm to Jesus.

Herod was tetrarch of Galilee (3:1), which made him responsible for preserving the emperor's interests there.[17] Mirroring Mark and Matthew, Luke holds him responsible for John the Baptizer's arrest and death (3:19–20; 9:7–9). Luke describes him as curious about Jesus (9:9) but soon reveals the dangerous nature of that curiosity when Pharisees inform Jesus of Herod's desire to kill him (13:31–35). Jesus' response to their warning, in which he insults Herod as "that fox," proves important for understanding his trial. That passage plays with the verb θέλω to contrast what the tetrarch *wants* (Jesus' death) with what Jesus *wants* (to nurture Jerusalem) before lamenting that this is not what the people of Jerusalem *want*.[18] Herod's murderous will cannot overwhelm Jesus' intentions and his desire to be about God's business. The trial will revisit the issue of conflicting wills and prompt readers to consider how certain wills prevail.

As it looks back at the trial, the book of Acts confirms that Pilate and Herod play important roles. Although Luke and Acts exhibit a measure of inconsistency in their stories and theological claims, their authorial unity and basic narrative unity invite us to consider these books as mutually informative.[19] We will consult several relevant passages from Acts when analyzing Jesus' trial, but for now we may note these:

- Acts 3:13 confirms that Pilate intended to release Jesus as it directs particular blame toward a group of the "people" (ὁ λαός; 3:12), those Peter addresses in the Jerusalem temple.
- Acts 4:27 lumps Pilate and Herod with "the Gentiles and the peoples of Israel" as arrayed against Jesus while resonating with Psalm 2:1–2 to affirm the fulfillment of God's plan.

- Acts 13:28 acknowledges Pilate's authority and role in the trial as it asserts that the people in Jerusalem and their rulers, although they had no basis for a death sentence, nevertheless pressed him to execute Jesus. (See a similar assumption about Pilate's authority in words directed to people dwelling in Jerusalem in Acts 2:23.)

To see these and other roles play themselves out among the characters who participate in Jesus' trial, we turn now to investigate the scenes themselves.

THE TRIAL

Scene 1: Jesus before the Jewish Leadership (22:66–71)

This scene emphasizes the hostility of the Jewish leadership and Jesus' disclosure of his authority as the Christ. As the action progresses, the former subsumes the latter: Jesus' statements about himself serve to underscore the magnitude of the authorities' opposition.

The scene's brevity and lack of clear accusations, witnesses, or definitive judgments lead some interpreters to liken it more to a preliminary hearing or interrogation than to a trial. But this misunderstands its role within the whole sweep of the action against Jesus. The scene plays an integral part in Luke's presentation of the opposition to Jesus and how that opposition finally results in a judgment against him. The scene offers a cutting characterization of the conflict at hand, for the content of the proceeding suggests anything but judicial diligence. The event, stripped of even a masquerade of orderly process, launches

> a stark attack upon him. No witnesses are called, for the council is itself the prosecution; no verdict is given, for the issue is already decided by them; no horror is shown at the alleged blasphemy, for any pretence of good motives on their part is gone. . . . It is . . . a case of deliberate refusal to accept what is acknowledged; what is evoked is a calculated rejection.[20]

It is a show trial without the show, a judicial farce.[21] The narrator adds to this impression by having the entire assembly speak and operate in a unified way, signified through third-person-plural grammatical forms, acting consistently "as a body" (23:1 NRSV). It appears that they all have made up their minds and need only a final impetus—Jesus' self-incrimination—to justify presenting him to Pilate. Later the narrator reveals that Joseph, a member of the council, had not consented to his colleagues' action (23:50–51). During the trial itself, however, the narrative gives the impression of complete opposition to Jesus.

The leadership's concern centers around who Jesus is, in response to the claims he has made in the temple.[22] When they ask whether he is the Christ, Jesus' initial response criticizes their refusal to believe anything he says. The grammar of his answer, "If I tell you, you definitely won't believe; and if I question you, you definitely won't answer," essentially declares that they refuse to accept what he tells them; he implies that dialogue or persuasion is pointless.[23] His words also closely resemble what Jeremiah says to Zedekiah in a climactic scene (Jer. 38:15); thus they reinforce Jesus' prophetic identity and intimate his demise.

The opinions of the council seem to matter little to Jesus, for he declares that his authority will soon be unmistakable. The process has begun, starting "now," which will result in his enthronement at God's right hand (recalling Ps. 110:1). Jesus does not refer to Daniel 7:13 (in contrast to Mark and Matthew) and says nothing about the council members seeing him in glory. When Peter later cites Psalm 110:1 during his Pentecost speech (Acts 2:34–35), he clarifies Jesus' claim. Jesus' exaltation results from his death, resurrection, and ascension. The presence of the Holy Spirit confirms this, says Peter: from God's right hand, Jesus pours out that Spirit (2:33). In the contrived examination by the high priest's council, Jesus therefore comes across as dismissive toward his interrogators, implying that he sees the trial not as an opportunity for them to weigh his claims but as part of a larger process through which he will be glorified to share undeniably in God's power.

The assembly hears Jesus' statement for what it is, a clear claim of his God-given authority. Their final question eagerly expresses the inference they make: "You're the Son of God, then?" This question essentially repeats their first; there is no clear significance in their switch from "Christ" to "Son of God," other than to include a fuller range of christological titles that appear throughout Luke–Acts.[24] The second, confirmatory question emphasizes both their delight at his willingness to admit as much and their refusal to accept what he claims as true. Jesus confirms all this by replying, "*You* say that *I* am." Similar to his words in Matthew 26:64, this accusatory answer throws the question back to the temple authorities. For all their concern about preserving an understanding of God, they are unable and unwilling to recognize God's Son, the Christ, in their midst. They do know the answer, Jesus suggests. They draw the correct inference between his supposed identity as *the Christ* and the declaration he made about his coming exaltation.

But this part of Jesus' story proves to be more about their determination to destroy him than it is about his desire to express exactly who he is. The scene quickly comes to a close with a final statement—in which the council exclaims that the clinching testimony has come from Jesus' own mouth—that ratchets up the irony. Their words, gleefully expressing their determination to reject Jesus, actually offer testimony on his behalf as God's anointed one. He gave them the information that they demanded. They understood but did not believe it. Now they will kill him for it.

Jesus' trial in Luke includes, then, an important christological revelation, but one configured differently from those in the Markan and Matthean trials. Jesus discloses his identity and authority precisely so he can be rejected for it and so the process can continue through which he will emerge enthroned at God's right side. His declaration of his identity causes him to become a rejected Christ, rejected summarily and directly by Jerusalem's religious insiders. By quickly cutting to the chase through the questions concerning his identity, the rapid scene sets up the anticipation that the leaders have spurned their prophet, the Christ, and now they can and will eliminate him by presenting him to Pilate. All they require is the governor's ruling.

Scene 2: Jesus before Pontius Pilate (23:1–7)

The narrative suggests that the council immediately brings Jesus to Pilate; their eagerness shows their dedication and perhaps their desire to accomplish everything before support for Jesus can emerge from the populace. No one appears to be present in this short scene other than the governor, the Jewish aristocracy, and Jesus. The "crowds" mentioned alongside the chief priests in verse 4 are not a mass of common folk but only the nonpriestly members of the council and their attendants.[25]

The Jewish leadership makes serious accusations that function on multiple levels. Their primary charge, that Jesus misleads or perverts (διαστρέφω) the nation, reflects their conviction that he is a false prophet, who aims to turn the Jewish people from God.[26] The statement probably suggests to Pilate that Jesus foments rebellion, as clarified through the restatement of this accusation in 23:5 and 23:14.[27] Two other charges offer examples of how Jesus stirs up the nation: he speaks against taxes and claims to be a king. These grave accusations deserve a provincial governor's fullest attention, but in them readers also see misinterpretations of Jesus and his ministry. First, Jesus did not technically forbid paying taxes to the emperor in 20:20–26. In that passage, however, he offers subtle criticism of the claims made by imperial propaganda, as it is inscribed on coinage. He also states that the scribes and chief priests have made themselves indebted to the emperor and his political patronage; therefore they are bound to give back (ἀποδίδωμι) what he has given them. Jesus implies that one's full allegiance belongs to God alone. Such talk has significant political consequences, but it falls short of the specificity alleged in 23:2.[28]

Second, while some aspects of Jesus' time in Jerusalem have evoked images of kingship (19:38; 22:28–30), Luke has also shown that Jesus does not come as a king intending immediately to claim or establish his royal prerogatives. Jesus' entry into Jerusalem in Luke 19:35–40, while regal, nevertheless evokes no mention of David (cf. Mark 11:10; Matt. 21:9). His question about the Christ as "David's son" in 20:41–44, read in concert with Acts 2:34–36, suggests that Jesus is fully recognized as "Lord" only after his death, resurrection, and ascension.[29] Readers suspect that the priests and other leaders are trying to ascribe to Jesus a vision of kingship that Pilate would find actionable but that the wider narrative has otherwise redefined in less recognizable or immediately majestic tones.[30] Their accusations, although certainly deeply held, come across as half truths and therefore add to the ironic impression that these people cannot recognize who Jesus really is.

Pilate seizes on the suggestion that Jesus is a king who would rival the emperor. Jesus' curt response again expresses contempt and suggests that he and Pilate have different understandings of kingship. He will say nothing else until on his way to crucifixion in Luke 23:28, not because he is indifferent or overwhelmed, but because the trial begins to become a story of him as the object of others' wills. Also, the issue of kingship dissipates, for Pilate does not use the title again as a sarcastic barb, as he does in Mark and Matthew. In any case, Pilate understands Jesus' answer as sufficiently vague or pathetic to communicate a negative response, even if readers spot ironic truth in it.

Pilate's next action is astounding. Despite the serious accusations, he barely conducts even a half-hearted interrogation before concluding that the charges have no basis. Is Pilate uninterested or careless? The volatile nature of the charge, which the priests' council redoubles in 23:5, makes that unlikely, for Pilate himself will later acknowledge that such an offense, if substantiated, would require death (23:15). It is possible but also unlikely that Pilate possesses unique insight about Jesus, that from their brief exchange he somehow emerges as the only one in the trial scenes able to discern Jesus' blamelessness and the true nature of his authority. Casting serious doubt on this are his willingness to send Jesus to Herod, his eventual consent to deliver Jesus to the cross, and the testimony of Acts 4:27.

Instead, Pilate's comment in Luke 23:4 intends to frustrate the chief priests and their associates. Jesus appears before Pilate beaten and probably appearing pathetic, prompting the incredulous question about whether he could be a king. Pilate assumes a relative harmlessness about him; Jesus may have done something wrong, but Pilate assesses him as fairly inconsequential, at least at this point in time. Besides, by refusing to continue the trial, Pilate may reap a political benefit. He perceives the vehemence of the aristocracy's aggression against Jesus and maybe also the embellishments in their accusations. In refusing to execute a relatively harmless royal pretender, he can prevent the eager Jewish aristocracy from having their way, from too easily imposing their will on him, and from presuming upon imperial muscle to punish their false prophets.

Pilate therefore issues an antagonistic taunt. As mentioned in chapter 2 of this investigation, Roman governors of Judea and the chief priests were allies, but it was hardly an alliance of equal power and mutual respect. Pilate's disdain for them and their inflated concerns about Jesus' influence leads him to halt the prosecution. The trial is not for them to declare what they found (εὑρίσκω) in Jesus (23:2); what matters is the governor's authority, what he can find (εὑρίσκω) in him (23:4). Pilate takes a calculated risk, since he figures that in this case there is more to lose by giving too much power to the Jewish aristocracy than by granting leeway to a potential (yet pathetic) instigator of unrest.[31] When it becomes clear that the priests and their associates will not back down, however, Pilate sends them and Jesus to Herod. They should bother him with their complaints and try to make him their collaborator.

Scene 3: Jesus before Herod Antipas (23:8–12)

This scene's opening verse signals little hope for a fair or open inquiry. Herod's desire to see a sign recalls the people's misguided demands that Jesus produce miraculous evidence of his divine authority (11:16, 29–32), demands that show them to deserve condemnation. It reveals Herod as glib, not a sincere seeker. His delight recalls his earlier interest in doing violence to Jesus (9:9; 13:31) and expresses his scorn. Despite repeated attempts, Herod can extract no information from Jesus, and the narrative reveals nothing about the nature of his questions. Meanwhile the chief priests and scribes strenuously accuse Jesus, trying to secure a judgment in their favor. The scene is ridiculous, but its ribald character points up inequities in power: an impertinent official and his soldiers delight in provoking a famous defendant while frustrated prosecutors waste their breath on repeated accusations. The chief priests and scribes suffer humiliation "by the absurdity of the scene," which serves as little more than entertainment for Herod.[32] At least Herod and the priestly aristocracy find common ground in directing disdain toward Jesus. We must understand what Herod's treatment of Jesus communicates: "Mockery is no statement of innocence; it looks rather more like a measured strategy, designed to undermine the public image of Jesus without creating a direct confrontation."[33] Herod uses the hearing to reduce the Jerusalem aristocracy through his stonewalling and to reduce Jesus through shaming him. Ironically visualizing the debasement he inflicts upon Jesus, Herod adorns him in fine clothing before returning him to Pilate.[34]

As the scene ends, the narrator comments that Herod and Pilate became friends that day. Possibly this suggests a grotesque irony about Jesus' trial's bringing about reconciliation between these two. More likely the friendship reflects the unity of purpose that emerges in Pilate's and Herod's treatment of Jesus in response to the Jerusalem aristocracy's repeated accusations. Herod does not make Jesus disappear but, like Pilate, realizes that the situation allows him to make sport of both the prisoner and the chief priests, who oppose their false prophet. Herod acts like Pilate by antagonizing the Jewish leadership. His theatrics also erode Jesus' image and standing. This pleases Pilate, for it emboldens his own strategy, and thus it mends the relationship between these two imperial officials. The trial of Jesus allows them both to retain a political upper hand over their Jewish subjects.[35]

This scene makes at least three key contributions to the trial. First, it confirms Pilate's assumption that Jesus is essentially harmless. No one in any of Luke's trial scenes claims that Jesus is entirely innocent, but Herod and Pilate agree that little risk results from their actions, especially if they can undercut his honor in the process. Something about the charges the Jewish leadership makes cannot hold up, especially insofar as they accuse him of capital offenses. It is a stunning development that even Herod, who previously expressed his intention to kill Jesus, cannot find a reason to justify executing him now that he has him in custody.[36] This leads to the second point, that Jesus comes across as unrecognizable in his trial. No one can quite grasp who Jesus is. In his current condition, beaten and silent, he appears much different from what his reputation had previously suggested, back when Herod was eager to kill him. Third, the scene again expresses the Jewish leadership's determination to do away with Jesus. Yet the more they accuse him, the more the Roman officials stymie them. Much has changed since the first trial scene, when the high priest's council encountered no obstacles. Their intentions run aground in the second and third scenes, as Roman authorities refuse to allow them to press their case any further. Readers may wonder whether the priestly aristocracy will be able to impose their will on the trial, and how God's will might finally be accomplished amid all the political jockeying.

Scene 4: Jesus before Pontius Pilate a Second Time (23:13–25)

As this scene moves from its beginning through verse 16, it appears that the trial is ending. Pilate convenes the session not so deliberations can continue but so he can announce his decision. He summons the chief priests and rulers, who participated in the previous scenes, along with a new group, the people (ὁ λαός). Later, through its comments about them in Acts, the narrative reveals the λαός present to be people who dwell in Jerusalem. They represent the Jewish populace of the city; nothing in Luke's use of the term suggests they stand for all Israel.[37] Pilate begins by addressing the Jewish leadership, indicated by his recalling the action of the second trial scene.[38] He needles his audience, overstating the depth of his interrogation and the seriousness of Jesus' hearing before Herod. In the people's presence, he noti-fies the Jewish leadership that their capital accusations have "no basis" (23:14 NIV). He obviously does not consider the complaints against Jesus entirely unimportant, for he intends to whip (παιδεύω) him as a deterrent against future offenses (v. 16, repeated in v. 22). With παιδεύω Pilate may indicate a form of punitive torture milder than the horrible scourging (φραγελλόω) that precedes crucifixion in Mark 15:15 and Matthew 27:26, but the narrative never reveals whether that is so. Pilate's decision does not entirely exoner-ate Jesus, for the humiliation of this purported "king" before Herod and the shameful whipping Pilate plans to inflict will likely damage Jesus' ability to influence the population. But Pilate evidently intends to chastise the Jewish authorities, too: by summoning representatives from "the people" to hear his pronouncement, he tries to embarrass and discredit the aristocracy publicly, declaring his will in the matter and in the process reasserting his own claim to power over the Judean people.

Then, with the final word in the Greek text of Luke 23:16, Pilate reveals that he intends to release Jesus. This marks the first time that he raises the prospect of setting Jesus free, a move certain to offend the Jewish aristocracy that so deeply opposes Jesus. But with the word "release" Pilate touches a tripwire also for the people.[39]

In verse 18, Pilate's audience reacts to his intention to release Jesus. Quickly the narrative reveals that the governor will not be able to dictate Jesus' fate after all. The Jewish leaders along with the people of Jerusalem effectively restart the trial, demanding in unison that Pilate release Barabbas instead and do away with Jesus. Luke offers no explicit rationale behind the people's participation. The chief priests and other leaders' opposition to Jesus is predictable; but the people, whose support for Jesus has consistently set them in contrast to the temple authorities, now surprisingly side with them. The only trace of expla-nation for their about-face resides in their insistence on release for Barabbas, a known insurrectionist and murderer. Calling for his release makes an incred-ibly bold demand, a strong assertion of their power. They do not respond to an either/or option, as in Matthew, for Luke is silent about a customary prisoner release or anything that compels Pilate to release *anyone*. The people simply insist. The sharp contrast sustained between Jesus' apparent harmlessness and Barabbas's clear participation in violence suggests that Pilate's audience not only renounces Jesus but also opts for a very different alternative. In rejecting Jesus, the people thus reject the kind of leadership he would exercise.[40] This is not fickleness on their part. Jesus stands before them now, looking silly in his radiant robe, by all appearances utterly powerless while the governor presumes to dictate his fate. At least Barabbas the insurrectionist tried to make tangible changes in the social order; Jesus, the political commodity being passed around by imperial officials who see nothing royal about him, appears not to be the kind of effective king some people had previously hoped he would be. When Peter speaks in the Jerusalem temple in Acts 3:11–26, he reiterates the contrast and indicts the people: "You denied the holy and righteous one and asked that a murderer be given to you. You killed the founder of life, whom God raised from the dead" (3:14–15a).[41]

The forensic roles therefore shift suddenly. Pilate, the governor, retains authority to make the final judgment, but he does so through a contest of conflicting wills. He must contend for his case, while the now-expanded circle of prosecutors contends for its case. As the aristocracy and people's united voice appears to grow stronger, Pilate's control over the scene appears to fade. His repeated objections prove powerless to alter the will of the people. In the process, Jesus becomes virtually invisible. The narrative becomes "a stark confrontation between Pilate on one side and the Jewish leaders and people on the other."[42] It is a confrontation between Pilate's desire (see θέλω in v. 20) and that of the leaders and people (see θέλημα in v. 25). In the background, readers remember Jesus' prayer that his Father's will (θέλημα) be accomplished (22:42). The postresurrection preaching in Luke–Acts will confirm that God's will is accomplished in the verdict. Readers' surprise at seeing the people join the opposition to Jesus now reminds them that the "authority of darkness" (22:53) is also at work. Somehow a theological drama of wills is also occurring even as Pilate struggles to hold court.

The trial concludes with the governor's will overrun. Truly he realizes that he has lost the crowd. He has overplayed his hand and capitulates. It is a clear and embarrassing concession of defeat for him to release a dangerous man such as Barabbas to stave off a more politically dangerous situation of popular unrest. The will of the people, people he himself summoned, is clearly strong, and now is not the time to exacerbate a schism between himself and them. Jesus is hardly worth that. The governor must figure that this Galilean can become a casualty of the political cat-and-mouse game that Pilate initiated with the Jerusalem aristocracy. At the end, Pilate never openly condemns Jesus but offers the oblique ruling that the priestly authorities and people's request be realized. Not even the Roman governor, with all his power, can resist the will that demands Jesus' crucifixion, a seditionist's death.

The immediate aftermath of the trial reminds readers that the narrative amplifies the people's role in the trial to such a degree that Roman responsibility becomes momentarily occluded. A strictly literal reading of the "they" who lead Jesus away in 23:26 (see also 23:32–33) suggests that the Jewish leaders and people bring Jesus to the cross and crucify him themselves. The historical context, however, confirms that the "they" must indicate Roman soldiers, yet the narrative's ambiguity momentarily invites readers to confuse the identities, roles, and power of these two groups. The emphasis remains more suggestive than definitive. Also, almost immediately after accentuating the people's agency in Jesus' death, the narrative mitigates it by distinguishing between the people and their priestly leaders. Many of "the people" lament Jesus' fate in 23:27, "the people" watch Jesus die while their "rulers" scoff (23:35; cf. 23:48), and Jesus' followers blame only their "chief priests and rulers" in 24:20.[43] Subsequently, in Acts, the narrative recalls that the people, their leaders, and the Roman authorities bear blame (see 4:26–28). Once the people of Jerusalem repent in large numbers (Acts 2–5), however, that responsibility gravitates primarily to the Jewish leadership (see Acts 5:27–30).[44] The aristocracy's concern about such blame pinned to them plays a role in the Jerusalem trials found in Acts and examined in chapter 7 (below).

As for Pilate, and to a lesser degree Herod, any suggestion that the crowd's ferocity exonerates him is misguided. Jesus means little to him. Pilate possesses the power to release Jesus; even if he does not think that Jesus is totally harmless, his capitulation to the will of the crowd shows him to be more interested in political survival than justice.[45] Pilate's inability or unwillingness to pursue justice makes him appear not morally weak or cowardly but in over his head. The unanticipated backfiring of his political stunt in this scene intimates that the process and scope of Jesus' case is larger than he can realize. Indeed, in that fact lies a surprise of even greater magnitude: Pilate cannot prevent his "court" from becoming the venue where his will does not dictate the outcome. The systems and officers of Roman rule and authority cannot fully control what they, given their place atop the local sociopolitical hierarchy, are supposedly empowered to control. Luke suggests that they are not the agents who ultimately manage (or thwart) justice, at least not in Jesus' case.

CONCLUSIONS

Luke's trial scenes would make little sense without the affirmations of fulfilled Scripture in Luke 24 and the commentary from speeches in Acts. The trial depends upon the rest of the story, as the rest of the story depends upon it. Viewed by itself, the trial looks like a clumsy and improbable drama in which a popular mob shouts down the will of its sovereign against all odds and expectations. Viewed within the whole of the Lukan narrative, however, the trial emerges as the surprising means by which God's prophet suffers rejection from his own people and the Christ moves toward an ordained fate that must end with his glorification. Such a trial has implications, not only for

Luke's depiction of the rejected Christ, but also for Luke's perspective on the Roman sociopolitical apparatus that sees that rejection take place under its supervision and despite its attempts to secure a different outcome.

Irony and Responsibility

Like Mark's and Matthew's trials, Luke's involves christological assertions. Jesus reveals and redefines his identity and authority, even as his adversaries ironically confirm those truths through their ignorance and actions against him. For Luke, the irony of the trial intensifies the sense of misperception that envelops the judicial drama. No one sees clearly: the aristocratic Jewish authorities cannot recognize the truth about Jesus; Pilate and Herod cannot quite discern the nature of his possible offenses; the people of Jerusalem cannot accept what looks to them like a failed or impotent bid for kingship on his part. The irony communicates truth about Jesus Christ while it stokes pathos around his thorough rejection. At last, it extends blame to all the trial's participants, even to the λαός of Jerusalem.[46]

The trial pivots on the people's surprising influence over Pilate, exercised when they assume an active role to bring about Jesus' ultimate rejection and force Pilate's consent. Luke's trial displays the political principals of Jesus' day conducting their business, but it also sees a wider social landscape. When the people step forward and oppose Pilate's will, this trial depicts Jerusalem society in microcosm. Beginning in its first scene with only the high priest's council in attendance, the trial grows to a much more visible and public event, finally showing that the exhibition of the Christ is met by public contempt and severe rejection. (Although the rejection is widespread, 23:27 shows it to be hardly universal.) This perspective differs from Mark and Matthew, insofar as those Gospels offer sharp warnings about the exercise of human power and its corruption. The Lukan trial includes its share of dirty pool, to be sure, in Pilate and Herod's attempted exploitation of Jesus for political gain.[47] Yet it also expresses a degree of resignation toward such authority being what it is while remaining powerless to derail God's ultimate design.

The Politics of Agency

Any claim that Jesus' death occurs as a fulfillment of God's will provokes countless more theological questions than it can resolve, but nevertheless the Lukan narrative makes such a claim (while simultaneously showing little interest in resolving the many questions that the claim may raise for us). New Testament scholar David Tiede observes that the Lukan trial scenes "are particularly important for determining exactly whose will is being accomplished in the story."[48] Jesus' trial poses not only the question Whose will? but also By what means is that will accomplished within Jesus' sociopolitical context? The trial scenes render Pilate's authority as far from absolute. Everyone, from Jesus' aristocratic conspirators to Luke's readers, enters the trial anticipating that Pilate possesses "rule and authority" (20:20) over Jesus and his case, but the trial itself demonstrates that they are mistaken. As Pilate tries to assert control, he finds it taken from him. In Acts, Jesus' followers confirm that *God* engineered God's design through the trial, even through the messy process of a struggle among the trial's other participants.

That struggle is vital to recognize, for the social setting in which the story's theological drama occurs, in which God's expectations are fulfilled, is nothing less than the arena of Roman sociopolitical authority within Palestinian society. The narrative anticipates that Jerusalem will reject Jesus. The trial shows us—amid great suspense generated when Pilate and Herod stymie the aristocracy's intentions and the trial fails to resolve itself after several scenes—the people and the priestly authorities harnessing the political authority of the day to make that rejection happen. Yet they do so in the face of great odds and political risk. Still, the trial's theological context insists that the story is not just about the people overpowering Pilate. Their surprising influence over him serves to press the question How can this be happening? In the end, what does it mean that the will of God is fulfilled in such a clumsy trial, presided over by people who represent the fullness of Roman power yet nevertheless resulting in a judgment they were disinclined to issue?

Many interpreters answer that question through appeals to an apologetic purpose behind Luke–Acts. They suggest that Pilate's desire to release Jesus shows the narrative to be at pains to demonstrate that Christianity's founder, although he died by crucifixion, was nevertheless acknowledged as unthreatening to Roman political stability, and that Christians continue to live peacefully and innocently within the imperial order.[49] Such interpretations, however, often render Pilate as much too sympathetic toward Jesus. They also downplay Pilate's final capitulation to the Jerusalem people and aristocracy, his desire to exploit Jesus for political leverage, and his failure to comprehend exactly who Jesus is and what he represents. Certainly Pilate and Herod treat Jesus as if he is relatively harmless, but this amplifies their lack of understanding and misperception more than anything else. If they really regard Jesus as totally innocent, the narrative shows them doing a poor job of expressing as much.

A better answer to the question acknowledges more ambivalence in the Lukan sociopolitical vision. By using the trial narrative to pose uncertainty about whose will prevails in Jesus' condemnation, and by using the wider narrative of Luke–Acts to answer that it is God's will, Luke indicates that the sociopolitical mechanisms of Roman-governed society and the sociopolitical interests and machinations of those empowered to maintain that society actually play roles in God's design. Pilate's imperium and political tactics are not facts that Luke dismisses or ignores. In Jesus' case, they provide a means through which God accomplishes God's will. This issues neither a divine endorsement of the Roman system nor a call for its destruction. But neither does it suggest that Jesus and his gospel leave the sociopolitical order undisturbed. When Luke–Acts implies that God's will trumps Pilate's and Herod's, precisely in the face of their deliberate attempts to control both Jesus' fate and his standing among the people, and precisely through the unanticipated insistence voiced by the people, the narrative relegates these Roman officials and their authority to subordinate status. Luke suggests that the mechanisms in place to regulate sociopolitical order are themselves manipulable and usurped to serve a larger purpose. The gospel finds a way.

If it were not so subtle, Luke's account of God's design playing itself out through a sociopolitical contest would appear almost determinative or suggestive of a God who overrides human initiative yet still assigns blame. But the subtlety remains and needs to be respected as subtle and hardly the only Lukan word on such issues. Furthermore, these observations about Jesus' trial do not stand alone. The other trial scenes in Luke–Acts, especially those that constitute Paul's trial in Acts 21–28, show similar dynamics at work and offer additional nuance to Luke's vision of judicial processes commandeered to serve God's will. Chapters 7–9 of this book will explore and revisit these points. Readers who want to continue exploring the Lukan writings may therefore opt to jump immediately to those chapters and return to the Gospel according to John (chap. 6) at a later time.

6

Jesus on Trial in the Gospel according to John

Jesus' trial in John's Gospel brings a juridical climax to a story full of interrogations, deliberations, and references to bearing witness and issuing judgment.[1] The prevalence of legal language and images has led some interpreters to propose that the whole Gospel functions as one extended trial in which Jesus responds to accusations, bears witness, and pronounces judgments against others.[2] But a preponderance of forensic rhetoric and terminology does not equal a trial. The trial motif that runs through John provides rhetorical foundations for the Gospel's depiction of a contest between the belief and unbelief that responds to Jesus' attempts to reveal his Father (see, e.g., 12:44–50). The motif, while it greatly anticipates Jesus' appearance before Jewish high priests and the Roman governor, never culminates in a formal trial against a specific defendant until after Jesus' arrest.

When the trial finally comes, it lives up to the anticipation that the narrative generates for it. In a unique setting, it presents an examination of what people—not just any people but the people at the top of the sociopolitical hierarchy in John's world—do in response to the truth that Jesus embodies. In ways not seen in any other Gospel, those people find themselves forced to make choices that define not only their theological commitments but also their political loyalties.

OVERVIEW OF THE TRIAL SCENES

The trial in John includes enough detail, literary artistry, and stock Johannine imagery that an analysis of it deserves an entire book, not merely a single chapter. This chapter must therefore stay content with treating those aspects of the trial scenes that pertain to our focus on narrative rhetoric and sociopolitical perspectives.

Jesus' arrest occurs in a garden, where Judas leads an apparently large group of Roman soldiers, as well as security personnel (ὑπηρέται) serving the chief priests and Pharisees (18:1–11).[3] The presence of Roman soldiers suggests prior collaboration between Roman and Jewish officials. The narrator identifies the relevant Jewish officials, the Pharisees and chief priests, as "the Jews" (οἱ Ἰουδαῖοι) in the opening verse of the first trial scene (18:12).[4] This expression, which occurs frequently in John, deserves comment. When used in John's trial scenes, "the Jews" refers only to the Jerusalem-based temple leadership, the Jewish aristocracy composed of the high priest and chief priests.[5] No common folk appear in Jesus' trial. Other than Jesus, the drama comprises only an exclusive group of people situated within the highest levels of Judean sociopolitical authority: Pilate and the Jewish aristocracy (accompanied by security personnel). In the trial scenes and elsewhere, but not everywhere (e.g., 8:31; 10:19; 11:45; 12:11), John refers to οἱ Ἰουδαῖοι as a symbolic representation of both that historical aristocracy (at least, those among them who opposed Jesus) and later authorities who were persecuting believers known to the Gospel's author (or authors). For John, together these groups stand within the wider sinful "world" that rejects Jesus. By using "the Jews" as a label, John surely spawned an interpretive history of damages and errors. Some interpretations have taken "the Jews" purely as an ethnic designation, thereby distorting the Gospel to make it condemn all Jews as enemies of Christ. Also problematic is the expression's capacity for rendering Jesus' own Jewishness almost imperceptible.[6] The quotation marks I use around "the Jews" in this chapter aim to highlight that it is John's expression and it must be understood in light of Johannine usage.[7]

Jesus enters and exits the first trial scene (18:12–14, 19–24) bound, suggesting that he remains so through all the scenes. He comes face-to-face with Annas, a former high priest and father-in-law of Caiaphas, the current high priest. Annas asks one vague question about Jesus' disciples and teaching, to which Jesus replies that Annas should interrogate "the Jews"—meaning the other leaders—not him. A slap delivered by a guard confirms the defiance in Jesus' voice. Jesus, again defiantly, complains that he has spoken rightly, and then the patriarch of the high-priestly family sends him to Caiaphas.

As the first trial scene transpires, John breaks away from it twice to describe Peter's denial. The narrator brings Peter into the high priest's courtyard with the help of "another disciple" (18:15–18). The anonymity of this character "is a Johannine literary technique for drawing the reader into the story as a participant in, rather than as an observer of, the action of the text."[8] Readers start to sense that many people will be on trial in what follows, perhaps even themselves, for they observe Peter denying his own identity as Jesus' disciple at the same time that Jesus tells Annas that he has no secrets. After Jesus goes to Caiaphas, the narrator returns to Peter in 18:25–27, again suggesting simultaneity in the juxtaposition of Jesus' boldness before Jewish dignitaries and Peter's own "trial" before slaves and guards.

The narrator offers nothing to describe what might happen when Jesus is with Caiaphas. No further action nor pretense of a legal hearing before Jewish officials is necessary in John, for they are going to bring Jesus to Pilate, no matter what. After all, Caiaphas has already spoken his mind about Jesus in 11:45–53, a scene that the narrator recalls in 18:14 and that we will examine shortly.

The second scene (18:28–32) begins in the morning, with Jesus inside Pilate's headquarters, called the praetorium, and Pilate outside, conversing with the Jewish authorities. The scene introduces the strong tensions that persist between Pilate and the Jewish aristocracy throughout the remaining scenes. Their feisty conversation about accusations against Jesus keeps specific charges unspoken, but it reveals that "the Jews" want Jesus to die by Roman hands, since they do not have the legal authority to execute prisoners.

Pilate enters the praetorium to begin the next scene (18:33–38a), asking Jesus if he indeed is "the king of the Jews." It is exactly the same question that he asks in the other three Gospels, and so its emphatic syntax again reinforces his disdain and incredulity. Yet Jesus qualifies Pilate's question by describing his "kingdom," or rule, as different from those Pilate knows, for it is derived "not from this world" and not according to the power struggles that characterize kingdoms "from this world." Pilate, apparently unimpressed with Jesus' distinctions, asks again, "*You* are a king, then?" Jesus replies, "*You're* saying that I am a king. I was born for this, and I came into the world for this: that I should bear witness to the truth. Everyone who belongs to the truth hears my voice." Pilate's next words, "What is truth?" are his petulant response to Jesus' voice, for he leaves the praetorium immediately without caring to have the question answered.

In the fourth scene (18:38b–40), Pilate tells "the Jews" that he finds no cause to execute Jesus. He proposes releasing this "king" to fulfill the custom of freeing a prisoner at Passover. "The Jews" refuse and ask for the release of Barabbas, a robber. Immediately after this, in the fifth scene (19:1–3), inside the praetorium, Pilate flogs Jesus. His soldiers dress Jesus as a king and inflict violent, sarcastic homage upon him.

Pilate returns outside to tell the aristocracy that he will present Jesus to them so they can know that he has found no basis for condemning him. It is a disputatious scene (19:4–8). Pilate displays Jesus, beaten and decorated like a king, and "the Jews" call for his crucifixion. Pilate reiterates, for the third time, that he finds no basis for execution. "The Jews" complain that their own law calls for Jesus' death, "because he made himself out to be God's Son." This fills Pilate with fear.

In the seventh scene (19:9–12), Pilate and Jesus return inside for their final exchange. Pilate asks where Jesus is from. Jesus remains silent. Pilate stands on the authority he believes is his, demanding an answer because he will be the one to decide whether to release or to crucify Jesus. Jesus says that Pilate's authority to do these things is not the governor's own but has been granted "from above." He accuses Pilate of sin. Immediately, Pilate begins seeking to release Jesus, but "the Jews" from outside call to him, accusing him of contravening the emperor's interests if he pardons someone who "makes himself out to be a king."

In the final scene (19:13–16a), Pilate returns with Jesus outside to face "the Jews." In a dramatic moment, Pilate issues a judgment from a judicial platform (βῆμα): "Here's your king!" "The Jews" cry out emphatically for his crucifixion. Pilate continues with a final question that highlights Jesus' identity as king. His question, paraphrased, reads: "It's your own king I'm going to crucify, right?" The chief priests respond, "We have no king except for the emperor," and Pilate gives Jesus over to them for crucifixion.

THE TRIAL WITHIN A WIDER PLOT

The plot of John's Gospel does not unfold as much as it reprises basic themes, probing deeper into basic questions about Jesus' identity as if following a helical route. One interpreter aptly describes John's iterative progression:

> Plot development in John, then, is a matter of how Jesus' identity comes to be recognized and how it fails to be recognized. Not only is Jesus' identity progressively revealed by the repetitive signs and discourses and the progressive enhancement of metaphorical and symbolical images, but each episode has essentially the same plot as the story as a whole.[9]

At the same time, Jesus' trial and death bring a definitive climax to a story about his efforts to reveal his Father to a world that responds with increasing hostility. Jesus' arrest and trial culminate his enemies' repeated attempts to eliminate him. Several times they try to arrest him (7:30–32, 44; 10:39; 11:57). Plots to kill him appear to be widely known (5:18; 7:1, 25; 8:37, 40). People try to stone him (8:59; 10:31).

Several times Jesus refers to his coming death (2:19–22; 10:17–18; 12:7–8), and his preparations for leaving his disciples in the so-called Farewell Discourses (John 13–17) occur because he knows "his hour" has arrived (13:1). In these discourses, Jesus sketches the kind of lives his followers will live in the same world that hates and rejects him (15:18–19; 17:14). But the preparations for death point toward an ordained path to victory. Concerning John's story, including the trial scenes, this is no overstatement: "Nothing in the passion and death happens against Jesus' will; all is an act of free obedience to the Father."[10] Nothing about Judas's betrayal surprises Jesus (6:70–71; 13:27). Although Satan plays a role (13:2, 27), he enjoys no power over the Son (14:30). Jesus asserts his unmistakable control over his fate in 10:17–18, saying that he lays down his life of his own accord and takes it up again. He announces his obedience to his Father in 12:27–28 and 18:11. John avoids much of the Synoptic Gospels' sense of Jesus' victimization and the passion's raw tragedy by telling readers in advance that through death, Jesus returns to the Father's glory (16:28; 17:5).

Nevertheless, for all of John's certain, confident, and glorious talk about Jesus' death, this Gospel still emphasizes Jesus' interactions with the political figures who conspire against him. He does not ride a conveyor belt to the cross but through the trial scenes enters and affects the halls of supreme sociopolitical authority in Judea. As mentioned previously, John overflows with language that evokes judicial drama and judgments, and at least two scenes set the political stage for the narrative's climactic judicial contest.

First, something like a trial erupts in 9:13–41, as Pharisees investigate Jesus' healing of a man born blind.[11] The Pharisees' deliberations provide a prelude to Jesus' trial especially in the clear dichotomy they pose between Jesus and the Jewish authorities. To side with one is to reject the other. Such a division issues a judgment on the Pharisees, whose ignorance about Jesus is incredible, as the formerly blind man emphasizes in verse 30: "*You* of all people do not perceive!"[12] The Pharisees' interrogations confront them with the truth about Jesus, making them all the more culpable for their sinful unbelief (cf. v. 41). A similar thing happens in Jesus' trial, for Jesus' Jewish prosecutors are like the others who oppose him throughout the Gospel, doing so despite their access to his signs and his true testimony. The Pharisees' investigation of the man born blind effects "judgment" (v. 39) upon themselves. The man they interrogate acts as "the judge and the authorities are condemned out of their own mouths and according to their own Law in a way parallel to the reversal of roles between Pilate and Jesus in the passion."[13]

Second, the high priest and his council (συνέδριον) meet in 11:45–53, in a scene that shows the controversy between Jesus and his principal antagonists (identified specifically as the chief priests and Pharisees in 11:47) finally coming to a boil still many days before Jesus' final visit to Jerusalem. The scene is more a deliberative hearing than a trial, but its conclusion—"From that day on they determined to kill him"—has the effect of a final judgment, for in subsequent verses Jesus must protect himself from them (11:54; 12:36). The council's action follows closely after 10:22–39, when Jesus answers the Jewish leaders' question about whether he is the Christ by equating himself with God ("The Father and I are one"). "The Jews" interpret this as blasphemy, and so the later meeting in 11:45–53 emerges out of no small theological concern about Jesus.

Yet the council's meeting reveals a motive other than countering blasphemy. The council fears that widespread belief in Jesus will also have serious political consequences, sure to result in the Romans' moving to "take away" their temple and nation. They fear that the enthusiasm of people who have already tried to make Jesus their king (see 6:14–15) will invite Rome's wrath. If the Jewish aristocracy cannot preserve social stability among the population, then they risk the destruction of Israel's national identity as symbolically rooted in the temple, the same thing that symbolically undergirds their Roman-granted authority as leaders of Israel. Even if the council's concern only raises the possibility that they fear losing their political advantages, Caiaphas's reply makes this more certain. He tells the group, "It is better for you"—not better for God, not better for Israel, but better for you—"that one person die" instead of the whole nation (11:50). His interest in preserving the nation comes across as rather contrived, given the self-serving character of "better for you." The narrator presents Caiaphas's assessment of the situation as unintended prophecy about a death for (ὑπέρ) the people (cf. 10:11, 15). At the same time, his statement and the council's fears also address their sociopolitical circumstances. If Jesus' death will squelch a widespread movement capable of eroding the aristocracy's ability to promote their religious tenets and will prevent an increase in political enthusiasm that would be perceived as counter to Roman sovereignty, it must happen.

THE TRIAL

Scene 1: Jesus before Annas (18:12–14, 19–24)

This episode marks Annas's only appearance in John. Although Annas ceased to be high priest in 15 CE, he retained the title and continued to be an influential figure among the Jerusalem priestly aristocracy, for five of his sons, plus a grandson, served as high priest after him.[14] He represents the high-priestly office in general, beyond merely the tenure of a single high priest, as well as the political and religious concerns of the entire community of priestly elites. His brief encounter with Jesus has a recapitulative effect, in that his general question about disciples and teaching brings the narrative of Jesus' ministry into view.[15] Also, several chapters have elapsed since Jesus has had contact with the chief priests and the rest of "the Jews," and so 18:14 reminds readers of Caiaphas's judgment in 11:45–53. Finally, Jesus' words in 18:20–21 confirm that there are no new issues on the table. The entire high-priestly circle, at least all those who have not already turned to believe in Jesus (e.g., 12:11), remains firmly set against him.

Although everything else about the scene in its narrative context confirms that an interrogation is, from a judicial perspective, a moot point, still Annas questions Jesus. Jesus testifies to the fact that the aristocracy has willingly rejected him, even as he issues an indictment of his own. In 18:20 he equates speaking "boldly to the world" (the "world" that hates him) with teaching in synagogues and the temple in the presence of "all the Jews" (meaning the Jewish authorities). Jesus has already made his case, publicly. In telling Annas to "ask them," Jesus is neither evasive nor resigned. He suggests that Annas try interrogating those who have rejected him.[16] They deserve the prosecution. Jesus, then, is hardly impressed with any semblance of curiosity or due diligence from Annas; this is no hearing (cf. 7:51). The charade can end so the real trial can begin. When Annas terminates the conversation and sends Jesus to Caiaphas, he thereby affirms that none of Jesus' powerful opponents have really "heard" what he has said to them previously (see v. 21). They are entirely against him, for they belong to the world. According to 15:24–25, they are without cause, and they are also entirely against the Father.

The meeting of the council in 11:45–53 and other previous conversations between Jesus and "the Jews" account for the relative emptiness of this first trial scene. The Jewish officials, under Caiaphas's leadership, have already judged Jesus. This scene thus quickly reveals itself as a sham prelude to the actual trial. Its judicial vacuity helps the narrative direct sharper focus toward the drama in the following scenes involving Pilate, Jesus, and "the Jews." Jesus' prosecution is hardly only a matter involving the will of the Jewish authorities. It depends upon, and will play upon, the relationship between those authorities and Roman power. In turn, Jesus' case will make a significant impact upon this strained relationship.

The Movement in the Trial

In the remaining seven scenes, Pilate is the only character who appears in each of them. He becomes the centerpiece. As we will see, as Jesus is tried, the narrative also puts Pilate and his authority on trial. As the official representative of the Roman Empire, he stands particularly for the empire and more generally for the "world" that cannot recognize Jesus' authority to reveal the Father. John's trial narrative will minimize Pilate's authority and the threat he poses to

Jesus and his gospel. It will also show Pilate responding to Jesus' claims by consolidating the semblance of Roman authority through efforts to extract greater loyalty from "the Jews" who demand a Roman execution for Jesus.

The trial's focus on Pilate shows him in motion across these seven scenes, shuttling between the praetorium's exterior and interior. Certainly this movement accentuates melodrama. As Pilate accumulates information and interacts with other characters, John stokes readers' eagerness to see how the governor will emerge from the trial. How does this depiction of Pilate's movement across an exterior-interior boundary contribute to the sociopolitical perspective of John's trial narrative? The analysis of the scenes will reveal that Pilate's locational oscillation does not reflect vacillating judgment; his movement is not a narrative depiction of hesitancy or neutrality on his part. To mistake movement for indecision is to miss the cunning and manipulative aspects of his behavior in these scenes.[17] The trial scenes instead suggest three effects of Pilate's constant back-and-forth relocation. First, the movement insinuates that he struggles to manipulate all the affairs. Given Jesus' claim that only he has authority to lay down his life (10:18), Pilate's judicial authority appears to be less than fully secure, especially as he tries to impose his will in two settings upon both Jesus and "the Jews." Second, the movement highlights the differences between Pilate and "the Jews." Pilate does not deal with the aristocracy as equal partners in their political alliance, and both parties seek to use Jesus against the other to gain political leverage. They occupy contrasting locations with respect to this prisoner and the threat he might pose. Third, the movement finally concludes with the threshold between outside and inside becoming pervious. Pilate, while inside, hears "the Jews" speak from outside in the seventh scene, and the trial terminates with all the parties together on the same stage.[18] In the final scene, Pilate and the aristocracy appear much alike and on common ground, for they express a similar exclusive loyalty to the emperor. When Pilate enters the narrative in the second trial scene, however, the differences between him and "the Jews" are much more stark.

Scene 2: Pilate with the Jewish Leadership, Outside (18:28–32)

As Jesus goes into the governor's praetorium, the narrator reminds readers that Passover begins later that evening. Frequent references to the Passover during the trial and crucifixion (see 18:39; 19:14, 31, 42) subtly recall God's triumph over Pharaoh in the book of Exodus. Is another nation about to be embarrassed by God's supremacy, or does the festival setting add an ironic touch to the story of Jesus' death? At this point, in any case, as a practical matter the imminence of Passover keeps "the Jews" outside the Gentile headquarters. This reflects the differences between them and Pilate while also painting them as hypocrites who see no contradiction between their efforts to destroy Jesus and their commitment to avoiding defilement.

Tension exists between Pilate and "the Jews." The words and context of their exchange hardly suggest an amicable relationship. The aristocracy refuses to present a specific charge, saying only that of course Jesus is "an evildoer." Pilate then challenges them to take him and conduct their own trial according to their own laws, something that both parties know is impossible if a capital offense is the issue. Multiple ancient sources confirm what verse 31 says, that Rome did not grant Jewish authorities the power to wield capital punishment, except in very specific circumstances.[19] "The Jews" do not want mob violence (cf. 8:59; 10:31) but a state-sponsored execution. Pilate presumably senses that "the Jews" are trying to exploit their alliance with Rome so that imperial authority will do away with Jesus on its own, thereby protecting them from any negative repercussions from elements in the wider Jewish population that support Jesus. Indeed, Pilate probably already knows the aristocracy's allegations. He has given them soldiers to assist in arresting Jesus, and so now the governor lets them know that he will conduct the trial according to his own demands. Rome's superior authority means that "the Jews" are essentially powerless to do otherwise.

The scene's closing verse (32), the narrator's aside that the previous dialogue fulfills what Jesus said about how he would die, sheds more light on the scene's dialogue. Jesus previously claimed he would be "lifted up" (ὑψόω), a veiled reference to both death and glorification (12:32–33; see also 3:14–15; 8:28). The use of ὑψόω in John indicates crucifixion, a form of execution certainly not usually suited to "draw all people to" its victim (12:32). The action and the aside therefore make plain that "the Jews" want Rome to be responsible for Jesus' death, that they want him *crucified* under the pretense of imperial security. They do not want to make his trial an issue of Jewish law. Pilate will make them pay an awful price for this, when the trial concludes.

Scene 3: Jesus before Pilate, Inside (18:33–38a)

Clearly "the Jews" and Pilate had collaborated prior to the arrest, for Pilate immediately asks Jesus whether he really is "king of the Jews." The idea of Jesus as king is not new in John, for his admirers have called him that in public settings (6:15; 12:12–16; cf. 1:49). Moreover, in the presence of "the Jews," Jesus has described himself as a shepherd (10:1–18), a metaphor for a king in Ezekiel 34:1–31 and elsewhere in the Scriptures. The issue of Jesus' kingship and authority will be the main focus of the trial from this point forward. Still, Jesus avoids Pilate's initial question and asks his own in reply. He refuses to adhere strictly to his forensic role of defendant and tries to examine Pilate. His question probes whether Pilate is really interested in understanding the truth of Jesus' reign, or kingship, or whether he simply follows what the Jewish aristocracy has told him.

Pilate's reply in John 18:35 expresses his insolence toward "the Jews" and their concerns. This suggests that Jesus might have a chance at receiving a fair hearing, if he cooperates with the process. Pilate appears to care little about why the Jewish leadership opposes Jesus, as long as Jesus does not threaten Roman interests. But the governor must take this case seriously, since the official representatives of Israel, Jesus' "nation," have given Jesus over to him.

Jesus then answers Pilate's original question by explaining what it means for him to be a king, but one whose rule is "not from this world." That statement indicates "not that Jesus' kingdom belongs to the other world rather than to this one. Although his royal power ($\beta\alpha\sigma\iota\lambda\epsilon\acute{\iota}\alpha$) derives *from* the other world, it comes *to* this one (see 14:18–19, 23)."[20] Jesus' kingdom exists in the same space and time as the emperor's, but his reign is an altogether different kind, one unfamiliar to the world and to Pilate. This explains why Jesus' followers, or attendants ($\acute{\upsilon}\pi\eta\rho\acute{\epsilon}\tau\alpha\iota$), do not employ violence on his behalf. His role as king is as a shepherd: to go before his sheep, to care for them, to give them life, and to lay down his life for them (10:1–18).

Pilate seems to grasp that Jesus is not a king in the usual sense. But the defendant's words still have political implications that concern him, and so he asks again about kingship. Again Jesus answers by contrasting Pilate's understanding of kingship with his own. His words in 18:37 point to several theological motifs in John, such as bearing witness (3:31–33; 5:30–39; 8:13–18; 10:25), the truth (e.g., 1:17; 14:6; 16:7; 17:17–19), and hearing ($\acute{\alpha}\kappa o\acute{\upsilon}\omega$) Jesus' voice (5:25; 10:3, 16, 27). Jesus thus offers the testimony of his entire ministry here in the trial. However, no one involved in this trial can really hear the truth he speaks. Pilate's final line, "What is truth?" is a flippant remark. Speaking these words in the face of Jesus—himself "the way, and the truth, and the life"—without waiting to hear an answer shows that Pilate is not one "who belongs to the truth"; he cannot "hear" Jesus' voice. John's readers understand that "the truth" at which Pilate scoffs is more than some philosophical ideal or the opposite of falsehood; it is knowledge of God revealed in Jesus.[21] Pilate belongs to the world, which cannot recognize this truth (see 14:17).

Scene 4: Pilate Back with the Jewish Leadership, Outside (18:38b–40)

Pilate returns to "the Jews" outside the praetorium and tells them he finds no case for a capital sentence against Jesus, thus suggesting that he finds Jesus' talk about a different kind of kingdom and belonging to the truth essentially harmless to Roman interests. Pilate could conceivably release Jesus without further discussion, but apparently he is not completely convinced of Jesus' total innocence and not willing to suffer the political consequences of so boldly enraging his aristocratic allies. Also, by making strategic use of Jesus and the question of his kingship, Pilate might benefit from gently feeding the flames of the smoldering tension between himself and the Jewish leadership.

In verse 39 Pilate speaks to the same people who gave Jesus over to him in the first place. They surely will not desire Jesus' release, and so he offers Jesus, whom he cleverly refers to as "the king of the Jews," as a taunt. This is not a test of the chief priests' loyalty, for Pilate already knows that they want Jesus destroyed. Pilate mentions Passover, and by pressing the title "king of the Jews" onto Jesus in this context, he belittles Jewish hopes that their God might provide them deliverance and political sovereignty. "The Jews" decline the offer and ask for Barabbas. By implication they call on the Roman governor to continue the case against Jesus.

John gives only this information about Barabbas: he is a robber (λῃστής). Barabbas is not mentioned again. This trial does not present a choice between these two men. It is not clear that Pilate ever releases Barabbas. Who is he, then, and what is the significance of "the Jews'" demand for him? The wider narrative context indicates that Barabbas and Jesus are hardly comparable figures in the eyes of both Pilate and the priestly aristocracy. Barabbas is not "a revolutionary" (NET) who "had taken part in a rebellion" (NIV). Such translations suggest undue influence from Mark and Luke. Asking for an insurrectionist, in John's perspective, would risk creating the situation like the one that "the Jews" explicitly feared in 11:48, something that could cause the Romans to "take away" their temple and nation.[22] Also, since they really want Jesus prosecuted by Rome, "the Jews" ask instead for someone whose crimes Pilate might find minimal. Barabbas, then, is a robber. The only other appearances of λῃστής in John's Gospel refer to the kind of person whose perfidy strikes contrasts to a reliable shepherd, like Jesus, who enters a sheepfold rightly via a gate (10:1, 8). "The choice between Jesus and Barabbas is thus the choice between the good shepherd and the bandit, and in choosing Barabbas 'the Jews' once again demonstrate that they do not belong to Jesus' sheep."[23]

Scene 5: Jesus Subjected to Pilate's Scourging and Mockery, Inside (19:1–3)

Neither frustration nor an arbitrary desire to placate "the Jews" prompts Pilate's decision to flog Jesus, for later (19:4) he will announce to them that Jesus' appearance—his wounds and his royal clothing—show that there is no cause to their accusations against him. The flogging, then, is Pilate's more thorough examination of Jesus, inquisitional torture meant to extract truth from the man in custody, in contrast to the penal torture seen before the crucifixion in Mark and Matthew.[24] Pilate initiates the torture probably out of suspicion that there is more to learn from Jesus. But he knows that even if there is not, and the brutality produces no confession or clarity, then still that will reaffirm his preliminary conclusion that Jesus poses little harm to Roman interests.

This brief scene makes important contributions to the overall trial, especially to later scenes.[25] First, it inscribes kingship upon Jesus in visible and ironic ways. Bruised, bloodied, and arrayed in mock splendor now and through the remaining scenes (see 19:5), the trial revolves around questions of his authority and what it means to submit to it or resist it. Second, the scourging is an expression of Pilate's power, not only to use force, but also to shape the proceedings. He has nothing to lose by torturing Jesus. Even if he elicits no confession, the debasement he inflicts on Jesus still provides an added benefit in that it allows him to parody his prisoner's reputation and the people for whom Jesus might claim to be king. The violent degradation expresses Pilate's opinion about any "truth" Jesus might represent. Finally, the scene maximizes the trial's objectification of Jesus. As Pilate shames and mocks him through wounds and sarcasm, Jesus becomes quiet. He has finished speaking in the trial, except for a final, definitive line to Pilate coming in 19:11.

Scene 6: Pilate Presents Jesus to the Jewish Leadership, Outside (19:4–8)

Pilate brings Jesus to "the Jews," expecting that having all parties in the same place will allow him to bring closure to the trial. His burlesque presentation of Jesus, still dressed in crown and robe, as "the man" (literally, "the person"), unintentionally recalls other Johannine references to Jesus as ἄνθρωπος (e.g., 7:46; 9:16; 10:33; 11:47).[26] Readers may also associate this ἄνθρωπος with the "one person" Caiaphas referred to so ominously in 11:50. In the spectacle, Pilate communicates several things to "the Jews." First, he expects that they will be satisfied by the inquisitional torture and "know" (v. 4) that he made a serious effort to examine and then disgrace Jesus by the means available to him. Second, it reminds them that he holds power over someone like Jesus, for Rome possesses authority to inflict such treatment. The degree to which Pilate tortures and humiliates Jesus is the degree to which he trumpets Roman authority. Third, it reaffirms his power over Jewish society in particular. If Pilate considered Jesus fully innocent *and* inconsequential, the royal theater would be unnecessary. But the beaten Jesus' crown and robe allow Pilate to discredit him and the claims of Jewish sovereignty that he may represent, even if Pilate ultimately finds him relatively harmless as a suspected revolutionary.

But the presentation fails to sway or intimidate the priestly aristocracy. When they see Jesus, they demand that Pilate's theater become real. "Pilate intends to display a torture victim. Instead, a king emerges."[27] They want Pilate not merely to dress Jesus like a political danger but to kill him like one. Thus, in the narrative's perspective, Jesus' appearance does not testify to Roman power over him; instead, and ironically, it comes to demonstrate Rome's inability to thwart the will of God that envelops the trial. John knows that Jesus really is a king. Jesus' appearance also means, again ironically, that Rome cannot finally discredit the truth of the gospel, a truth that "the Jews" declare when they complain that Jesus made himself to be equal to God. Indeed, they have put on trial not just a "person" but also the authority that belongs only to God.

Everyone knows (recall 18:31) that the Jewish leadership cannot execute Jesus, and so Pilate's response to them in 19:6 sounds like angry sarcasm; he almost dares them to defy his authority, an authority underlined by his emphatic statement, "*I* don't find a basis" for a such a punishment. "The Jews" still want Rome to put Jesus to death, but they change their approach in verse 7, talking about what their own law requires and imploring Pilate to respect that. Pilate may not consider Jesus threatening to certain imperial interests, but he also has a responsibility to tend to the legal traditions of the people in his province.[28] What the aristocracy says deeply affects Pilate and causes the trial to change directions. But as the narrative presents it, Pilate does not respond to their appeal to Jewish law; he responds to the statement that Jesus "made himself to be God's Son." At these words, Pilate suddenly becomes "exceedingly fearful."[29]

There is an inexplicable dimension to Pilate's fear. Trying to offer a reasonable basis for it, as some interpreters do, through appeals to Greco-Roman traditions about gods appearing in human form misses the point. Pilate's response to the idea of Jesus as "God's Son" is as strange yet unintentionally insightful as when those who arrest Jesus—Jews and Romans alike—fall down when he tells them, "I am" the one they seek, taking the divine name for himself (18:6). In John's Gospel, Jesus' identity as God's Son means that he is the very revelation of God (1:18; 5:19–27; 14:8–11). Pilate's fear is a mysterious yet appropriate response to the implications of Jesus' authority, expressed in that title.[30]

Scene 7: Pilate and Jesus' Exchange concerning Authority, Inside (19:9–12)

Pilate's question about Jesus' origins confirms his fear that Jesus might possess an authority with real implications. In John, "to know where Jesus comes

from is to know *who* he is."[31] Those who do not know where he *really* comes
from do not belong to him (7:27–29, 41–42; 8:14; 9:29). Readers know that
his true origin, and thus the source of his authority, is divine and primordial
(1:1–4). But Jesus does not grant Pilate an answer. He has already given him
a strong hint in 18:37 when he spoke of coming "into the world." His silence
emboldens Pilate. But, given the governor's lingering fear, his demand for a
response in 19:10 comes across as based on irritation mixed with desperation.
He waves his imperial fist in Jesus' face, confident but less than absolutely sure
if the authority he claims over Jesus' fate is as certain as he supposes. What
does the empire's authority mean in light of this "Son of God"?

Jesus, in verse 11, tells Pilate that his authority over him is provisional.
It is not Pilate's; it comes from God, "from above." He refers not to the
authority vested in the governor's office, but to Pilate's particular authority
over Jesus in this instance, authority to release or to crucify him.[32] It is Jesus,
empowered by his Father, who lays down his life; Pilate cannot *take* it or *grant*
it (cf. 10:17–18). Given who Jesus is across the breadth of John's Gospel, his
statement in verse 11 is rather unsurprising. Within the drama of the trial,
it is a strong and deeply ironic claim for a bound defendant, on trial for a
capital offense, to make before the emperor's representative. Pilate, after all,
has been conducting the whole trial in ways that enhance his own authority
over Jesus. Jesus' statement, however, issues his judgment on Pilate and on
the entire trial. He punctuates this assertion about God's ultimate authority
by leveling his own accusations. Pilate is guilty of sin, even though the sin of
Caiaphas, the leader and personification of the priestly aristocracy and the
one who gave Jesus over to Pilate, remains greater.[33]

John does not explain the governor's next move but only says that in
response to Jesus' words, "Pilate began attempting to release him."[34] This
is the only instance in the trial where Pilate seriously pursues this option.
Although he will soon have to abort it, it nevertheless seems to be a serious
undertaking, much different from the stunt in an earlier scene when he mock-
ingly offered Jesus for the prisoner release. Pilate perhaps finally considers
Jesus to be little more than a harmless babbler of ideas not worth his time.
But, against this reading, he never again protests to "the Jews" that he finds no
cause to kill Jesus. More likely fear continues to motivate Pilate, inexplicable
fear that Jesus is more than he appears to be. In any case, the fear and Pilate's
effort are both extremely short-lived. The indoor setting suggests that he
considers releasing Jesus without the Jewish aristocracy's knowledge. But they
detect something, and their voices penetrate the praetorium, catching him in
the act. "The Jews" remind him that if Jesus claims any royal authority for
himself, then he is by definition opposed to the emperor. Everyone accepts
this as a true statement, whether Jesus is truly a king sent by God or a pathetic

pretender with little more than a title and a penchant for mysteries. "The Jews" force Pilate to choose once for all between the emperor and Jesus, and Pilate snaps out of his fear. He will deal with Jesus as he knows a provincial governor must.

Scene 8: Pilate Brings about Condemnation, Outside (19:13–16a)

In verse 13, Pilate hears (ἀκούω) the words "the Jews" speak in 19:12, and they sink in.[35] They affect him more finally than any word he has heard from or about Jesus (cf. 5:24; 18:37). "The Jews" insist anew that Jesus die a humiliating death at the hands of the empire. They demand that their alliance with Rome shall provide the machinery that kills Jesus. They force Pilate's hand with political pressure, reminding him that the duties of his imperial office dictate what he must do, unless he wants to side with Jesus. In a dramatic response, Pilate brings Jesus outside and moves to the judicial bench to deliver his judgment.[36] If this aristocracy wants to claim the benefits of an alliance with Rome, they will live with what that entails. Pilate may not be fully able to control Jesus, and his authority over him remains limited by Jesus' refusal to acknowledge it, but Pilate can unite "the Jews" more closely with Roman sovereignty and call them to account as they did with him. He will make them confess their loyalty to Rome to obtain a Roman execution. If Pilate cannot occupy middle ground with respect to Jesus and the emperor, neither will he allow the Jewish leadership to do so.

So Pilate announces from the bench, "Here's your king!" Pilate's theatrics, Jesus' reminder of his Father's ultimate authority, and political pressure exerted by "the Jews"—all have led to the ordinary person (ἄνθρωπος) of 19:5 now becoming "king" in 19:14. Pilate manipulates the judicial spectacle to denigrate Jesus in particular even as it also denigrates the general notion of a Jewish king in the face of Roman authority. The irony is that Pilate's scornful declaration actually makes Jesus into a king, so to speak.[37] Pilate formally pronounces the declaration and sets into motion the process that Jesus has anticipated and even designed throughout the whole Gospel, a process toward crucifixion. Pilate's authorized pronouncement only underlines Jesus' own authority to reveal the Father and draw all people to himself (see 12:27–33).

"The Jews" respond appropriately, calling for crucifixion, the punishment for sedition. Pilate pushes again, emphasizing "your king" in the phrasing of his final question (v. 15). Then the union between "the Jews" and Roman authority becomes complete.[38] The chief priests confess, "We have no king except for the emperor," denouncing Jesus as a pretender, denouncing hope for a Jewish king, and agreeing in principle with what Pilate said to Jesus in

19:10 about his authority. The political implications of this confession are clear. The priestly authorities state their fealty to Rome to get what they want. But there are also profound theological implications to this oath, for "affirming Caesar's exclusive lordship means rejecting God's lordship"; "the Jews" submit themselves to the Roman emperor, who was referred to as "son of God," over the Father who sent the true Son.[39] A hymn sung during Passover, at least as early as the second century CE, says to God, "We have no king but you." In light of this prayer and other familiar Jewish affirmations of God's unique lordship and rule over all, the aristocracy's statement before Pilate is extraordinary and devastating.[40] They greet the Passover, a celebration of God's deliverance of Israel, with a blasphemous declaration. They deny God's unique authority, having themselves accused Jesus of doing the same by making himself equal to God.

The narrator accentuates the political convergence of Pilate and "the Jews" in 19:16a, where the grammar indicates that the chief priests conduct the crucifixion (cf. Luke 23:26). Subsequent narration (see 19:19–25a) confirms what the historical context would require, that Roman soldiers actually crucify Jesus. John nevertheless invites readers to see both parties as acting in tandem. Still, it is an uncomfortable partnership. The inscription that Pilate places on the cross chafes the chief priests because it declares Jesus to be "King of the Jews" and not merely one who claims the title. Pilate's refusal to change the sign offers ironic testimony to the truth and demonstrates his commitment to holding the Jewish aristocracy accountable to their confession about the emperor's unique authority. In the trial of Jesus, Pilate reaps a political benefit: the opportunity to crucify Jewish hopes for another Passover deliverance by their God.

CONCLUSIONS

Some interpreters question whether the Johannine trial really occupies itself with political concerns. It is difficult to understand how that is even up for debate, given scenes that include such statements as "You would have had no authority over me, except for what was given to you from above" and "We have no king except for the emperor." Our analysis of the trial has focused on the political calculations at work in the scenes, passing over many other points of the trial's theology and symbolism. In the process, we have seen that Jesus claims an authority quite different in kind from Pilate's and Rome's. The difference lends ambiguity to John's depiction of the relationship between Jesus' authority and the Roman sociopolitical system. Yet, within that ambiguity, John also depicts characters confronting polarizing choices between Jesus and the emperor, choices that cannot help but have political ramifications.

The Politics of the World

In John, Jesus characterizes his reign as foreign to the "world." The violence and mockery of the trial confirm this otherness, making it stark when Pilate declares Jesus to be the Jewish king and has him suffer the consequences. John's distinctive revelation of Jesus' kingship during a politically charged trial shows that the "world" that hears Jesus' testimony and rejects it is not merely a "world" marked by spiritual dullness or violent opposition. Pilate and his interactions with the Jewish aristocracy show the "world" also to be one of political power—the kind of power that is rightly made fearful of Jesus' claims to divine authority, the kind of power that does everything within its reach to suppress "the truth" about Jesus, the kind of power that forces false confessions to protect its own interests.

This is the "world," represented by Pilate and "the Jews," that is on trial in John. The narrative judges this "world" through Jesus' statement in 19:11, through Pilate's forcing "the Jews" to confess the emperor's ultimate authority, and through their blasphemous willingness to do so. These dimensions of the trial indicate that Jesus and his message encounter a "world" that knows that any claim to truth has potential to be absolute. In turn, the authority Jesus represents minimizes Rome's claims to power, even subverting those claims through John's ironic portrait of Jesus becoming king in relationship to Passover. There is a clear incompatibility between Jesus and the Johannine "world," not because they are diametrical opposites, but because Jesus' reign is such a different thing. The truth to which Jesus bears witness can abide no other master and finally permits allegiance to God alone. The "world" that opposes Jesus recognizes this and resists it. Just as siding with Jesus in 9:13–41 is to side against the Pharisees, in the trial siding with the emperor entails rejecting Jesus, and rejecting Jesus makes one to side with the emperor. Pilate is forced into this choice. He forces the Jewish leadership into this choice. John's Gospel presents this choice to its readers.

An Ironic Connection to the World

Dramatic irony saturates the trial, from Pilate's cynical "What is truth?" through the governor's pregnant introduction of Jesus as "the man," to the final mocking pronouncement of Jesus' royal identity. Through their attempts to suppress the truth, the authorities actually declare and reaffirm it. They play a part in making it visible.

An ironic contrast between the way of Jesus and the ways of the "world" does not posit an *antithetical* relationship between the two. Irony involves more than pitting two articulations of reality against each other; irony creates a dynamic relationship between the two and draws attention to that relationship as the place to discover a new, ironic significance.[41] Thus Jesus and his claims are not only different from the "world's" articulations of authority; they also retain an intrinsic relationship to the "world" by virtue of their ironic contrast to it. Irony keeps Jesus' authority and the hostile "world" related, so that the trial indelibly stamps Pilate's authority as provisional and violent. Despite the choice the trial poses between Jesus and the emperor, Jesus himself neither calls for nor prophesies Rome's destruction. Instead, Johannine irony establishes him and the community of his followers as perpetually displaced from the "world" that judges them because that "world" already opposes Jesus. They are unrecognized by this "world" and hated by it; yet they are also charged to give life to it (1:10; 6:33; 15:18–19). The irony casts Jesus as an *alternate* to the "world," an alternate who remains in the "world" and whose incompatibility with that "world" cannot be erased.

What do the "world's" judgment against Jesus and Jesus' judgment against the "world" indicate? John's wider narrative reminds readers that the same "world" that uses its power to destroy Jesus is also the "world" that God loves (3:16–17). Negatively, the trial exposes the distance between the "world's" modes of ruling and the rule that Jesus brings to the "world." Other parts of John's Gospel positively reaffirm a commitment to the "world." Jesus' so-called Farewell Discourses (John 13–17) define the alternate culture that he makes possible. This "world" is a dangerous place for Jesus' disciples (see 15:18–21; 17:14–16), but they are to engage it (17:18). The trial's judgment, then, simultaneously offers both warning and invitation.[42]

That "world," for John's earliest readers, was particularly Roman, as the dominant political force. At the same time, John gives no indication that the "world" that chooses a human sovereign over Jesus is a uniquely Roman phenomenon. John's depiction of a "world" eager to accrue loyalty in the face of attempts to minimize its claims to authority extends to any sociopolitical system that demands inordinate allegiance and prominence, when it does so to the exclusion of the truth that Jesus brings.[43]

7

Trials in Jerusalem in Acts 4–8

A large amount of the Acts of the Apostles describes people in legal jeopardy. The trial scenes provide climactic and telling moments, for much of Acts can be characterized as, among other things, a story about conflicts that erupt when Jesus' followers bring their claims about the crucified and risen Christ to the people of the first-century northeastern Mediterranean world. While not all of these conflicts result in trials, nevertheless groups of opponents make accusations so frequently that confrontations eventually seem likely in practically every scene.[1] Trials are deeply significant for the structure and meaning of this conflict-riddled narrative for at least four reasons.

EXPERIENCING OPPOSITION AND LEGAL CONFLICT

First, arrest and accusation were realities for some early Christians, so that enduring legal conflict became imbedded and even valued in Christian self-understanding as the first century ended and the second dawned. Even earlier, the apostle Paul was no stranger to this kind of conflict, for his writings include language of legal defense to describe his imprisonment as a means by which he bore witness to Jesus Christ (Phil. 1:7, 12–17). When the imprisoned Paul adopts for himself the moniker "prisoner of Christ Jesus" (Phlm. 1, 9), he takes the shame associated with ancient imprisonment and inverts it into a badge of honor to suggest that incarceration for the sake of the gospel validates his faithfulness to Christ.[2] Paul's imprisonments remained a key part of his legacy, for later writings continue to celebrate his legal troubles as evidence of his faith (Eph. 3:1; 4:1; Col. 4:3; 2 Tim. 1:8). Other Christian texts from the late first or early second centuries also valorize the realities of conflict, custody, and defense (Heb. 10:32–34; Rev. 2:10), and Christians began to spiritualize notions of arrest and constraint.[3]

Language of courtrooms and testimony was thus more than a theological motif for the early readers of the Gospels and Acts. For some ancient Christians, but certainly not all of them, it mirrored their lives because to be Christian for them meant defending their faith in public venues and contending against perceptions that this faith leads to social deviance. By including many trial scenes, Acts acknowledges the opposition that its early readers may have known. The trial scenes positively instruct them by portraying exemplary ways in which they might face their struggles and by subtly destabilizing the imposing magnitude of Roman authority.

CONTINUING THE MINISTRY OF JESUS

Second, the trials of the apostles and others connect them to Jesus and his trial. Their tribulations and conduct in Acts make a theological statement about the nature of the gospel and Jesus' presence with his followers.

As previous chapters have argued, the trial of Jesus has great significance for understanding the whole story of the Gospels, including their presentations of who Jesus is and why he was opposed. Acts attests to the importance of Jesus' trial; often when believers proclaim Jesus' story, they remember him not only as one who was crucified and raised but also as one tried and condemned by the authorities (3:13–17; 4:26–28; 13:27–31). By narrating the juridical struggles of Jesus' followers, Acts further emphasizes that their ministry and the conflict it generates mirror Jesus'. As the authorities in Jerusalem opposed Jesus, so they oppose his followers (4:27–30). Moreover, their trials do not introduce altogether new charges; they function as continuations of Jesus' trial, for the characters in Acts appear on trial specifically as Jesus' witnesses.[4] Therefore, theirs is not a new or separate gospel ministry but the continuation of his.

The point goes beyond noting that the apostles and other characters in Acts resemble Jesus in facing accusation, trial, and judgment. Acts intensifies the connection by relying upon the terminology of judicial confrontation to depict people's fundamental identification with Jesus. When the risen Jesus makes his programmatic declaration to his followers in 1:8—"you will be my witnesses in Jerusalem, in all Judea and Samaria, and to the end of the earth"—he uses a word, "witness" (μάρτυς), from the legal spheres of both the Greco-Roman world and the Jewish Scriptures, referring to people who provide public statements about their experiences and convictions to settle questions about truth and authority.[5] Through the term's wide use in the book of Acts, the notion of *witness* extends beyond courts of law to indicate the public roles of Jesus' followers, even when they are not standing before the bar of judicial authority. The frequent use of the term draws even more attention to the trial scenes in Acts. It also beckons readers to consider ways in which the whole of Acts reflects the dynamics of a trial, in terms of the book's interest in depicting public debates concerning the gospel and its potential to impact society.

Jesus' mention of "witnesses" in Acts 1:8 hardly marks a new development in the broader narrative of Luke–Acts. In Luke 21:12–19, Jesus gives warnings that play out during Acts. In those verses he tells his followers that arrests, persecutions, and appearances before "kings and governors" will not be evidence of defeat or failure but opportunities to act as witnesses, to offer testimony (μαρτύριον). The testimony Jesus has in mind for his followers will not be the product of their well-crafted legal defenses; it is the speech and "wisdom" that Jesus himself provides. Given Jesus' similar promises about the Holy Spirit in Luke 12:11–12, along with the other ways in which Luke–Acts connects the risen Christ to the Spirit that fills believers (e.g., Luke 24:49; Acts 2:33), the point is that the Holy Spirit and Jesus are active in the legal experiences of the human witnesses in Acts.

THE PLOT OF ACTS

Third, because trials are so prominent in Acts, they frame and shape the plot. In previous generations Acts scholars paid attention to the trials mostly out of their interest in analyzing the speeches that defendants give—where they came from and how the author might have used them to offer theological commentary on the history recounted in Acts.[6] But this angle of inquiry largely ignored the rest of the narrative in which the speeches are located, and how the speeches spoken in trials (and in other scenes) work integrally with the rest of the narrative to create a meaningful story. For example, it is one thing to analyze the speech that Stephen gives in his defense in Acts 7:2–53 by exploring its theological claims and connections to the LXX. It is also necessary to recognize that the speech's ideas connect to what occurs in the surrounding narrative, especially Acts 6–8. When Stephen emphasizes that God cannot and will not be restricted to a single place, he does not merely criticize his accusers' devotion to the Jerusalem temple and rebut their charges against him. He also offers a theological interpretation of what is about to occur in the plot, for in 8:1b–4 the church's preaching of the gospel will expand beyond Jerusalem for the first time in Acts.[7] Stephen's speech in his defense assures readers that God will remain present in the locations where believers will bring their proclamation after his trial concludes.

As this and the following two chapters will show, the trials in Acts show Jesus' representatives addressing new audiences and facing new obstacles that come from the social settings in which they find themselves. What the protagonists say, how they are treated, and the judgments that emerge from their trials all work together to contribute to the narrative's vision of what it means to proclaim the gospel and be faithful to Jesus amid the conflicts that inevitably arise. The trials also contribute to the book's understanding of how the word of God perseveres as believers cross new horizons of ancient society.

THE SOCIOPOLITICAL VISION OF ACTS

Fourth, the trials in Acts allow the bearers of the gospel to make their claims in the presence of sociopolitical elites. Jesus' followers defend themselves and their actions in a variety of locations, against different accusations, before both Jewish and Roman authorities. Because trials are public contests over ideas and their acceptability, they matter greatly for understanding Luke's perspectives on the gospel's relationship to both Jewish and Roman values.

Most of the trials and much of the public conflict in Acts emerge from the Jewish context in which Jesus and his earliest followers were firmly situated. As Acts insists that the gospel is the fulfillment of God's longstanding promises to Abraham's offspring, the Jews, it endeavors both to make clear theological sense of the actions of those Jews who actively oppose the gospel and to offer a consistent message about what this means for Jews who are not convinced by the proclamation they hear. Many of the trials come across as high-stakes disagreements about theological claims and whether the gospel that Jesus' followers proclaim is indeed consistent with Jewish hopes. This interpretive issue touches nearly every passage in the book of Acts, and it is an issue that will be considered in each trial scene for which it is relevant.

Among the New Testament writings, perhaps only Revelation gives as much sustained attention to the struggles that Christians face when they encounter the sociopolitical structures of the Roman Empire, although the perspective in Acts is certainly more ambiguous and textured than the resistive tone that pervades Revelation. The vast majority of late-twentieth-century Acts interpreters held that Luke–Acts was guided by an apologetic agenda, that its efforts to depict Christian existence in the Roman world aimed to defend Christianity against suggestions that it posed a threat to Roman social order. The fact that Roman officials in Acts, following Pilate's precedent in Luke 23:13–25, continually declare Jesus' followers to be harmless (e.g., Acts

18:12–16; 23:28–29; 25:25–27; 26:32) plays an important role in this position, particularly when interpreters consider the trials.

While recent scholarship has complicated the once-dominant view by proposing multiple, nuanced categories to identify exactly how Luke–Acts might manifest an "apologetic" purpose, and toward what end, nevertheless a widespread attitude persists that assumes Acts portrays Jesus' followers as nonthreatening to the social and moral order of the cultures they encounter, even though some of their opponents claim that they are malfeasants. These comments reflect the common view:

> Luke portrays an unstoppable, non-subversive religion. Those who disrupt society are the Jewish leadership who have misappropriated Jewish tradition or magistrates or the hoi polloi, who for economic gain, or political expediency, or misguided religious allegiance, circumvent the norms and laws of the empire and of God. Luke reaffirms that Christians from the beginning have been innocent bystanders.[8]

A handful of interpreters, however, reject suggestions that Acts consistently portrays harmony between church and Rome. They see much more conflict in the story, with some asserting that the church in Acts takes a decidedly "nondeferential" stance against the empire.[9]

As the following two chapters will demonstrate, the trial scenes do not reflect a "non-subversive religion" or an utterly conciliatory stance toward Roman power and social welfare. Nor do the trials communicate wholesale opposition or a complete lack of deference. Acts assumes a much more ambiguous perspective toward Rome. This perspective is shaped largely by trial scenes involving Paul, which in subtle ways deny the empire full authority to manage dimensions of social existence and his proclamation of the gospel. As they affirm the gospel's ability to challenge and perhaps delicately undermine Rome's sociopolitical authority, these trial scenes evoke memories of Jesus' trial in the Gospel according to Luke, in which God's will becomes actualized through a judicial process ostensibly under Pilate's control. The trials' primary function is certainly not to issue Luke's "theology of Rome"; but one of their functions in the narrative is to contribute to Luke's depiction of how one can bear witness to Jesus within (and sometimes over against) the Roman world's channels of authority and social contact.

A few comments will clarify our approach to this topic in light of similar scholarship on Acts. That scholarship is vast, and in recent years studies of the sociopolitical perspective of Acts have become increasingly detailed and varied, dissecting the literary, rhetorical, and cultural world of the first century in ways that problematize even the widespread use of the term "apologetic."[10] Many of these discussions require engaging debates about the book's genre and the social location of its author and original audiences. Our analysis will not delve into questions of whether or how Acts might *formally* defend the church, criticize Rome, or commend one party to the other. Our focus will remain more narrowly set upon the theological claims in the trials that impinge upon questions of human authority, specifically that authority's potential to confine, define, or issue judgments upon Jesus' followers and their message. What will become clear is that the trial scenes, within their narrative context, reflect a greater degree of ambivalence toward the Roman world than some previous studies have allowed.

INVESTIGATING THE TRIALS IN ACTS

The investigation of the trial scenes in Acts will occur over three chapters. The current chapter treats trials involving Peter, John, Stephen, and others. These scenes build upon one another, and all occur before the Jewish high priest and other members of the Jewish aristocracy in Jerusalem. The next chapter explores two trials in which people in Philippi and Thessalonica accuse Paul and Silas of anti-Roman activity. Finally, chapter 9 deals with Paul's extended trial in Acts 21–28. Separating the investigation into three chapters acknowledges the different issues and parties involved in the various trials, yet the chapters work together just as the trials do. The narrative relies on no single judicial episode to make all its points in isolation from the other trials.

The climactic point in the series of trials is actually not a moment but a process: Paul's long-term custody under Roman authority forms the conclusion to Acts, and its duration and legal maneuvering make it unique among the New Testament's trial scenes. The other trial scenes in Acts come across as much less formal, usually more chaotic. The chaos comes from the immediacy with which accusers and authorities convene these trials. None is a planned affair, and all—as well as Paul's extended trial in Acts 21–28—involve violence or the threat of violence against the accused. The dangerous climate of these scenes contributes to their verisimilitude, heightens the narrative drama, and also spotlights the readiness of Jesus' followers. Their poise and ability to confound their opponents without much preparation in a perilous context further testifies to God's power at work in them.

Any investigation of the trial scenes in Acts stands on the shoulders of other scholars who have labored over this same ground and given substantial attention to legal history, Luke's sources and redaction, the rhetoric of speeches, and the genre and literary milieux of Acts.[11] While these interpretive concerns are vital, the present work follows different angles. I draw from other studies that shed light on the trials, but this book does not pretend to be a comprehensive treatment of these scenes. We will pay close attention to more than just what characters say, considering also the subtleties of their narrated situations and the functions of these scenes within the wider plot.

PETER AND OTHER APOSTLES ON TRIAL

Scene 1: Peter and John before
the Jewish Leadership (4:1–22)

After a handful of foundational scenes that depict Jesus' followers as empowered by the Spirit to proclaim Jesus, to call people to repentance, to form a community of service and fellowship, and to heal, it does not take long for the apostles' ministry to attract the attention of Jewish authorities in Jerusalem. While Peter and John preach to a crowd in the temple, a group of priests, the captain of the temple guard, and some Sadducees arrive to arrest them. Obviously these people are not sympathetic to the apostles' message, for parallels with Jesus' arrest present themselves through the similarities between this group and the people who seized Jesus in Luke 22:52 (cf. those identified in Luke 22:66 and Acts 4:23). Only after the two apostles spend a night in custody does the narrator provide two important points of information, in Acts 4:4–6. First, about five thousand people believed "the word" that Peter and John proclaimed just before their arrest. Their message makes a notable impact among the Jewish population. Second, the concern about the apostles' acts extends throughout the high-priestly family and its closest allies.[12] The Sadducees collaborate with the high priest and the others who are present, an arrangement that is fully consistent with other ancient texts that include the Sadducees among the Jerusalem Jewish elite.[13] The leaders who assemble and question the prisoners therefore constitute the height of religious and political authority within Jerusalem Judaism, authorized by their offices, the temple, and the will of the Roman provincial government. The narrative thus makes it clear: the defendants and their message disrupt the status quo, and their prosecutors and judges are people inclined and empowered to prevent such disruptions.

Peter and John face questions from the Jewish leadership, who want to know "by what power or by what name" they have healed a man who could not walk. Since it introduces two key Lukan themes about the proclamation of the gospel, the authorities' question perfectly sets up a response that allows the apostles to continue preaching, now to the authorities. The apostles' response lets the leaders catch up with what readers have already seen in previous scenes, and the narrative indicates that this response is no spur-of-the-moment statement but a confirmation of the Spirit working within them. Peter and John's boldness (4:13, 29, 31) before the authorities signals that the Spirit energizes them with power from God (Luke 24:49; Acts 1:8), just as it did for Jesus (Acts 2:22). As for the name at work in the apostles' action, the name of Jesus has been a centerpiece of the apostles' proclamation so far in Acts (2:21, 38; 3:6, 16; cf. Luke 24:47), and so they inform their interrogators (Acts 4:10–12). In addition to answering a question, their words introduce a countercharge against the Jewish officials: this Jesus is a man whom the leadership crucified and God raised from the dead (4:10), a charge of opposing God that will emerge again and receive greater attention in the second trial scene, in Acts 5:17–41. The brief exchange thus gives the apostles an opportunity to offer a pointed summary of their message before the highest-ranking Jews in the city.

This scene has a preliminary character. No additional questioning ensues. No accusations are made, and what kind of jeopardy Peter and John face remains unclear. From a juridical perspective, the scene stages the conflict and leaves it unresolved, unless the authorities imagine that their threats will prove effective. Yet the narrative depiction of the hearing illuminates important details. The Jewish elites are annoyed (4:2) by Peter and John's activity and obviously concerned about the setting in which the apostles have been preaching: within the temple, the locus of priestly authority and activity. The idea of "the resurrection of the dead in Jesus" understandably provokes opposition from the Sadducees (see Luke 20:27; Acts 23:8).[14] However, even though Peter returns to Jesus' resurrection in Acts 4:10–11, when he cites Psalm 118:22, and again alludes to it by speaking of "what we have seen" in Acts 4:20, it is striking that neither the veracity of Jesus' resurrection nor the hope of a general resurrection emerges as a matter of debate. Readers hoping for a theological dispute must wait for this issue to reemerge later in Acts. For now, the foundation of the leaders' objections is the influence that these men possess among the Jewish "people" (λαός, a term that appears frequently in Acts 3–5).[15] Emphasizing his awareness that the masses' receptivity to his preaching is what the leaders find objectionable, Peter addresses the officials as "rulers *of the people*" (4:8, with emphasis added). In doing so he distinguishes them from the population they represent, from the people who responded positively to the healing of a man and the preaching of the word. The people understand; their leaders do not.

In arresting Peter and John, the Jewish officials place themselves in a bind by concretizing the contrast between the people's receptivity and their own opposition to the apostles' message. Lest the affair evolve into an extended interrogation or a prosecution that could backfire because of the popular support the apostles enjoy, the authorities end the encounter by exercising their power to issue threats and censure.[16] But even this move manages to minimize the rulers' authority vis-à-vis the apostles, for Peter and John's response in

4:19—"You judge whether it is right before God to listen to you rather than God"—insists that the root of the conflict is not about who has power to determine what is and is not proclaimed in the public sphere. They tell the high priest and others that the contest really is between competing voices of authority, "you" or "God." Again, the people praise God as the agent behind Peter and John's activity (v. 21); the authorities endeavor to bully the apostles into ceasing their influence. Likewise, the sheer fact that Peter and John speak "in the name of Jesus" shows them to be bound to a different authority (a difference highlighted in the leaders' refusal even to voice the word "Jesus," saying instead "this name" in v. 17). These details set the stage for the narrative to put religious authority—that authority supposedly possessed by the Jewish leadership—on trial, a move that will happen more vividly in the second scene, in Acts 5:17–41.

The scene ends without much closure. Peter and John return to their community and pray that they might continue their ministry with boldness (4:29). This request, along with the divine confirmation it receives (v. 31), demonstrates that they speak with God's own authority, as Christ's agents, again minimizing any suggestion that the Jewish leadership can really exert influence over them and their actions.[17] The authorities do not pursue a formal judgment against the apostles, but God's positive judgment of the apostles' deeds is clear. The scene's lack of formal resolution generates suspense and emphasizes at least two additional things. First, the priestly aristocracy find themselves in a difficult position, caught between their own concerns about these influential apostles and the opinions of the Jewish people. The apostles' preaching chips away at foundations of the leaders' authority among the people who have been receptive to that preaching. Second, the countercharge spoken by Peter and John remains only that, a charge. They name the leaders' culpability in Jesus' death but do not pronounce any judgment upon them. Opportunity remains for the high priest and others to repent, just as other Jews in Jerusalem have previously done in response to such a charge in Acts 2–3.

Scene 2: Peter and Other Apostles before the Jewish Leadership (5:17–41)

The arrest of Peter and others in 5:17–18 presents itself as the resumption of the first scene, with the conflict now more intense.[18] Again the ministry of healing and preaching in the temple complex attracts great, even stunning attention from the people (5:12–16); it is public activity that the Jewish leadership considers to be a violation of their previous warnings (5:28, referring to 4:18). All that has changed since the previous trial scene is that Peter's power as God's messenger appears to have grown and become more undeniable. Peter likewise remains the focal figure throughout the apostles' encounter with the Jewish officials. The roster of concerned authorities is essentially the same as it was in the first scene: the high priest and his advisers, referred to collectively by the general term "council" (συνέδριον; see also the related if not synonymous word γερουσία in 5:21). In 5:33–39 the presence of Gamaliel, a Pharisee, brings a new perspective to the second scene, for he appears willing to keep open the possibility that the apostles are indeed about God's work. A degree of openness among Pharisees will contrast with Sadducean resistance again when Paul appears before the high priest's council in 22:30–23:10. Luke thus indicates that not all of the Jewish authorities in Jerusalem are fully opposed to the apostles' ministry.

More than anything else, the foundation of the conflict unites this scene with the first. The authorities and apostles hardly debate proper belief or the legality of the apostles' public witness; instead, once again the exchange wrestles with the question of whether the leaders will accept the apostles' continuing preaching and influence among the Jewish populace. The high priest, Sadducees, and others in the religious aristocracy recognize that they have much to lose if this new movement attracts more attention and possibly erodes their ability to manage public activity and sentiment. At face value, then, the episode functions as an expression of the conflict over who will exercise religious authority and be recognized as authoritative; for all parties concerned, these things stem from the question of who rightly speaks on behalf of God's purposes. In this regard, the episode holds much in common with Synoptic accounts of Jesus' trial and all that those scenes have to say about his identity and the source of his authority to heal and teach.

Three features of the narrative contribute to its ability to express a contest over power and public influence. First, the great popularity and increasing success of the apostles' visible ministry prompt their arrest. The leaders are filled with "jealousy" (ζῆλος; 5:17) because of the honor and esteem the people give (μεγαλύνω; v. 13) to the apostles. This indicates personal envy and dishonor on the part of the aristocracy but also more, for a measure of religious zeal probably also motivates their actions. The apostles' popularity goes beyond matters of their good standing in the community; the signs they perform and the positive response to their message (5:12–16) suggest that people glimpse the same divine power at work in them as was in Jesus (see 2:22; 4:16, 30). Such acknowledgment of divine activity does not mesh with the established religious leadership's understanding of God. The matter of their "authority" is therefore not merely about the sociopolitical privileges they enjoy. As will become clearer later in Acts, the apparent obstinacy of these officials stems from their unmovable convictions about how God might act. (As Paul cries out in exasperation toward his Jewish accusers during his final trial in Acts, in 26:8, "Why do any among you judge it unbelievable that God raises the dead?") Still, because they hold priestly offices or stake their credentials on a priestly theology, their unresponsiveness to what the narrative depicts as divine activity threatens to reduce their standing and practical authority in the eyes of the Jewish public.

Second, the leaders immediately move to place the apostles into confinement, a sharp contrast to the dramatically public context of 5:12–16. The apostles are, borrowing New Testament scholar F. Scott Spencer's words, "quarantined in a marginal time and place outside the realm of normal, everyday life. Clearly the temple authorities want the apostles out of the spotlight, off the stage."[19] Thus the authorities do not later address the apostles' miraculous escape as a breach of law or an act of defiance, nor do they try to determine how they were freed. Their frustration comes because the liberated apostles repeat the same offense: returning to public, preaching to the people again in the temple.

Third, Acts depicts the miraculous deliverance from custody as divine authority one-upping the officials' power, not an escape for the sake of escape or fleeing confrontation. The angel sends the apostles back to the temple, the very place where they will certainly be rearrested. The humorous portrayal of authorities who cannot keep track of their prisoners shapes the scene as a contest about power:

> The primary interest here is not in miraculous rescues as such but in the impotence of human authorities to control the course of events. Although the apostles end up just where they would have been apart from the prison release—standing before the Sanhedrin accused of disobedience—the threat from the Sanhedrin has been undermined by irony and burlesque.[20]

If the contest between aristocracy and apostles were solely a struggle over who may influence the public's hearts and minds, the suitability of considering it a trial could be questionable. An additional issue is at work here, however, one that concerns the content of the apostles' preaching. Although the narrative does not present this as the chief impulse behind the apostles' arrest, the leadership recognizes that the gospel message has the potential to indict or implicate them in Jesus' death, bringing his "blood" upon them (5:28). Their supposition appears well founded, given Peter's earlier words to them in 4:10 and the fact that this council seems to consist of the same men who prosecuted the case against Jesus in Luke's Gospel. Yet thus far in Acts nothing in the apostles' *public* preaching has singled out the Jewish leadership for unique blame. Instead, all society bears some responsibility for rejecting and eliminating the Christ (see 2:23; 3:13–17; 4:27).

The leadership misunderstands if they presume that the apostles' preaching indicts only them, as if it were merely a matter of understanding Jesus' rejection only in terms of political jurisdiction. Nevertheless, the more the general public responds to the message of Jesus' death and resurrection with repentance, the more the authorities' lack of repentance distinguishes itself. What began in the narrative as widespread blame concerning Jesus' death begins to focus slightly more narrowly on the officials who do not discern God's hand in the message and ministry of the gospel.

Peter seizes an opportunity created by the council's protest in 5:28, affirming their fears and emphatically (signaled by the pronoun ὑμεῖς) accusing them of causing Jesus' execution (v. 30). The blame may not belong *solely* to them, but Peter assigns their share of guilt. He further claims that the apostles' ministry itself confirms what they proclaim about Jesus' death and its role in God's salvation to Israel, because this ministry reveals the Spirit that empowers and thereby confirms all that they say and do.[21] Peter's short speech thereby holds together both the contest over authority and his accusation concerning the leaders' guilt. His point is clear: just as God raised and exalted the one whom they killed (vv. 30–31), so also God's commission to him and his associates to bear public witness (v. 32) overrules the authorities' warnings to stay silent. The wider narrative context also adds this point: just as God's commission overrules the authorities' warnings, so also God's ability to free the apostles from custody overrides the authorities' ostensible power to control access to the public sphere. Peter's defense is that he and his friends are simply obeying God. The simplicity of his argument hardly belies that larger dynamic of God overriding the authorities' ability to control the apostles. This dynamic indicts the religious authorities by judging the council as hostile toward God's plans, resistant to God's authority (v. 29).

Once Peter finishes speaking in 5:32, the conflict threatens to escalate. Before desires to execute the defendants can be actualized, Gamaliel delays any final verdict with a theological consideration. While stopping short of endorsing the apostles' actions, the Pharisee explains the risk that the council assumes by opposing these men at this stage. His words lay down a programmatic criterion for the rest of the book of Acts and a characterization of the conflicts that will continue to present themselves: those who will oppose the proclamation of the gospel from this point onward will indict themselves as "people at war against God" (θεομάχοι; v. 39). Gamaliel's warning effectively delays the council's judgment concerning the apostles—and by extension, any judgment concerning the "plan" or "activity" (βουλή or ἔργον; v. 38) in which the apostles are engaged—until the leaders can gain better perspective on whether the apostles' activity is destined to fail.[22] The judicial delay reminds readers that the trial is not merely about Peter and the others' guilt or any danger that they pose; it also serves as a forensic inquiry into God's activity in the world and the perils of opposing it. On the temporal level of the narrative, Gamaliel's warning issues a provisional judgment in the contest between the two parties, for it allows the sides to separate without reaching conclusions on any issues.[23] Surely the conflict will have to be resolved, but not in this hearing, not until more history can play itself out under the council's watch. Yet on another level, readers of Luke–Acts discern an ironic self-condemnation in what Gamaliel says.[24] Thousands of people have repented in response to the apostles' message and demonstrations; Gamaliel's desire for more evidence and his wait-and-see approach pronounce him and his colleagues unable to read the testimony taking place around them. In effect, Gamaliel brings incriminating evidence against himself and the council as people at war against God in their refusal to embrace the apostles' call to repentance.

The two scenes in Acts 4–5 essentially set the stage for conflicts that persist through much of Acts between Jesus' witnesses and certain Jewish audiences, as that conflict moves from these private settings to more public venues. Acts 5 ends with little promise that opposition and persecution will cease: even after Gamaliel's counsel, the authorities cannot refrain from beating the apostles and enjoining them to cease their proclamation. The apostles interpret the whole episode as a privilege and confirmation of their faithfulness; obviously their public conduct will not change. The conflict will soon reignite in Acts 6, when Stephen comes to the forefront of the narrative. For the time being, however, Peter and the other apostles' travails have highlighted their boldness, allowed them to affirm their commitment to God's commission even against the desires of human authorities, and made the Jerusalem religious leadership appear to be impotent and motivated by a desire to protect their own standing. These early trial scenes also imbue the conflict with theological concerns, for the apostles and even Gamaliel frame the issue in terms of who expresses fidelity toward God.

STEPHEN ON TRIAL (ACTS 6:7–8:1)

What begins as a trial with an authoritative body set to weigh charges against Stephen devolves into a lynching when antagonism boils over into mob violence that overcomes any sense of process or justice that the initial circumstances might have promised. His is a trial gone wrong, and his ugly demise makes a strong statement about the intensity of the conflict between Jesus' followers and the Jerusalem religious establishment that opposes their claims.[25]

This is Stephen's trial, but in the narrative trajectory of Acts the scene connects to the trial that began in Acts 4–5. The description of his works among

the λαός (6:8) closely resembles the narrator's words about the apostles in
5:12. However, unlike the apostles in previous scenes, Stephen encounters
resistance among the general public and Jews from beyond Jerusalem, which
may give the Jerusalem authorities the political cover they need for more
decisive action against Jesus' followers. Fellow Jews in a synagogue try to
refute Stephen and concoct false testimony against him before bringing him
before the high priest and his council (συνέδριον). While Peter and the others in Acts 4–5 enjoyed the support of the people during their trials, Stephen
stands isolated during his, with no advocates in sight until the heavens open
to him in 7:56. The origins of the charges against him are difficult to discern,
but their severity may explain why no one among those present supports him.
He is accused of being against the temple ("this holy place") and the Mosaic
law. These serious charges will give rise to serious persecution against the
Jerusalem church, once Stephen's life is taken from him.

By the time Stephen's opponents bring him before the council, the narrator has made it clear that readers should not anticipate a fair contest. By
contrast, the mention of Stephen's angelic appearance in 6:15 enters decisive evidence on his behalf. The image suggests fierce boldness, not cherubic
innocence. Instead of showing fear in response to the deck stacked against
him, his face might inspire terror in others because it reflects God's glory.
Stephen, the narrative implies, is not about to be overwhelmed. He will speak
on God's behalf, with words of divine wisdom, just as Jesus predicted in Luke
21:15, a promise that Acts 6:10 recalls through the words ἀνθίστημι (resist)
and σοφία (wisdom) (cf. Luke 12:11–12).

Stephen's speech has attracted much attention from interpreters, mostly
because of its theological claims and meandering rhetoric. It adds a great
amount of complexity to a scene that raises more than its share of questions
about the historical realities and authorial agendas that might reside behind
Acts. Our focus must direct itself toward the ways in which the scene communicates its judgments about the conflict that engulfs Stephen, as the narrator
presents it.[26]

As a selective retelling of events from the stories of Abraham, Joseph,
Moses, David, and Solomon, drawn largely from the language of the LXX,
Stephen's speech appears almost to ignore the charges against him. Throughout the first fifty verses of Acts 7, he hardly directly refutes accusations that he
is against the law and the temple. Yet a broader view of the speech, its conclusion, and its aftermath suggests that Stephen is more engaged with the charges
than some interpreters have recognized.[27] At the end of his speech, in verses
47–50, Stephen makes a strong statement about the temple (the "house" that
Solomon built), verging close to equating reverence of the temple with idola-

try when he describes the building as χειροποίητος, something made with human hands. Although the LXX sometimes uses this term to refer to idols, Stephen's point is not to characterize the temple as inherently idolatrous, as if on par with the golden calf (see 7:41). Instead, he accuses his audience of treating the temple in an idolatrous manner, telling them that they mistakenly view the temple with reverence so narrowly focused that it constrains God, for their reverence implies that God might be confined to that or any other place.[28] Just in time for Acts 8 to relate the expansion of the gospel outside of Jerusalem, the bulk of Stephen's speech underscores two relevant truths: the gospel that Stephen preaches cannot be detached from all that Jerusalem represents in the history of God's dealings with Israel, and Judaism's history of encountering God in various places provides proof that God cannot be confined to a particular locale.

Stephen says nothing about the law, the other thing he was accused of opposing, until his speech's concluding verse, when he accuses his audience of disobedience: "You received the law as ordinances of angels, and still you did not keep it!" (7:53). This is not a temperamental outburst with no connection to what precedes it. Rather, it is part of a more expansive and pointed accusation that he brings against his accusers (7:51–53), which portrays them as disobedient to God. His accusation points both backward and forward in the narrative.

By telling the high priest and his council that they are doing just what "your ancestors" have always done, Stephen looks backward into history, associating them with the faithless activities of others who resisted God by opposing God's representatives (note the speech's frequent reference to the people in Israel's past as "our ancestors"). Stephen's recitation of Israel's history devotes more attention to Moses than to any other figure, and the speech's concluding references to persecuting Israel's prophets and not keeping the law imply that Stephen stands firmly in Moses' line.[29]

Stephen's indictment of his opponents also points forward by anticipating and interpreting what happens next in Acts. The violence unleashed upon Stephen confirms what he says, providing decisive evidence to support his characterization of his opponents:

> Unlike Stephen, who is explicitly said to be "filled with the Holy Spirit" (7:55), the accusers oppose the Holy Spirit (7:51), they are about to persecute Stephen, they will kill him as "they" did the prophets and Jesus (7:52); finally, this type of action is amplified in terms of violation (7:53), where it is said that while the people received the law from angels (a good thing), they have not kept it. From this it is clear that by killing Stephen the adversaries are the ones who have broken the law of God.[30]

The accusation that concludes the speech in 7:51–53 understandably puts Stephen's opponents on the defensive. His words provide much more than a "counter-accusation" meant to impugn the council's qualifications to sit in judgment of him.[31] Seen in light of the entire speech—in which Stephen implicitly groups his activity with the obedient conduct of Abraham, Joseph, Moses, and others—his indictment claims that he himself now stands in the line of Israel's heroes of faith.[32] To be resisted by the council, Stephen implies, would only confirm that this is so, and that they are the ones who have done violence in and to Israel's tradition. The irony of the violence that will kill Stephen is that—according to the argumentative logic of his speech—it exonerates him of the charge that he has set himself up against God, that he has voiced blasphemous ideas.

Stephen's speech calls the luminaries of Israel's legacy to the witness stand against the current Jerusalem authorities. Self-defense is only a secondary concern of his rhetoric; primary is bringing the authorities into close association with those who perpetrate violence against God's representatives and wrongly revere the temple so as to deny God's freedom to act in other ways and venues. From beginning (7:4) to end (7:51–52), Stephen's rhetoric heightens the sense of distance between him and his audience.[33] We miss the point if we presume the speech to be an explanation of how to understand past history. It is an argument about the present, the time in which the speech is delivered. The high priest and his closest associates' resistance to the gospel perpetuates, according to Stephen, a distortion of the theological affirmations confirmed by the stories of Israel's "ancestors." Stephen contends that the gospel and his behavior as a servant of the gospel more accurately correspond to Israel's story and the theological inheritance of Israel than do the resistance and theological presuppositions of the high priest. Considering that Acts was written after the temple's destruction, Stephen also affirms God's ability to be present apart from the temple, throughout the world. His vision of the Son of Man standing at God's right hand calls Jesus himself as a witness to confirm his testimony.

The scene ends as it does in an ironic confirmation of Stephen's innocence and his opponents' guilt. The hostility will have it no other way. The authorities and now an emerging segment of the Jewish population in Jerusalem have made their judgment. The wider narrative makes its own judgment, that Gamaliel's hypothesis of 5:33–39 has proved itself to be true and revealed the gospel's opponents as θεομάχοι. In the trial's concluding violence, however, Acts insists on a positive dimension: Stephen and Jesus become correlated in their righteous suffering and faithfulness in death (cf. Luke 23:46; Acts 7:59). Moreover, the conflict and violence in Jerusalem is not finished. The narrative will reintroduce it when Paul returns to the city for the final time in Acts 21.[34]

CONCLUSIONS

Judgment by Characterization

The trials of Peter, John, Stephen, and others allow Acts to characterize the supreme Jewish authorities in Jerusalem based on their negative attitudes toward the gospel, their strained connections to the Jewish people at large, and their faulty spiritual perception. Roman officials are nowhere in sight; the trial scenes revolve around the defendants' popularity within the temple and their perspectives toward the temple and the law.[35] The extremely critical characterization is accomplished through the scenes' ability to indicate that the religious leadership is also on trial. The narrative intimates judgments being rendered against this leadership when roles shift in the forensic drama, such as when Peter and Stephen issue accusations about the authorities' roles in killing Jesus and resisting the prophets. An evangelistic spirit flavors the apostles' and Stephen's statements in their defense. The narrative indicates that what they say to the high priest and his council is essentially on par with what they preach in public, yet the authorities remain unconvinced. The consistent violence of the council (4:3; 5:18, 40; 7:58; cf. 23:6–10), the ironies of Gamaliel's statement, and the stoning of Stephen in response to his claims and criticisms make the council's opposition all the more egregiously self-condemning.

Such judgments against the council discredit the high priest, the Sadducees, and their allies. The narrative does not imply that these authorities need to be overthrown or replaced, but it does discredit their theological credentials. The point goes beyond highlighting their spiritual blindness; the criticism of the council exposes matters at the root of their privileges—cultural assumptions concerning the temple and the law, things that add to the legitimacy of their priestly offices and therefore to the power endowed upon them by Rome. If the gospel has potential to erode a particular understanding of the temple and the law held by members of the Jewish community, then these leaders can expect their own high standing and influence to erode as well. The miraculous opening of the apostle's confinement in 5:19–20 furnishes a symbolic expression of the officials' inability to inhibit the gospel's widespread impact among the population.

Setting the Political Stage

The extended drama of the three passages, which begins with the authorities' annoyance in 4:2 and culminates in "a great persecution" in 8:1, accomplishes several ends beyond amplifying suspense. It tends to a gap in opinion between the Jewish leadership and elements of the wider λαός, something we observed also in Luke's account of Jesus' passion. In almost comical ways, the drama establishes the authorities' limited ability to control the influence that Jesus' followers have on others, rendering their detention facilities ineffective and leaving them with violence as their desired option. God's actions, expressed in both miracle and the Jerusalem masses' embrace of the gospel, deteriorate the leadership's ability to manipulate the social arena, which is a dangerous thing for authorities whose political power and high social standing depend in part upon their ability to maintain public order. Similar things occurred when authorities lost control in Jesus' trial in Luke. They will happen again later in Acts.

Finally, the verdict against Stephen and the implied verdict against the high priest and his collaborators remain provisional, for the real end of this conflict is not yet clear. The narrative will pick up the same questions concerning the Jerusalem aristocracy and the gospel's connections to Israel's traditions when Paul is put on trial in Acts 21–28. That trial allows Acts to treat these matters with more complexity, for the marks of zeal and social privilege that the high priest's council enjoys are also inscribed upon Paul's own person through his privileged history and previous contributions as a persecutor of the church. He looks a lot like the council members; rather, he looked that way once.

Trials in Philippi and Thessalonica in Acts 16–17

The persecution that scatters members of the Jerusalem church after Stephen's death (Acts 8:4) and the commissioning of Barnabas and Saul (13:1–3) are two of the impulses that propel the ministry of the gospel across new cultural horizons within the Roman Empire. Conflicts involving the Jerusalem aristocracy fade to the background for a time while new conflicts arise around new issues. In two parts of Macedonia, Philippi and Thessalonica, accusations against Paul and his associate Silas attract attention from local Roman officials.

PAUL AND SILAS ON TRIAL IN PHILIPPI (16:16–40)

Paul's story in Acts begins in conflict. While still known as Saul, he enters the narrative to approve the killing of Stephen (7:58; 8:1). In his encounter with the Lord on the road to Damascus, Jesus accuses Saul of warring against him by persecuting the church (9:5). After that meeting, Saul soon finds himself on the other side of the escalating opposition to the gospel, for in the next two scenes Jews in Damascus then Jerusalem seek his death on account of his bold and public proclamation about Jesus (9:19b–30). After taking a short break from the narrative spotlight in Acts 10–12, Paul reemerges and consistently faces opposition in various points of his travels in Acts 13–14. In those conflicts there is nothing that resembles a trial in any formal sense, and no political authorities are involved except for a brief incident in Iconium. There people call local officials to join their opposition, perhaps to provide legal sanction for violent persecution, but Paul and Barnabas's escape short-circuits the initiation of any kind of juridical process, either formal or improvised

(14:5–6). At last, in Philippi, Paul cannot avoid falling into channels of legal authority that bring him before local magistrates.

In Acts 16 we again encounter a scene that at first glance seems not quite a trial in a full or formal sense. On their surface the events in Philippi suggest sanctioned brutality, more like harsh arrest and degradation in advance of any kind of formal hearing, if the Philippians who are responsible even intend to initiate a judicial process. Since there is no conversation and no exchange of perspectives for authorities to weigh, either before or after an earthquake destroys the local prison, it might appear that the substance of the charges brought against the accused men receive neither elaboration nor rebuttal. But there is more to this scene. The miraculous opening of the prison, the conversion of the jailer and his household, and the public apology of the magistrates all serve to legitimate Paul and Silas and render judgments in ways reminiscent of the juridical debates that make up more conventional trial scenes.

Of all the trial scenes that this book investigates, this is the only one in which all the interested parties—except, of course, Paul and Silas—are Gentiles.[1] Accordingly, the conflict touches on issues raised as the gospel encounters the Roman world beyond Palestine. When Paul casts a "Python spirit" from a slave girl, he takes himself, Silas, and their ministry into powerful currents of the Roman religiopolitical waters. Deprived of the income that her capacity for divination could generate, the girl's owners spring into action against the travelers. They bring Paul and Silas into a center of public life in Philippi, into the marketplace, and into the presence of the local authorities (ἄρχοντες).

Because the narrative offers virtually nothing about the content of Paul and Silas's teaching in Philippi, the accusations that the slave girl's owners make against them may appear disconnected from the previous action, unless the general claim about disruptive activity (ἐκταράσσω) refers to the destruction of personal property (the spirit being the source of the slave girl's unique value).[2] On the other hand, Paul's mastery over the spirit—which itself audibly confirms the gospel message that Paul and Silas bring to Philippi—has far-reaching implications, as the owners' accusation realizes. By vanquishing a spirit connected to the powers of Apollo, the god who gained divinatory abilities by killing the Python of the oracle at Delphi, Paul's action suggests that the name of Jesus Christ possesses superior power.[3] This makes no small statement in such a place as Philippi, a Roman colony, whose cultural ethos was very Roman. Given the integral connections between Roman religion and the rhetoric of imperial power, to overpower a spirit associated with Apollo implies the potential to challenge values and power close to the heart of Roman identity.[4] Moreover, the well-crafted accusation against Paul and Silas appeals to familiar prejudices that immediately elicit broad support among the crowd. No one explains exactly which Jewish customs or principles threaten Roman culture and loyalties. Readers might detect a measure of truth in the charges, in that the missionaries certainly are about the business of propagating their good news concerning the God of Israel. But it is hardly clear that readers should agree with the charge that Paul and Silas's efforts and what they advocate are, in and of themselves, legally questionable.

Opposition to Paul and Silas immediately overwhelms them, and the colony's chief magistrates (the στρατηγοί, whose authority includes the power to decide ordinary civil and criminal matters) treat them as common criminals by beating them harshly without benefit of any kind of formal hearing, not necessarily an unusual tactic in Roman governance.[5] Meant at every step to shame and intimidate through nakedness, flogging, binding with stocks, and incarceration "in the innermost part of the prison," this treatment communicates the will of those charged to maintain local sociopolitical stability: not merely to banish the two travelers from public view but also to discredit them and their teachings. Paul and Silas do not speak in their own defense; their statements come later, when they sing hymns to God in the middle of the night. Although just a small audience hears the songs, they serve as one means by which the narrative defends the accused as indeed faithful "slaves of the most high God" (cf. 16:17). God's opening of the prison and the subsequent conversion of the jailer also defend the legitimacy of Silas, Paul, and their actions while issuing a warning to any who would oppose them.

After an earthquake destroys the prison, Paul's repeated refusals to leave (vv. 28 and 37) reveal that he desires neither escape nor immediate release from his situation. Apparently God also has other purposes for the miracle, for clearly God is the agent who sends the earthquake that can open doors and release chains without apparently injuring anyone.[6] The earthquake offers a decisive statement of God's power in defense of the apostles. It alone does not release them; it demands their release. The name of Jesus Christ has enabled Paul to cast the powerful spirit out of a slave girl; now God negates human efforts to hold Paul and Silas securely and remove them from public view. Just as in Acts 5 and 12, a miraculous opening of a prison plays a divine trump card over human authorities' efforts to halt the influence and vitality of the public witness that Jesus' followers offer. The ruined prison also has effects beyond frustrating and embarrassing human resistance, in that the means—literally, the structure—by which the authorities enforce their resistance to Paul and Silas is broken open and rendered impotent. To deny the authorities their instruments of social quarantine is to deny them their ultimate authority to manage the public sphere.

The trial has not yet concluded. Just as Habrocomes in *An Ephesian Tale* is not judged innocent until the Egyptian prefect recognizes his ordeal as a divine endorsement, the Philippian prisoners in Acts 16 require authoritative voices to acknowledge what readers can clearly see. The narrative thus mimics a trial through two consequences of the earthquake, which render two separate judgments concerning the gospel and the magistrates.

One consequence is a conversion. Certain he has lost the prisoners whom his superiors ordered him to keep secure (v. 23) and therefore facing the prospect of his own execution or dishonor, the jailer intends to kill himself. When he learns that his prisoners are still there, he asks about the possibility of his own salvation.[7] His word "saved" carries a double meaning that perfectly fits both his current jeopardy and the "way of salvation" (v. 17) that Paul and Silas proclaim. Paul and Silas continue their missionary work there in the prison. When the jailer leads them away into his home, the exit from the prison represents a new, hospitable openness toward them expressed by his positive assessment of them and their god. In leaving the prison and washing their wounds, the jailer reverses the harms previously inflicted upon them and relinquishes his authority as their keeper; authority over him now resides with the ones whom he refers to as κύριοι (v. 30).

The second judgment comes the following morning, in the ruined prison, to which Paul and Silas return. Paul insists that the same place where they were incarcerated be the site where they are vindicated. The narrative implies that the magistrates initially order freedom for Paul and Silas because the earthquake has made them afraid of these men and their god. Paul's response highlights the public shaming that he and Silas endured at the order of the magistrates and dramatically reveals that he and Silas are Roman citizens and therefore legally protected from such degrading treatment in the absence of a formal judgment against them (v. 37).[8] His words sharply contrast their public shame with the magistrates' hope for a private discharge, implying that his and Silas's release must be anything but discreet or out of the plain view and knowledge of the wider citizenry. They will not leave before seeing official acknowledgments that the way they were treated was unjust and that they have not found their way out of prison without formal sanction. Paul demands not only the restoration of their honor but also the tacit recognition of God's power. The magistrates come to the prison to apologize and excuse the prisoners because they fear what could happen to them for mistreating Romans. But it also remains quite significant that they do this in public and personally escort Paul and Silas out of their place of detention.[9] The narrative suggests a spectacular sight, one declaring that no human authority can restrict these "slaves of the most high God." The magistrates' action in effect declares the futility of anyone pursuing the charges of anti-Roman activity originally leveled against Paul and Silas.

Both judgments come at the local magistrates' expense. Their persecution of Paul and Silas, perpetrated in ignorance of the prisoners' Roman citizenry, violates Roman values. That creates an ironic twist, given that Paul and Silas were accused of advocating anti-Roman behavior. Also, the jailer and his household strike sharp contrasts to the magistrates. As a result of the events, the former become baptized believers while the latter come off as unscrupulous, eager to make the problem of Paul and Silas disappear, and unwilling to inquire further into the power of the gospel. Indeed, when the magistrates come to the wrecked prison to give official sanction to the prisoners' release, their actions appear almost ridiculous. The miracle of the opened prison has already divinely vindicated Paul and Silas. The presence of the apologizing magistrates admits the victory of the gospel over the forces that had resisted it and actually testifies to God's incursion into the city.[10] As the magistrates and their prison stand humiliated and gutted, the implication is not that Paul and Silas's ministry is harmless to Roman values and prerogatives, but that this ministry will not heed these things if they are construed against the gospel. The gospel enters Philippi and shows its ability to overturn any prerogatives or systems that might cause obstacles, whether they be lodged in the power of Roman religion, the voice of a mob, a Roman prison building, or the will of Roman magistrates.

PAUL AND SILAS ON TRIAL IN THESSALONICA
(17:1–10a)

The events in Philippi initiate a sequence of scenes in which municipal authorities in various locales are called to hear accusations concerning Paul's behavior and message. With the exception of 17:1–10a, none of these accusations is able to generate enough momentum to result in a trial, according to the definition put forth in this book's introduction. Even the trial initiated in Thessalonica is brief and perhaps incomplete. Nevertheless, along with the Philippian affair and the accusations that that will dog Paul and his associates from this point through Acts 19, the events of 17:1–10a reinforce the narrative's message that characters perceive Paul's witness to the gospel as having serious ramifications for Roman society and interests.

Paul's preaching in Thessalonica involves themes familiar in Luke–Acts: the Scriptures demonstrate the necessity of the Christ's suffering and resurrection, and Jesus is the Christ. Paul's proclamation in the synagogue convinces men and women (some from the higher social ranks, whose influence among others in that cultural context could be quite extensive), including Jews and Greeks; yet it again arouses opposition. Some among the Thessalonian Jews exhibit jealousy, echoing the motivations of other Jews in 5:17 and 13:45. Spencer observes:

> The issue is not so much a doctrinal dispute over Paul's handling of Scripture as it is a social conflict arising from Paul's popularity in the community. With honor and social standing inextricably tied to finite public opinion, Paul's sudden jump in the polls—especially among high society folk—means a slump in rank for the synagogue elites. And so they fight to restore their honor, not by arguing against Paul's biblical exegesis, but by aiming to downgrade his social reputation.[11]

Again, religious convictions cannot be considered in isolation from matters of social organization.

The instigators assemble a mob of people with not much else to do—17:5 implies that these are unemployed day laborers waiting around the marketplace—and seek Paul and Silas. When they cannot find them, they bring Jason, who has hosted the missionaries, and others before the city officials (πολιτάρχαι).[12] This initiates a short hearing in which Jason and other believers stand as surrogates for Paul and Silas.

The accusation resembles the one lodged in Philippi in 16:20–21: disturbing the public order and violating imperial precepts. The phrasing of the charges looks beyond the social realities of Thessalonica alone, for it claims that Paul and Silas stir up unrest (ἀναστατόω; see Acts 21:38) across the Roman Empire.[13] They do so as a result of their belief in another king, the accusation continues, whose purported kingship directly challenges Caesar's unique authority.[14] That Jewish opponents here employ nearly the same accusation as Gentiles in Philippi underlines the volatility of the issue and the seriousness of the charges. Although the claim that Paul and Silas bring an anti-imperial message fails to capture or address the principal thrust of the gospel proclamation, as it is described in 17:2–3 and elsewhere in Luke–Acts, it nevertheless exploits a perceived implication of that message. Roman officials and crowds are rightly concerned by claims of a king who might rival Caesar, and so the accusation raises the stakes very high, just as a similar accusation did in Jesus' trial in Luke 23:2. As for the claim about disturbing the social order, this ironically appears as a matter of perspective; from another point of view, the jealous Jews' decision to organize a mob proves that their actions are what most upsets the peace.

The accusations target Paul and Silas. In the trial, Jason faces trouble because he has given hospitality to the accused. The narrator does not indicate that Jason speaks to defend himself or the missionaries. Still, when he pays money to the magistrates, this indicates his view of the matter. The payment is not a fine or punishment in admittance of any wrongdoing. It is a statement of surety, guaranteeing his responsibility for the behavior of his absent guests.[15] Jason's payment suggests that he acknowledges the gravity of the charges concerning Paul and Silas's actions and motives, yet he is willing to risk his money and honor in the confidence that the charges will not be substantiated by the future activity of his associates. This satisfies the magistrates, who appear more interested in making the problem go away than in prosecuting Paul and Silas. Perhaps they know something of what recently occurred in Philippi. The charges nevertheless leave them unsettled (ταράσσω; v. 8) about Paul and Silas's behavior, meaning that their concerns exceed simple anxiety.[16] In receiving the surety, the magistrates issue a stern warning and draw a line in the sand. The case remains open, pending any future basis for judgment, but friends nevertheless respond to the risk by spiriting Paul and Silas out of town, an act that both acknowledges the hostility of the missionaries' opponents and suggests that the emerging accusations would be difficult to refute in Thessalonica.

What looks at first like a narrow escape from danger soon proves to be otherwise. In Beroea, Paul and Silas's proclamation continues, finding success that is both similar and more impressive than what happened in Thessalonica. But the opposition also continues when the group of hostile Jews from Thessalonica arrives and resumes an attempt to sway the masses against the missionaries (Acts 17:10b–13). Although the narrative does not describe the outcome of this particular conflict, when believers convey Paul to safety in Athens (17:14–15), readers suspect he cannot hope to escape those who seek to silence him and his associates and who insist on opposing the gospel's claims in the name of Roman values.

The explicit claim that the gospel is hazardous to Roman interests is a new development in Acts, beginning with the events in Philippi. Later scenes renew the accusation (17:16–34; 18:12–17; 19:23–41), yet none of them culminates in an actual trial, according to the definition offered in the introduction. In Athens (Acts 17), no expectation of a formal legal judgment is implied, for the narrator offers no indication that Paul is compelled to address the Areopagite Council, nor that he goes there facing the prospect of legal jeopardy or censure.[17] In Corinth (Acts 18), the Gentile proconsul Gallio perceives the issue as one of intra-Jewish disputes outside his jurisdiction, and so, perhaps out of his contempt for both accusers and accused, he discontinues the assembly before Paul can address any charges. After the outbreak of a riot in Ephesus (Acts 19), a grand public rhetorical showdown nearly occurs, but the town clerk diffuses the volatile situation by insisting that those with a complaint initiate a *real* trial.[18] No believer speaks against any accusations, and no human authority offers a judgment, either de jure or de facto.[19] More concrete judgments concerning the substance of these accusations will have to wait until Paul's arrest and defense in Acts 21. Clear already, however, is that certain accusations generate heat and are effective for both Gentile accusers (Philippi) and Jewish ones (Thessalonica).

The events in Thessalonica and beyond therefore function not to settle anything but to fuel the volatility associated with Paul's ministry. The ease with which opposition arises and the recurrence of dramatic, narrow escapes across several interconnected scenes have multiple effects for our understanding of the sociopolitical conflict that fills the narrative.[20] Paul comes across as quite able to elude serious confrontations, even when violence remains a constant threat. Powerful people in local politics become involved, some more willing than others to weigh in on the issues. Consistent prospects of danger sound a note of adventure as the protagonists in Acts struggle to fulfill their objectives; from a theological perspective, this underscores the ability of the word of God to persist in finding avenues for its proclamation despite opposition and political pressure. Through all the scenes, opponents occasionally come across as vindictive or motivated by self-interest, but the repetition of accusations nevertheless lends gravity to the charges and suggests that resolution of some kind is inevitable—not to end the conflict once for all, but to make a more definitive statement about the character of the conflict and the witnesses swept up into it. All this points us toward Paul's final, extended trial in the book of Acts, in which the narrative at last permits him to defend himself against specific accusations.

CONCLUSIONS

Evolving Opposition

Compared to the other trial scenes in Acts, the trial scenes in Philippi and Thessalonica strike quite different chords. Situated among other episodes in which Paul and others' ministry incites challengers desirous to preserve social, religious, and economic aspects of Roman culture, these scenes illustrate a range of ways in which the gospel makes its presence known among people. Both scenes involve high-ranking Roman officials—not exactly governors but still high-ranking figures who possess sociopolitical authority in key cultural centers—who hear complaints that Paul and Silas threaten Roman values. Both involve angry mobs, and neither includes any kind of formal verdict. The two incidents characterize the reactions of some people in Macedonia, both Gentiles and Jews, as hostile and hasty. The Thessalonian affair gives a glimpse into the political alliances that Jewish groups and Roman officials might form against Paul. Groups of Jews have been able to arouse Gentile opposition to Paul's ministry previously (Acts 13:50; 14:2, 19); in Thessalonica they manage to do so in the presence of the governing authorities, specifically by casting the gospel as contrary to Roman interests, a tactic that will appear again (in Acts 24:2–6) during Paul's extended trial in Acts 21–28.

Both scenes make use of irony to criticize the accusations. In Philippi, charges that Paul and Silas transgress Roman law bring harsh treatment that itself violates their legal rights, an irony that emerges only after the late and dramatic revelation of Paul and Silas's citizenship. In Thessalonica, Jewish accusers express their offense at assertions about Jesus' kingship, as if they themselves are so fond of the emperor's majestic status. Through the irony the scenes emphasize the extent to which the gospel's opponents will turn to mechanisms of sociopolitical control in their attempts to halt the proclamation of the gospel.

Further Setting the Political Stage

Although Paul and Silas leave both cities uncondemned, the narrative refuses to provide an unambiguous answer to the question of whether their deeds and teachings violate Roman values. Is their message then really "non-subversive" of Roman interests? They may not have done anything illegal in a technical sense, but they do manage to upend certain Roman values and humiliate local officials through the power at work through and around them. The significance of this dynamic must not be underestimated, especially in Acts 16, given the integral connections between Philippi, a Roman colony, and Rome itself.[21]

Because in neither of the two cities do Paul and Silas have opportunity to speak in response to the accusations, readers need to look to other parts of the narrative to see how it might address the charges. Certainly the opening of the prison and the public restoration of Paul and Silas's honor in Philippi speak volumes. Paul and Silas's God has come to the city and successfully established and legitimated "the Christian message and community within both the physical and social spaces of Philippi."[22] The magistrates' authority to govern civil society, expressed symbolically in the prison structure and in their ability to have prisoners beaten, shamed, and constrained out of public sight, becomes turned on its head through the course of the account. When the magistrates come to excuse their former prisoners from the prison, they enact Paul and Silas's acquittal and their own inability to manage the gospel's effects in the public sphere.

At the same time, answers to general questions concerning the gospel's place within Roman society remain only provoked and less than fully resolved in these scenes. Is it just the hasty Philippian magistrates, the greedy owners of the slave girl, and the unsettled or misled city officials of Thessalonica who should be concerned about the gospel? Any implied judgments or verdicts in these trials need to be brought into conversation with the ends of the larger story, specifically as it plays out in Paul's future. For he will again find himself in Roman custody, addressing high-ranking Roman officials in Acts 21–28. The events in Philippi and Thessalonica contribute to expectations for what that trial will address.

9

Paul on Trial in Acts 21–28

Although Paul almost evenly divides his time on the narrative stage in Acts between living as an itinerant evangelist and detained in Roman custody, a careful reading of his trial in Acts 21–28 does not support interpretations that neatly split his story into two separate ones. Paul's identity or career does not shift from missionary to prisoner, if that would suggest that accusations and incarceration curtail his ability to bear witness about Jesus Christ to others. Paul's role does not change after his final arrest. Rather, his trial creates distinctive venues and opens unique avenues for his work as Jesus' emissary. The trial scenes of Acts 21–28 demonstrate his ability to manipulate the organs of sociopolitical power for the purposes of proclaiming the gospel. In doing so, they also manifests the gospel's ability to commandeer and thus destabilize the mechanisms designed to exercise imperial authority.

Paul's trial unfolds over seven scenes that span approximately four years, the final years of his life. That duration is only part of what makes his trial so prominent. The trial also brings together a number of major themes from Acts. Particularly through Paul's speeches, the trial addresses charges that he has betrayed his Jewish identity, offers justification for his ministry among Gentiles, displays his rhetorical skill and high social standing, and highlights his exemplary boldness before imperial authority. Paul is a unique defendant in Acts; his Roman citizenship affords him protection from certain forms of coercion and maltreatment, and his history of zeal shows him as one who once shared much in common with some of his high-profile Jewish accusers. When Paul's speeches in his defense repeatedly mention and even elaborate his past deeds—as Saul, the persecutor of the church—the narrative keeps attention on the suspicions that persistently swirl around his identity and trustworthiness, as well as the history of conflict depicted up to this point in Luke–Acts.[1]

Through it all, Paul comes across as the quintessential defendant, one who offers a witness that consistently stymies the arguments and schemes of those who seek his destruction. Truly Acts puts forth Paul as one well suited to illustrate how the Lukan theme of bearing witness to the gospel of Christ generates conflict with those who reject that gospel or who remain wary of its sociopolitical implications.

Paul's trial does not exist in isolation but shares integral connections with a larger story about conflict, trials, and witness. For example, once Paul's trial commences, the narrative relates it to Stephen's previous trial. Both men face accusations brought by Jews from the Diaspora (6:9–14//21:27–28), and similar language describes the encounters each has before a crowd and the council in Jerusalem (e.g., 6:12//21:27; 6:15//23:1; 7:57//22:23; 7:58//22:23).[2] Also, as we will see, Paul's defense finally, in Acts 28, concludes with him moving from defendant to judge, just as Stephen concluded his defense with a judgment that indicted his opponents as disobedient to God. One dimension of Paul's trial, then, is that it resumes the intense conflict that arose earlier between the Pentecost-era believers and the Jerusalem establishment. Stephen serves as a kind of forerunner for Paul, and Paul is hardly exempt from the hostility that other, less socially privileged believers have faced throughout the story.

The previous two chapters emphasized that the trial scenes in Jerusalem (spanning Acts 4–8) and those in Philippi and Thessalonica (Acts 16–17) leave many questions unanswered and conflicts unresolved. The narrative anticipates more to come. The whole of Acts perpetuates these expectations through some Jews' ongoing opposition to Paul (e.g., 20:3) and repeated unrest among those who perceive the gospel as dangerous to Roman interests (throughout Acts 16–19). By bringing together on the same stage Jewish and Gentile authorities and their various concerns about Paul and his message, the final trial in Acts presents itself as a crucial piece for understanding the significance of the gospel's encounter with the complex world of first-century Judaism and the sociopolitical structures of the Roman Empire. Through the whole process, Paul issues judgments on behalf of the gospel against both unbelief and assumed prerogatives of imperial authority.

ANTICIPATING PAUL'S TRIAL

Not only the lack of resolution achieved by the other trials, but also other aspects of Acts point to the climactic function of Paul's final trial. Certain passages anticipate this trial by highlighting details of his distinctive commission and thus creating specific expectations. Just as the Gospels repeatedly signal that Jesus will be brought before the governing authorities, so Acts does with Paul. At least three passages foreshadow the serious opposition that awaits Paul: Acts 9:15–16 (a declaration that Jesus makes about Paul's future); 20:17–38 (Paul's final address to elders of the Ephesian church); and 21:8–14 (an oracle and sign performed by the prophet Agabus).[3]

Paul's reputation as a persecutor of the church resounds throughout Acts (see 9:13, 21; 22:4; 26:9–11). His encounter with Jesus in Acts 9:1–19a not only ends that phase of his life; it also thoroughly upends it by depicting him as dependent and vulnerable, inverting the image of Paul's wielding power over others.[4] One piece of this reversal comes when Jesus tells Ananias what it will mean for Paul to bear Jesus' name "before Gentiles, kings, and the children of Israel." Jesus promises, "I'm going to show him how much he'll have to suffer for my name's sake" (v. 16). What makes this a chilling claim is the sentence's final word, παθεῖν (suffer), which Luke rarely employs to indicate physical harm or death in a general sense (only in Luke 13:2; Acts 28:5). Instead, it usually refers specifically to the final events of Jesus' life—his passion (Luke 9:22; 17:25; 22:15; 24:26, 46; Acts 1:3; 3:18; 17:3; see also παθητός in Acts 26:23). By characterizing Paul's future with a term that serves nearly as a technical designation for Jesus' demise, the narrative strengthens the association between these two men. The prospect of conflict and suffering is clear.[5]

Other words in Acts 9:15–16 lead readers to expect that Paul will encounter upper-echelon political authorities. Jesus' statement that Paul's suffering will come on account of his connection to Jesus' name recalls Jesus' promise that his followers will be arrested and persecuted, handed over to authorities in synagogues and prisons, and brought "before kings and governors because of my name" (Luke 21:12). As observed in chapter 7 (above), connections between Jesus' name and juridical environments emerge earlier in Acts, when authorities in Jerusalem try to prohibit the proclamation of Jesus' "name" (4:17–18; 5:28, 40–41). In Paul's case, however, Jesus' specific mention of bearing his name "before Gentiles and kings" (9:15) recalls Luke 21:12–15. Acts further reinforces this connection when a number of key terms from Luke 21:12–15 recur in Acts 21–28.[6] For example, language of making a "defense" (ἀπολογέομαι and cognates; see Luke 21:14; Acts 22:1; 24:10; 25:8, 16; 26:1, 2, 24) makes itself at home in the story of Paul's trial.[7] The verbal resonances among Luke 21:12–15 and Acts 9:15–16, punctuated in Acts 22–26, indicate that Paul's work as Jesus' representative will have him defending himself and the gospel before powerful figures.[8]

A second passage arousing expectations that Paul will find himself in dangerous confrontations with authorities comes as he bids farewell to the Ephesian elders who meet him in Miletus (Acts 20:17–38). Paul looks back on his faithful endurance of various hardships and turns to gaze forward into what will transpire after he returns to Jerusalem.[9] While he remains ignorant of exactly what will happen to him, the Spirit has repeatedly told him to expect "imprisonment and hardships" (v. 23).[10] Nevertheless, he expects to continue his efforts as a "witness" (διαμαρτύρομαι; v. 24). The gravity of this scene, Paul's comments in verses 24–25 and 29, and the concluding verses (vv. 37–38) indicate that Paul also announces his impending death.[11]

The third passage that raises expectations about the finality of Paul's coming custody describes an oracle performed by the prophet Agabus in 21:8–14. This scene plucks at the tightening narrative tension as Paul, nearing Jerusalem, sees Agabus bind his own limbs with Paul's belt and announce, "Thus says the Holy Spirit, 'In this way, in Jerusalem, Jews will bind the man to whom this belt belongs and give him over to the Gentiles'" (v. 11). Although Agabus declares Paul's arrest to be certain, he does not mention anything about a trial. Yet the language of his prophecy recalls Jesus and what he experienced after his arrest and "giving over" (παραδίδωμι) in Luke's Gospel. Agabus's words recall Luke 18:32, Jesus' prediction that he will be given to the Gentiles.[12] Agabus, then, contributes to expectations that Paul's experience in Jerusalem will mirror Jesus' arrest, trials, and ultimate penalty. A grave outcome looms. As we will see, these expectations make certain aspects of Paul's trial all the more dramatic and surprising. For despite all the expectations for suffering that Acts generates before Paul's arrest, the actual narrative of his custody and trial downplays any real sense of hardship and accentuates the prolonged and unresolved character of Paul's legal adventure.

PAUL UNDER SUSPICION FROM BOTH JEWISH AND ROMAN AUTHORITIES

Most of the trial scenes earlier in Acts, as we have seen, center around either Jewish or Gentile opposition to the actions of Jesus' followers. None of the points of opposition is exclusively religious or political; theological assertions and public influence are virtually inseparable in the narrative's accounts of conflict. Also, in most scenes, Jewish leaders deliver judgments on accusations from Jews, and Roman (Gentile) authorities deliver judgments on accusations from Gentiles. Events in Acts 17:1–10a present an exception and thereby reflect a coalescing of opposition to Paul and the gospel he preaches. By contrast to most of these earlier scenes, in Acts 21–28 both Jewish and Roman interests are present and intertwined. Jewish concerns about Paul first bring him before high-ranking Gentile representatives of Roman power, representatives who are puzzled by the details of the conflict (see 23:28–29; 25:18–20,

26–27) but nevertheless aware of Paul's importance for their political calculations. Confusion and conflicting judgments arise also among Jewish participants in Paul's trial (see 23:7–10; 28:21–22, 24). The frequent disarray and difference of opinion reflects the multiple and sometimes competing interests that emerge out of the conflicts that have been simmering throughout Acts and now come to a boil in Paul's trial.

There can be little doubt that the primary focus of Paul's defense in Acts 21–28 falls upon his faithfulness to God and the theological heritage of Israel. Paul repeatedly rebuts accusations that he opposes Judaism and its values (see 21:28; 24:6; 25:19). New Testament scholar Jacob Jervell correctly observes that Paul both defends himself and accuses his Jewish opponents: "Paul is not an apostate; the leaders of the Jews are. Paul, not his accusers, has the right to speak on behalf of the people and to represent Israel."[13] At the same time, interpreters must recognize that Paul does not speak these assertions in a vacuum. The trial setting allows him to address them directly to various Jewish audiences—including the popular (a crowd at the temple), the high-ranking (the Jerusalem council, the high priest and other leaders, and King Agrippa), and the relatively uninformed (representatives of the Jewish community in Rome). As Paul repeats his claims of innocence and reaffirms his faithfulness to the traditions and hopes of Israel, what he puts forward for judgment is less his own character and more the identity of the gospel itself as good news to Israel. Given the previous trials in Acts, especially the point at which Gamaliel provides his commentary (5:33–39; subtly recalled through Paul's words in 22:3), those who remain unconvinced by Paul show themselves to be more than poor students of theology; they actually are wayward leaders who refuse to acknowledge that God might be at work in Jesus and his followers.

Paul's speeches thus restate the insistence made throughout Luke–Acts that God's visitation in Christ and the calls issued to and carried out by Jesus' followers are fully consistent with God's foundational promises to Israel. Our investigation of these chapters cannot go into detail about the means by which the speeches make this case. Rather, the investigation will contend that there is more to Paul's trial than speeches and expressions of fidelity. We distort the trial if we imagine it to be only about contested theological ground. It is not true that the Roman authorities "are simply brought in as external arbitrators" for disputes about Judaism.[14] Although the Romans do provide safe cover for Paul to have these conversations with the Jewish elites, they do much more than occasionally express opinions about Paul's guilt. By their presence in the scenes, Roman authorities represent their own set of concerns about Paul and the effects he has for their social order, concerns that have appeared earlier in Acts and never entirely dissipate throughout Paul's trial.

The narrative presentation of Paul's custody, our analysis will reveal, suggests that the Roman officials' concerns are well-founded.

The Roman authorities who appear in Paul's trial deal with him in different ways. They do not judge him to be a lawbreaker, but they clearly realize that his release would incite unrest in Judea, and so their solution consists of exercising their power to keep him out of public circulation. Put simply, Roman officials incarcerate him because they can, believing that keeping him in custody is the best way for them to arrive at some beneficial outcome, whether that outcome be social stability, bribes, or political favors. In this, the Romans purport to exercise their authority over Paul's activities. They appear to be correct when they judge his only offense to be a religious dispute with his fellow Jews, but they turn out to be very wrong in their tacit assumption, expressed through their actions, that they can hold sway over Paul's ability to exercise influence over others. Similar to Jesus' trial in the Gospel of Luke, the gospel finds a way.

THE TRIAL

The drawn-out character of Paul's trial is hardly unique. Schwartz sees similar dynamics in Greek novels that divide trials into multiple segments and observes: "The expectation of a final verdict keeps the reader reading. The skillful narrator leads the readers on by continually holding out the promise of closure."[15] In Paul's case, this intensification of suspense magnifies the significance of the trial and the events or claims that provoke it. Reading the events of Acts 21–28 as a single, extended trial in seven scenes reveals changes, uncertainties, and transitions that come into view over the course of the entire process. Our exploration of the trial will proceed with a scene-by-scene overview followed by more extensive comments on the significance of the trial as a whole.

Scene 1: Paul before a Jerusalem Crowd (21:27–22:22)

Having been back in Jerusalem for about a week, Paul performs purification rites, attempting to counter a reputation among some local believers that he disregards the Mosaic law and Jewish customs. His willingness to perform rites publicly in the temple and to associate with a Gentile believer from Ephesus attracts the attention of a group of "Jews from Asia," perhaps people familiar with the schism that resulted when Paul came to an Ephesian synagogue in 19:8–10. This group stirs up a crowd against Paul, accusing him of "teaching everyone everywhere against our people, our law, and this place" (21:28). The accusation is severe in this Jewish context, and it sets the stage for the issues that dominate the trial scenes from this point through the end of the book:

> It is a charge that Paul is anti-Jewish, attacking the very foundations of Judaism, the special role of the chosen people, called to live by the law and worship in the Jerusalem temple. The charge refers to Paul's teaching. That is, it relates not just to Paul's personal behavior but to what he advocates in his mission. His mission is an anti-Jewish movement, the accusers claim.[16]

The accusers become more specific when they claim (erroneously, by the narrator's implication) that Paul has brought a Gentile into the temple and thereby "defiled this holy place." A larger mob assembles against Paul and drags him from the temple, while the shutting of the temple doors expresses their contempt for his apostasy. The mob beats Paul, intending to kill him, and it looks as if Paul might suffer the same fate as Stephen, but without having the luxury of rebutting accusations first.[17] The mob's frenzy is, however, interrupted by the auspicious arrival of the Roman tribune and a collection of soldiers, who save Paul from death when they bind him and carry him from the crowd toward their nearby barracks.

At the top of the stairs leading into the soldiers' barracks adjoining the temple compound, Paul easily persuades the tribune to let him take charge of the volatile situation by speaking to the crowd below. His decision to address the people in their common tongue secures a point of common ground with them while likely signaling that he has no interest in persuading the Roman soldiers with this speech. His words do not address Roman law or concerns about social unrest. He introduces his oration as a "defense" (ἀπολογία), then offers an explanation of his fidelity to God, his encounter with the risen Jesus, and his work among the Gentiles as nothing less than a faithful response to God. While making this case, he equates the mob's zeal for God with the zeal that has characterized his whole life, testifies to the disciple Ananias's fidelity, and describes a vision that he experienced in the same temple that he is accused of defiling. The speech aims to assure the crowd that he once expressed his zeal for God as they do now and to convince them that his new perspective on the gospel is an obedient response to God. This proves to be too much for them; as soon as he says that Jesus sent him to bring this message "to the Gentiles," he reignites the crowd's fury. Their response is not an expression of blind anti-Gentile bigotry. For them, Paul's mention of his mission to Gentiles only lends credence to the suspicions voiced in the original accusations concerning the vital place of the law and temple. Unable to accept Paul's position, the people issue their judgment: he deserves death.

Scene 2: Paul before Claudius Lysias, a Roman Tribune (22:23–29)

Paul's speech to the mob, although it inflames the situation, is hardly a wasted effort from the reader's perspective, for Paul introduces themes that will return later in his trial. His location during his speech, standing at the threshold of the Roman barracks, with a mob of angry Jews in front of him and the strength of the Roman military presence in Jerusalem at his back, emphasizes the multiple dimensions of his predicament. Because Paul has been unable to calm the crowd in the temple, he is wrenched into the very Roman environment of the barracks. The soldiers' control over his circumstances now comes in a new way. Previously they protected him; now they assert their power to extract information from him, to learn who he is, and to assess what he has done to arouse such fierce opposition. But Paul shows little interest in explaining himself. Then, in a moment of high suspense, after waiting until he is tied up to provide a still target for the inquisitional torture, Paul announces that he is a Roman citizen. This news strikes fear in the tribune and his men, for they realize that they have unlawfully bound a Roman and almost further assaulted his rights and honor.[18] Paul's declaration quickly brings this scene to an end with little dialogue, only enough for him to one-up the tribune by declaring his superior status through citizenship by birth. All that is settled is the fact that Paul possesses the ability to set some of the terms of his incarceration.

Paul offers no explanation to the tribune. He says neither "Look, this dispute is just a Jewish affair," as an attempt to calm the tribune's concerns about his possible offense, nor "I suspect that you are an extremely religious man, and so I want to tell you about Jesus of Nazareth," as an attempt to evangelize the soldier. He does nothing that might help him secure his release, probably because neither he nor the tribune is eager to have him again face the zealous crowd outside. Moreover, his strategy of nondisclosure introduces a sense of defiance. If the Roman military is willing to employ power to extract information from Paul through torture, he will make his own power play by insisting on his rights as a Roman citizen. Playing this card requires the Roman authorities to figure out what to do with him without being able to resort to their default tactics of brute force and intimidation. This scene thus provides the first indication of Paul's intention to use his social status and legal circumstances to his advantage in this scene and those to come.

Scene 3: Paul before Jewish Authorities in Jerusalem (22:30–23:11)

What were essentially kept separate in the previous two scenes—the accusation of Paul's apostasy and the Roman desire to decipher the controversy surrounding him and the unrest he generates—begin to come together in this scene. Lysias does not seek the instigators of the mob in the temple to help him understand what has happened. He instead goes to a quite different set of Jews: the current high priest (named Ananias) and his council (συνέδριον). As the highest ranking Roman military official in Jerusalem, Lysias orders (κελεύω; 22:30) the Jewish aristocracy to assemble and assist him. Paul begins the session by declaring his own clear conscience before God, but this earns him a slap on the mouth. His sharp words in 23:3 accuse the high priest of hypocrisy, claiming that Ananias's strong-arm response betrays his own lack of concern for Jewish law. Paul's words also accuse Ananias of corruption, and thus challenge the high priest's credentials both to judge Paul's fidelity to Judaism and to hold authority over the Jewish people.[19] In striking Paul, the high priest and others reaffirm the continuing hostility against Paul and suggest that his Roman citizenship cannot secure him any favors with the Jewish aristocracy. When Paul moves, in 23:6, to characterize the charges against him, he does not dwell on his own fidelity, but defines the contest as one concerning the heart of Jewish hope, which for Paul is centered in the resurrection from the dead. His words refer to the eschatological hope that God will raise people from the dead, a hope that he believes to be assured and actualized specifically in Christ's resurrection (see 13:32–37; 17:30–31).[20] Paul's statement, although it instantly forces an early and violent end to the hearing, is not only a calculated attempt to divide his opponents. It also resumes and reshapes his defense from Acts 22, asserting that his ministry of the gospel is nothing but an expression of his loyalty to the God of Israel and the hopes of Judaism. He will return to these ideas later in the trial (see 24:15; 26:22–23; 28:20). Paul is less interested in talking about the law and the temple than he is about the resurrection of Jesus as a fulfillment of God's promises to Israel; this is more evangelism than legal defense.

His statement in 23:6 surely includes an implied counteraccusation against those who deny that resurrection is at the heart of Jewish hope, and even more broadly against those who deny Jesus' resurrection. This ignites violence in the assembly as Pharisees and Sadducees fight over an issue that divides them. As the situation degenerates into chaos, some judge Paul's words to be plausible, while others do not. Clearly, not *all* Jews are portrayed as Paul's antagonists. The distinction between these two parties extends beyond theological tenets.

Those in closest collaboration with Roman power, the Sadducees, seize this opportunity to denounce Paul while the Pharisees, who for the most part reaped substantially fewer sociopolitical advantages from the Roman system, voice qualified support.[21] The dividing line suggests that matters of status and political advantage play a part in dividing the assembly, just as matters of theology do.

In any case, the hostility stemming from the sudden schism requires the Roman soldiers to take Paul where he will be safe and cannot incite additional disturbances—to their barracks. From this point forward, Paul can persuade audiences only while under the oversight of high-ranking Roman officials. Also, until he arrives in Rome in Acts 28, Paul will speak to those Roman authorities instead of engaging in head-to-head debates with other Jews. Following the current scene, when the revelation of a plot against Paul suggests that it is too dangerous for him to remain in Jerusalem, Lysias dispatches an escort of stunning magnitude to ensure the safe transfer of his prisoner to a higher authority, hoping that the governor will be able to conduct a more appropriate hearing in the provincial capital, Caesarea (23:30).

Scene 4: Paul before Antonius Felix, the Roman Governor (24:1–27)

In the trial's fourth, fifth, and sixth scenes, Paul finds himself before the highest-ranking members of the Jewish and Roman political elite in Judea, parties that share many mutual interests and depend upon a degree of collaboration for their successful governance. The first twenty-three verses of this scene describe a hearing convened by Felix, the ruling governor of Judea. The final four verses summarize Paul's condition and his relationship with Felix for two years after the hearing concludes.

The presence of the high priest and elders signals that Paul's case remains a high priority for those at the highest echelons of Jewish political power. Paul's removal from Jerusalem does not satisfy them. They press their case against him and accuse him of activity that the governor would interpret as dangerous. To do so, they enlist the services of a professional legal advocate named Tertullus; he is "major-league talent."[22] Yet Paul proves to be up to the task of a rhetorical showdown with an impressive opponent, for his polished response minimizes the danger that Tertullus poses. Both men give speeches well suited to the formal judicial setting.[23] For his part, Tertullus does not focus on whether Paul adheres to Jewish traditions. In summary fashion he paints a picture of an agitator who foments public unrest and leads a sect, charges designed to arouse the governor's concerns about social disorder and potentially rebellious activity.[24]

Paul's defense (ἀπολογέομαι; 24:10) is rather brief, although it addresses each of the accusations that Tertullus brought and recasts them in language that Roman ears would find less threatening, emphasizing his fidelity to Judaism and the consistency between Jewish beliefs and the gospel. Along the way he reasserts his (Jewish) hope of the resurrection as founded in Jesus' own resurrection (vv. 14–16, 21). Perhaps the most critical part of his defense is his claim that none of his opponents has been able to substantiate a specific accusation (vv. 18–21). In a contest over ideas, they cannot establish their own position. This implies that they fail in their role as legal combatants and that the true cause of their opposition to them must be jealousy, enmity, or stubbornness (cf. 4:2; 5:17). By adjourning the hearing until Lysias can arrive from Jerusalem and provide information, Felix confirms Paul's ability to articulate a skillful defense.

Lysias apparently never comes to Caesarea, however, and so Felix effectively delays Paul's case for two years. The custody in which he keeps Paul is not especially harsh or oppressive, as indicated by the emphasis given to Paul's freedoms (24:23–26). Even though the trial involving his adversaries from Jerusalem has been suspended, Paul continues to bear witness in a different venue when he speaks repeatedly about "faith in Christ Jesus" with the governor and his wife, Drusilla.[25] In this way Acts indicates that Paul's long trial is not only about reasserting the gospel as the fulfillment of Jewish religious hopes; it remains good news for a Gentile like Felix, as well.[26] Even though Felix's motives for conversing with Paul come across as mixed at best and perhaps not based on a sincere curiosity (v. 26), Paul still preaches to him boldly enough to arouse fear (v. 25). The governor's nervous response to talk about "justice, self-control, and the coming judgment" exposes his unbelief, the injustice he is perpetuating through Paul's prolonged imprisonment, and the lack of self-control for which his Roman contemporaries criticized him.[27] Paul's evangelistic efforts do not persuade the governor, but they do render a judgment against him, which the narrator intensifies by explaining that Felix hopes to receive a bribe and intends to keep the Jewish leadership indebted to him. Although Felix makes no formal judgment concerning Paul's innocence or guilt, he does judge Paul to be more valuable to him in custody than free. Felix is not confused by Paul's case. He sees the importance of this prisoner for his ongoing alliance with the Jerusalem Jewish aristocracy.

Felix supposes that keeping Paul removed from contact with the general public will benefit him and his sociopolitical interests as governor. This poses an odd contrast to the narrator's claim that his knowledge of "the Way" was quite accurate (24:22). This statement means that he is better informed about the Christian movement than the Jewish prosecutors think he is. Yet the statement also compounds the narrative's negative judgment of Felix: he chooses to hold out for a bribe, even though his knowledge about the gospel should lead him to know that believers do not regard imprisonment as failure or an insurmountable obstacle. He should know better, but still he acts as if imprisoning Paul might prove financially lucrative.

Scene 5: Paul before Porcius Festus, the New Roman Governor (25:6–12)

Paul's two years in custody do not assuage some Jews' determination to do away with him, and so they see the arrival of a new governor as an opportunity to spring a trap. Festus hears a request from the Jewish chief priests and leaders in Jerusalem to transfer Paul there, and he responds by convening a hearing to learn more about the specific accusations against his prisoner. The narrator presents this trial scene with little detail, summarizing the Jewish leadership's case as "many significant charges" that "they were unable to prove." Paul offers a defense (ἀπολογέομαι; v. 8) that merely denies his having transgressed Jewish law, the temple, or the emperor. Again, he is not anti-Jewish. He also says that he does nothing contrary to the emperor. This is true insofar as in his public ministry in Acts, Paul never set out to criticize the emperor or destabilize Roman society, although he must know that what he *did* set out to do—bear witness to Jesus Christ—often resulted in an uproar about what that witness implies for Roman society and its religiopolitical values. Certainly the judgment of many others in Acts is that the gospel does not leave imperial values or structures unchallenged.

Festus still refrains from ruling Paul guilty or innocent of any charges brought by the Jerusalem crowd, probably because he sees the weakness of their case. At the same time, he also refrains from releasing Paul. His inaction reveals his own ambivalence. But when the governor raises the possibility of moving Paul to Jerusalem for a more substantial trial, Paul sees the danger that lurks in the indecision of the Roman official. Recognizing that such a transfer would mean his death (cf. 25:3), Paul appeals his case to the Roman emperor, again asserting his innocence.[28] Paul plays a legal trump card to avoid being offered as a gift in a game of political favors. His appeal also ensures that he will remain a defendant before the bar of imperial power, for his castigating words in 25:10 emphasize that his legal status properly locates him before the judgment seat of the emperor himself. He will not allow Festus to pawn him off to the Jewish leadership; if the governor will not judge Paul in his role as an imperial representative, then Paul insists that the emperor himself will have to do so.[29]

Through his appeal, Paul remains confined yet free from victimization. Even the machinations of his powerful enemies and the political maneuvering of the Roman governor cannot keep him from influencing the future of his trial. He contests their moves and continues to make use of avenues available to him to exercise substantial control over his fate. The promise of Jesus in Acts 23:11, that Paul will yet bear witness in Rome, certainly stands in the background and suggests that more is at work in the current action before Festus than mere cleverness on Paul's part. God's design is working itself out.

This scene briefly serves a transitional function. It concludes with Festus's endorsing Paul's appeal, which he elsewhere says he must do (25:21; 26:31–32). Paul's appeal will warrant one more hearing in Caesarea, for it requires Festus to send the emperor a letter explaining Paul's case, something he is not equipped to do (25:25–27). His solution to this problem comes when King Herod Agrippa II and his sister Bernice arrive in Caesarea.

Scene 6: Paul before Agrippa, Bernice, Festus, and Other Roman Elites (25:13–26:32)

This last scene in Caesarea begins with a preliminary conversation between Festus and Agrippa, in which Festus reviews the events of 25:1–12 and identifies the struggles between Paul and the Jerusalem Jewish leadership as disagreement over religious matters. Once the assembly begins, Festus overstates the charges against Paul when he says that "the whole Jewish population" in Jerusalem and Caesarea petitioned him concerning Paul.[30] Agrippa quickly becomes the focus of the assembly and Paul's defense speech, for the great pageantry of the hearing connotes a royal affair, and Agrippa's words in 26:1 show him to be presiding over the spectacle. Agrippa makes for a fitting authority figure in this scene. Paul's trial has gradually taken him up the ladders of local sociopolitical authority and involved an interplay between the interests of both Jewish and Roman leaders. Although Agrippa was a Herodian client king who answered to the governor of Judea, he appears in Acts 26 as a unique blend of both Roman and Jewish interests and authority. Others refer to him as knowledgeable about Judaism (25:26; 26:3, 27), yet in speaking to him Paul uses language appropriate for one situated outside the religious discourse (26:3, 5). In this scene Agrippa—just as Paul does in his trial—has his feet in two worlds, one of mainly Roman concerns and one Jewish.[31]

Because Paul faces no accusers in this scene, and because Festus only casually refers to any specific accusations that Paul's Jewish opponents have raised, his defense speech is essentially a monologue. Paul refutes no specific charges; he only lays the gospel before his audience in light of his own encounter with and commissioning from Jesus Christ. His speech is the capstone of all his speeches in Acts 22–26, clarifying the foundations of his witness to Christ among Jews and Gentiles and demonstrating the continuity between Jewish hopes and his proclamation of the resurrected Christ.[32] Here we cannot devote detailed attention to the speech's impressive rhetoric and content, except to observe that it pulls together a number of themes that have emerged throughout Paul's trial, including his fidelity to God, the gospel as the fulfillment of the Scriptures, and the resurrection of Jesus as God proclaiming light to Jews and Gentiles.[33]

Perhaps the most notable aspect of Paul's speech emerges at a point of transition where it becomes clear that Paul intends to lay the gospel before his audience, not to gain his release but to proclaim Jesus' name before these "Gentiles and kings." Bible scholar Robert C. Tannehill remarks:

> When his life story reaches the present, he says, "I stand bearing witness both to small and to great" concerning the fulfillment of the scriptural promise of the Messiah (26:22–23). The past story of being called to witness merges into the present act of witnessing, and the defense speech becomes a missionary speech. This shift in function is reflected in Paul's language. In 26:6, on the one hand, Paul describes his situation by saying, "I stand being judged (ἕστηκα κρινόμενος)"; in 26:22, on the other hand, he says, "I stand bearing witness (ἕστηκα μαρτυρόμενος)." The shift in self-definition reflects the shift in the function of the speech.[34]

The trial affords Paul opportunity to bear witness before the most powerful political figures in the region. Greatly confused or dismayed, Festus interrupts. Paul and Agrippa engage in a brief dialogue that shows Agrippa understanding that Paul is trying to persuade him to believe the Christian gospel. As the audience disperses, all agree that Paul has done nothing wrong and could have been released, if he had not appealed his case to the emperor.

For the first time in Acts, a trial scene does not include violence or the threat of violence against a defendant. The irony is that Paul escapes impending violence, at least for a season, by wrapping himself in the protection provided through his appeal to the emperor's judgment seat. Also, after five scenes in Paul's trial that were unable to produce any decisive judgments, other than those expressed by some Jews who seek Paul's death for what they regard as apostasy, finally a Roman authority, one who is "especially knowledgeable about all the customs and disputed issues of the Jews" (26:3), declares Paul's innocence. However, even as Agrippa and the other notables make this declaration, they acknowledge the limitations of their authority over Paul. No matter what they think, Paul will go to Rome, which fulfills the divinely authorized promise of Acts 23:11 and keeps him liable to legal judgment. The trial is not finished.

Scene 7: Paul before the Leading Jews
in Rome (28:17–28)

Agrippa's pronouncement of Paul's innocence in 26:32 makes for a climactic moment, but one movement remains in Paul's trial, and at least one more judgment to be pronounced. Following a thrilling voyage, shipwreck, short sail from Malta to Syracuse (on a ship whose figurehead is a representation of the gods Romans knew as avengers of perjury, no less), and warm welcome from believers in Italy, Paul arrives in Rome and soon summons the leaders of the local Jewish population.[35] He has two separate conversations with these people; together, the conversations constitute the final trial scene in the book of Acts. It does not matter that no recognized official appears in this setting; the subject matter and terminology set the stage for Paul's trial to conclude in his Roman residence.[36] The judicial character of the scene is further confirmed at the end of Paul's exchange with the Jewish leaders when, as we will see, Paul himself assumes the role of a judge.[37]

The scene begins with Paul summarizing his recent legal history (28:17–20), albeit with some slight departures from the earlier narrative, including the claims that he was "given over" (παραδίδωμι; v. 17) to the Romans and that certain Jews opposed a Roman decision to release him (v. 19). Paul's summary includes several details that cast this scene as a resumption of his judicial proceedings. First, Paul's language, opening in v. 17 with the emphatic pronoun ἐγώ, resembles other introductory remarks he has made while defending himself against accusations in front of Jewish audiences (see 22:3; 23:1, 6). Second, Paul's reference to the Romans who deemed him undeserving of death recalls important moments in the story of his prosecution, a prosecution initiated by the actions of the Jewish mob in Jerusalem (23:29; 25:25; 26:31–32).[38] Third, his claim that he was innocent of anything that might be "contrary to the people [of Israel] or the customs of [Israel's] ancestors" (28:17) reintroduces themes regarding his reputation that ignited the opposition against him in Jerusalem (21:21), the mob's rallying cry before his arrest there (21:28), and a central theme of his defense throughout Acts 22–26. Fourth, his concluding reference in 28:20 to "the sake of Israel's hope" recalls the key theological claim that divided the council in 23:6 and other related remarks in subsequent scenes (24:15; 26:6–8). Paul therefore introduces himself to his audience of Roman Jews as one actively maintaining a defense both against accusations made during the previous scenes and in support of the gospel as the fulfillment of Israel's hopes. We should also recognize Paul's stature in this scene. Not only does he convene the meeting and speak first; his declarations of innocence, mention of the Romans' desire to release him, and reference to his desire to appeal his case also underscore the rhetorical and political advantages he enjoys.

Only after Paul reopens his defense does he discover that reports of accusations against him have not reached Rome. When his guests tell him, giving readers no small surprise, that he has no negative reputation among them, the narrative recasts the scene as an opportunity for Paul to enjoy a fresh start by contending for his story in new, relatively unprejudiced legal territory.[39] At the same time, however, these people reveal that they know something about the "sect" to which Paul belongs, that "everywhere it is opposed" (28:22). Their statement does not say they are ignorant of Christianity; they probably know quite a bit and are interested in Paul's take concerning the controversial movement.[40] Although Paul will not have to defend himself against personal charges, he will continue to make a case for his message against an assumption that Jews "everywhere" are refusing it. This occurs in the second part of this scene, in verses 23–28.

The narrator does not divulge the specific arguments and deliberations that occur in the second conversation. All readers get is a short summary that emphasizes the duration of the event ("from morning until evening") and its size ("even larger numbers," perhaps not unlike the impressive turnout before Agrippa described in 25:23). Paul's Jewish audience reaches a split decision: some are persuaded and others not. His defense of the gospel leads to a choice, not between acquittal or conviction, but between belief or unbelief. His defense against charges is once again thoroughly evangelistic.

The greatest amount of detail in this conversation comes in Paul's final statement (vv. 25b–28), where he cites the LXX's version of Isaiah 6:9–10, ratifying the words of the Holy Spirit to Isaiah's audience. Paul has the scene's final word, a word of judgment. He does not declare that God has cut Israel off; his judgment states that these particular listeners, these representatives of Israel living in Rome, will not accept Paul's message. What makes Paul's statement a *judgment* against his audience is that it quotes Isaiah and claims to speak in concert with the Holy Spirit to identify these people as those who rejected Isaiah's message in the eighth century BCE. Here, in what Bible scholar Daniel Marguerat calls "an inverted trial," a noteworthy shift in narrative roles takes place: Paul moves from defendant to judge, and some in his audience move from judges to the ones judged.[41] When some respond to Paul's defense of the gospel with unbelief, he appeals to the Holy Spirit's authority and declares a portion of his audience to be dull-hearted, hard of hearing, and refusing to see. Paul does not issue this judgment as his personal repudiation of Judaism; after all, he has already told his audience that his struggles and his current status as a Roman prisoner demonstrate his resolute commitment to Israel's hopes (Acts 28:20). A prophetic verdict hardly negates that commitment, and nothing about this scene suggests that Paul regards himself and his audience as anything other than the same "people" with common "ancestors." Paul's negative judgment on the recalcitrance of some Jews remains, however, in sharp contrast to his positive statement that Gentiles will listen to the message of God's salvation.[42]

SHIFTING ROLES IN PAUL'S TRIAL

Over the course of seven scenes, Paul moves from his seizure in Jerusalem, to a declaration of exculpation from King Agrippa, to his own judgment of Jews in Rome who remain unconvinced by his witness to the gospel. Multiple episodes of accusation, defense, deliberation, and skullduggery weave their way through the process. Having reviewed the individual scenes, we can now reflect on the image of the whole trial that emerges, taking as our point of departure Paul's shifting forensic roles with respect to other participants in his trial. For when the seventh scene effects a shift in Paul's role, from defendant to judge, it does not come as an unexpected or inconsistent development. Instead, Acts uses this moment to accentuate the means by which the whole of Paul's judicial struggle serves to advance the word of God in new directions.

From Accused to Defendant

The initial shift in Paul's roles comes with a transition from accused to defendant, when the tribune Lysias spirits him away from the angry crowd in the temple and permits him to offer a speech in his defense. This is a rather obvious transition; there would be no trial scenes at all if Paul remained only accused and voiceless and was killed by the mob. Nevertheless, it warrants notice that Paul is able to speak in his defense precisely because Roman intervention ensures it. Later, when he declares his citizenship to the soldiers inside the barracks, Roman policy ensures that he will receive relatively humane treatment and, the narrative implies, have additional opportunities to defend himself. From that point, then, throughout his time in Jerusalem and Caesarea, he is able to be an active defendant because, ironically enough, the constraints of Roman authority provide him the privileges and avenues to do so. Roman custody defines Paul as a defendant. No other place—no other social context—is safe for him, for from the first scene through the sixth nearly all the Jewish characters who appear (except for some of the council in Jerusalem, Drusilla, Agrippa, and Bernice) show no desire to hear Paul's defense. They demand or plot his death.

Paul exercises his role as a defendant with great aplomb. He comes across as crafty, for he is able to exploit the theological and sociopolitical divides between Pharisees and Sadducees in the third scene, which is more than Luke's attempt at a humorous display of the council's propensity for violence. The chaos there shows that the opposition to Paul among Jews is not monolithic. As long as some Pharisees insist on his innocence (23:9), openings of support for him and the gospel he proclaims exist among the Jewish leadership.[43] Paul's effectiveness as a defendant also manifests itself in the rhetoric of his speeches, which contain formal elements found in other defense speeches from contemporary literature and conform to instructions found in ancient rhetorical handbooks.[44] Paul's rhetorical skill shows him to be well equipped—perhaps as a conduit of Jesus' own words and wisdom, according to Luke 21:15—to negotiate his legal challenges. This is consistent with the stunning amount of control he exercises over his environment from his position as defendant, something that contributes to his transition from defendant to judge.

From Defendant to Judge

When Paul meets with the leading Jews in Rome, he assumes a judge's role. One way to glimpse and further appreciate the subtle yet significant transition of Paul's role from defendant to judge is to recognize that other material from Acts 21–28, apart from the trial scenes investigated above, is also germane to the depiction of Paul's legal situation, especially the roles he assumes in the contest. Perhaps the most important place to look is Acts 27:1–28:16, a series of scenes that offer much on top of grand adventure, dramatic interlude, and miraculous preservation from natural forces.[45] Marguerat correctly observes that the story of Paul's travel from Caesarea to Rome puts forth a "glowing image" of Paul as it emphasizes his commanding presence in preparation for the culminating point in the trial scene in which "the prisoner reaches the capital and stays there with the authority of one who will not be judged, but will deliver a judgement."[46] Marguerat finds this image specifically in the leadership and direction Paul exercises during the sea voyage (27:9–10, 21–26, 31–37, 42–44), the triumphant portrayal of Paul on Malta (28:1–10), and his reception in Italy as an honored guest or arriving dignitary (28:14–15). This Paul commands respect and makes it possible for the journey to proceed as it does. He hardly appears as one under the authority of other persons or imperiled by the vicissitudes of life and legal status.[47]

Marguerat might also have looked back even farther into Acts 21–26, however, for the image of Paul as both confined prisoner and authoritative agent is also present elsewhere in his trial. We have already seen that Roman authorities and the benefits of citizenship provide him opportunities to leverage his case, but there are also instances in which he himself exercises significant authority over how others treat him. Paul works to exploit his circumstances under Roman custody, securing privileges and opportunities when he orders a centurion to inform Lysias of the plot against his life, resulting in an impressive escort (beginning with 470 soldiers!) from Jerusalem to Caesarea (23:16–24). While enduring the delay imposed by Felix, he has frequent conversations with the governor about the gospel (24:24–26).[48] One effect of this portrayal of Paul as a defendant who claims prerogatives and attracts special attention from his custodians is that he comes across as one with the authority of God's representative, a characterization that the narrator explicitly reinforces through the supernatural reassurances Paul receives (23:11; 27:23–26).

This commanding characterization of Paul must take account of the theological light in which Acts casts it. Paul wields such influence precisely as God's representative, for throughout the trial and journey his power reflects the perseverance of the word of God. Luke therefore presents Paul not primarily as a wily rhetorician, a man of distinguished rank who boldly towers over his social inferiors, or a triumphant hero of the faith. God guides and ensures his steps throughout his trial.[49] Such divine assistance precedes Paul's impressive talents and standing, yet it does not make him untouchable. (The promise of his imminent death, from his meeting with the Ephesian elders in 20:17–38, is a clear statement of how touchable he is.) It affirms that God empowers Paul's defense even within the putative confines and restrictions of Roman custody; God can and will use these things to advance the witness of the gospel.

CONCLUSIONS

The Trial and the Wider Narrative

Paul's trial has great significance for the overall story that Acts tells. For one thing, it contributes to a unified understanding of Paul's commission to serve as Jesus' witness, whether as a free man or as an accused prisoner. As we have seen, Paul eschews prolonged defense speeches that appeal to points of law or specific Roman values and repeatedly bears witness to Jesus and offers evangelistic proclamation to his audiences.[50] Paul's overriding concern is not to secure his own release (although nothing indicates he would not appreciate that); it is to capitalize on the opportunities that his trial places before him to present the gospel to new audiences composed of elite figures who lead and represent the social and political powers of his day. For

Paul to give a defense of himself is to continue to offer testimony about Jesus Christ. Paul's experience on trial suggests that Jesus' followers do not change their identity, nor do they alter their message, when they are brought for judgment before authorities. Nor is their ability to bear witness totally removed by legal jeopardy and the restrictions placed upon them. In this regard, Acts views accusations, custody, and trials with little concern. Likewise, the book casts a rather indifferent eye toward the particular tactics of specific authorities. Governing authorities might dictate the mode and audience for believers' witness, but nevertheless that witness persists and finds new venues.

Second, Paul's witness results in the rendering of multiple judgments. Members of the Jewish aristocracy in Judea who oppose him show themselves to be thoroughly committed to killing him, recalling the Gospel of Luke's portrayal of Jesus' opponents in Jerusalem. A larger point Luke–Acts makes is that these opponents' rejection of Paul's message, which itself is embodied in his own experience with the risen Christ, is a rejection of the fact that a core hope of Jewish faith—the resurrection of the dead—has been fulfilled in Jesus Christ. In the narrative's perspective, the Jerusalem leadership's negative response to the Christian message betrays the bankruptcy of their identity as leaders of the religious and sociopolitical lives of Judean Jews. Their willingness to employ all sorts of overt and covert means of doing away with him demonstrates as much. Paul's trial therefore helps Acts explain why Jewish opposition to the gospel persists. With the trial, Acts thus distances its early Christian audiences from the Judean Jewish aristocracy that held power in the years before the Jewish-Roman War of 66–70 CE.

Third, the end of Paul's story speaks more loudly than any delayed human verdict from his trial. Paul's end in Rome has him continuing to bear witness to Christ for a two-year, home-based missionary venture even within the constraints of his detention. Paul proclaims the reign of God "with the greatest boldness and without hindrance" (28:31), an expression that describes him operating with legal and spiritual freedom as he awaits his appearance before the emperor.[51] Throughout the seven scenes the Romans consistently mean to keep Paul situated in a custodial netherworld: incarceration tries to regulate a person in a liminal existence where governing authorities exercise power to keep elements of a society quarantined from the wider social world.[52] Yet Paul continues in his efforts *in spite of* and even *because of* his legal predicament. It is an ironic situation, then. The process that was meant to keep him out of sight and restrained from influencing others actually becomes the means by which he preaches openly in Rome. Through a prisoner awaiting his legal appeal, the proclamation of God's word perseveres in Rome.

Manipulating the Means of Control

It is perhaps tempting to consider these three points and conclude that Acts directs only a dismissive glance toward the sociopolitical powers of the first century, as if the narrative is not interested in considering what it means to live in light of the gospel within such a world. But Paul's trial, in its fullness, registers a more ambivalent opinion about the Christian faith's relationship to Roman authority. We have seen that Paul exercises significant control over his conditions and assumes an increasingly authoritative role as his trial progresses. Also, as Paul finds ways to proclaim the gospel to various authorities in Acts 21–28, Acts suggests that they cannot silence him or keep him from doing what Jesus has called him to do. To be sure, many other interpreters have seen how the Roman judicial process in these chapters functions as Paul's protector and conveyor. It is inaccurate, however, to move from that observation to conclude simply that Acts thus contends that the church is "politically harmless, no threat to the state," or that "Rome is not only just and powerful; Rome can abide the Christian message."[53] Interpreters who follow these routes often claim that Acts views the gospel's ascendency over the empire only in an eschatological vein, that the church makes no claims of defiance against the sociopolitical structures of this world but merely waits for all this to be accomplished in the coming reign of God and prefigures such a state of affairs through the ethical life of the Christian community.[54]

Such a perspective rightly recognizes that no one in Acts openly advocates or declares the upending of the imperial system; yet it ignores the subtle ways in which the narrative of Paul's trial relegates that system to subordinate status in the face of the gospel. There is a reason why the preaching of the gospel disturbs the Roman social fabric repeatedly in Acts 16–19, as chapter 8 (above) explored, and why the Roman officials who hold Paul in Acts 21–28 equivocate concerning him. Paul's trial asserts that Roman structures of sociopolitical authority can be made to serve God's will at the same time that they expend their energies and prerogatives in trying to limit Paul's ability to proclaim the gospel. We observed a similar dynamic in Jesus' trial in Luke. Paul's trial in Acts thus deteriorates Roman dominance on an ideological level, even though Acts does not imagine the gospel giving immediate rise to an alternate form of governance. Such an ideological deterioration can be threatening, given that it calls into question the state's own ability to maintain and rely upon the structures it uses to maintain itself.

Paul's story prompts readers of Acts to consider those implications. Bible scholar Eric Franklin observes, concerning the Roman authorities:

their very inability to comprehend witnesses to the fact that they are responding to the action of God which has been released in their midst through the exaltation of Jesus of Nazareth. Luke does not suggest that God's final action inaugurated by that event will win over the Roman state. What he does maintain is that the Roman state is compelled to co-operate in something greater than itself, that God uses it to achieve his purposes.[55]

Reflecting further on what it means for the Roman state to be compelled to cooperate or to be used by God allows us to see that Acts depicts the gospel arrayed against values and interests of the Roman Empire in particular, as well as other human construals of sociopolitical authority more generally.

Bible scholar Gary Gilbert's analysis of the theological rhetoric of Acts shows that Acts communicates its sociopolitical vision in indirect ways. Gilbert compares that rhetoric to Roman imperial language and imagery and concludes that Acts imitates aspects of Roman propaganda as a means of legitimating the nascent Christian churches and shaping their communal self-understanding. Important for us is Gilbert's realization that such borrowing of ideological rhetoric to promote Christianity can hardly avoid provocation; it "also deconstructs the Roman world in the process" by deftly staging a confrontation between Roman authority and the church concerning the nature of true dominion.[56] The judicial drama in Acts 21–28 effects a confrontation that is similar in its subtleties to the one Gilbert traces in the book's religious rhetoric. The trial scenes do more than reiterate Paul's innocence over the span of multiple chapters and propel him to Rome as a fulfillment of God's design. Even though he rarely speaks to or about imperial assumptions of dominance, the fact remains that Paul's long trial is entirely set under the protective eye and power of increasingly powerful levels of Roman authority. When Paul is consistently able to navigate and even manipulate the Roman custodial and judicial apparatus, to assume the role of a prosecutor, and to conclude with a two-year "unhindered" ministry in Rome, he contests the power arrayed against him. In this way, Acts portrays the government's judicial tools as not merely advantageous or neutral to the gospel but ultimately *ineffective* in light of the gospel. This does not call readers to construe the gospel as revolutionarily defiant or treacherously subversive; yet it does minimize the empire's sociopolitical privileges, contravening its intentions and exposing its power as less than absolute.

This is oblique communication from the narrative, to be sure. But oblique criticism still criticizes. That Paul and others express neither passive compliance nor revolutionary defiance in the face of Jewish and Roman authorities should not take us by surprise, for in that context such tactics could doom them and their movement. Their modes of criticizing and contesting domination are like those employed by others in different social systems. Subordinate groups live their public lives between the extremes of compliance and defiance, and ambivalence within that middle ground provides them a tool of creative and discreet resistance. Subordinate groups' "vulnerability has rarely permitted them the luxury of direct confrontation. The self-control and indirection required of the powerless thus contrast sharply with the less inhibited directness of the powerful."[57] Subordinates therefore express resistance publicly yet subtly—openly voicing a "hidden transcript" in the face of the authorized, civil "public transcript" of open communication—by exploiting available loopholes, veiling true intentions, inverting symbols, and acting out reversals.[58]

In Acts, these kinds of encoded expressions of nonconformity manifest themselves, not only in believers' private statements (such as in 4:23–31, when their community meets in isolation), but also in the public discourse of the trials, performed before the authorities themselves. For example, Paul exploits a legal advantage when he appeals his case to the emperor. He only slightly veils his intentions or subverts others' when he offers evangelistic speeches to defend himself. His assumption of different roles in the forensic drama, seen most vividly with the Jewish leadership in Rome, inverts judicial expectations. When describing Paul's transportation from one judicial venue to another, the narrative imagines a reversal of Paul's condition: the massive military escort to Caesarea (23:23–24), the authority he commands during the sea voyage (27:9–10, 21–36), the goodwill he secures on Malta (28:7–10), and the freedom he exercises when visiting believers in Puteoli (28:13–14)—all make him appear as more the traveling dignitary than the chained prisoner. None of these are overtly insurrectionary expressions, but they do not need to be so for them to depict the mechanisms of Roman power as exploitable and manipulable. Such enacted inversions of the prerogatives and instruments of the governing powers do not merely *prefigure* what the reign of God will accomplish. They also *demonstrate* it with subtle but nevertheless effective results.

10

Conflict, Power, and Identity in the New Testament's Trial Narratives

The contents of the New Testament's trial narratives and the high-profile figures who appear in them should discourage us from underestimating the depth and breadth of the conflicts that the Gospels and Acts describe. These conflicts had deep foundations in the religious and sociopolitical currents of their time, and they escalated because Jesus, his followers, and his opponents understood that he and his claims posed considerable implications for how his followers would understand and live amid those currents. In the Gospels, each in its own way, Jesus' trial also provides a critical moment for presenting or re-presenting Jesus' identity as Christ and king. Although he is the defendant, the narratives nevertheless allow readers to perceive his divinely authorized authority through the trials. Generally speaking, trials say something about societies. In particular, according to the Gospels, Jesus' trial also says something about who he is *in relationship to human society.*

The trials in the Gospels portray the Christ in relationship to his society and the authority that rules it. These episodes have a climactic effect not merely in a literary sense but also in a theological one. Clearly Jesus' trial occupied a potent place in the early church's memory: Christians used it as a theological resource, as seen in its varied reappearances along multiple trajectories. Some New Testament authors remember Christ's behavior in his trial as exemplary for Christian conduct (1 Tim. 6:13; 1 Pet. 2:20–23). When the Gospels predict legal hardships for Jesus' followers and use these predictions to foreshadow Jesus' own trial, they suggest that Jesus' appearance before authoritative figures was only the first of many in the history of Jesus and his followers (Mark 13:9–11; Matt. 10:17–20; 24:9; Luke 12:11–12; 21:12–15; cf. John 15:20; Rev. 2:10). Comments about imprisonment in multiple Pauline writings (e.g., Eph. 3:1; 4:1; Col. 4:3; 2 Tim. 1:8; Philemon) confirm that

Christian proclamation can count on attracting such opposition. No doubt many among the first generations of Christians who heard and cherished the stories of Jesus' trial and his followers' trials would have found them exemplary for their own judicial travails. The Acts narrative goes even further, however. There, Jesus' trial serves as more than inspirational memory: it actually continues in the lives and witness of his followers. Jesus' trial recurred in the early church's existence; traditions about it gave Christians language and concepts by which to interpret both their place in the world and their means of bearing witness within their sometimes hazardous sociopolitical contexts.

In this way, stories of trials, stories of contesting truth claims in the face of the agents and structures of sociopolitical power, provided a means by which early Christian readers—and after them, Christian readers through the centuries—could engage in self-definition. The first readers of the Gospels and Acts were negotiating their place within various pockets of Roman-governed society, and sometimes over against Jewish communities that only recently had seemed much like their own. This means that they were constructing their sense of identity, their sense of themselves as Christians, as imperial subjects, as members of societies. Negotiating a place is a political process; at least, it requires groups to define themselves and articulate their values in comparison and contrast to their neighbors' values and their rulers' values. Identity formation therefore involves forging both connection to and differentiation from other communities. The New Testament's trial scenes assist in such a process, although they do not prompt readers to position themselves according to unambiguous political postures as much as they illustrate both dangers and opportunities that their sociopolitical context presents to them.

The New Testament's trial scenes make their individual points in their individual ways, but our exploration has frequently emphasized their use of irony, misperceptions, confusion about charges, and contested ideas. These features allow the narratives to employ ambiguity and subtlety in their representations of the trials. No scene is so simplistic that we can plainly label it "resistant toward Rome," "conciliatory toward the empire," or "politically indifferent." Such labeling was not our goal to begin with, and attempts to affix such labels nevertheless run aground on the basic observation that different ancient audiences would have encountered the trial scenes in varied ways. Not all first-century Christians were directly touched by the Jewish-Roman War. Few experienced concentrated persecution from Rome. Even into the second century, Christians' experiences with Roman power were hardly uniform. Some would find comfort in the trials' dramatically depicted warnings about abusive power and promises of future vindication. Others might hear a startling, prophetic summons in these same scenes. We might better observe the fabric of these complexities and bring our study to a close by posing two general questions that point to ways in which these scenes might contribute to Christian self-definition: What do the trials assert about political power? What do they say about God and the gospel?

As for political power, the trials of the Gospels and Acts reject any notion that human authority effectively rivals God's. Such a perspective is hardly surprising. For Mark and Matthew, God gives Jesus over to experience the abuses of human power. Luke and John suggest that God's will somehow works itself out through the trial and all the political posturing that it includes, ultimately leaving the human authorities not fully in control but nevertheless scrambling to secure whatever political gains they can manage. These dynamics certainly raise profound theological questions when they lead some to ask whether Jesus' condemnation might itself implicate God, insofar as God permits the destruction of God's Son and holds human beings accountable. For the purposes of our investigation, however, it is important to observe that the subjugation of Jesus to human authority becomes a means by which Jesus' opponents—along with Gamaliel and the Philippian magistrates in Acts—acknowledge Jesus' authority and God's supremacy, ironically, without intending to do so. As we have seen, this keeps Jesus' identity as the Christ simultaneously related to and displaced from society's ability to comprehend him and his ways.

When trials—as especially with Jesus' trial in Mark and Matthew and Stephen's in Acts—expose human authorities' propensities to overwhelm and tyrannize others to protect their convictions or privileges, they set the way of Jesus and his gospel in sharp contrast. The claim that Jesus is Christ has a way of bringing these abuses to light, and so these trials implicitly warn readers against seeking political power or becoming overly friendly with those who hold it. The tactics of the authorities in the trials discourage Christian communities from co-opting the values and systems of empires. Further, when the trials in Luke–Acts insist that the sociopolitical authorities of this world are ultimately powerless to thwart God's design, and that their attempts to do so actually backfire and become means by which God advances God's purposes, they take focus away from the strength of those authorities and redirect it toward God. In Luke–Acts, the provisionality of human authority results in an almost indifferent perspective toward it, because of the narrative's insistence on God's ability to manipulate the structures and tools of that authority. Jesus' trial in John's Gospel keeps vivid the hostility of the "world" that requires an entirely different kind of king to bring into it an alternate way of living.

The Gospels and Acts, given their basic historical context, take account of the sociopolitical arenas involving the Roman Empire and the Jewish priestly aristocracy of pre-70-CE Jerusalem. The particular historical conditions we see reflected in the New Testament's trial scenes have passed away. The criticisms at work in these narratives have their roots in those conditions, but their relevance also extends beyond that historical context to sustain a critical perspective toward the trappings of human authority in other contexts. Together, these trials assert that all political power is provisional and capable of being made to serve God's purposes. This must not be taken to imply that all political power is corrupt, dangerous, or arrayed against God. It must also not be taken to characterize God as a Master Puppeteer or history as determinism. Neither experience nor the New Testament writings support such extreme conclusions. But the New Testament does depict a variety of political stratagems and values that come across as contrary to the good news of Jesus Christ.

What do the trials say about the Christian gospel? When God's will prevails in the Lukan trial, and when Paul's activities in Roman custody frustrate the intentions of those in Acts who presume to wield authority over society, these trials suggest that God can make the gospel to do its work within all social contexts, even potentially hostile or restrictive ones, making them fitting for God's purposes. Even in the Markan and Matthean accounts, where Jesus appears thoroughly victimized, the trials perform the positive function of defining him within and over against the heart of the systems that make him such a victim. Jesus gently but definitively leverages the constellations of sociopolitical power by exposing them and imagining a different kind of rule. Jesus, by sheer weight of his access to these authorities in his trial, and according to the ends of the Gospel narratives, has the potential to shape the social realities that the trial represents. This is what makes these scenes so powerful and worthy of ongoing attention.

The Gospels and Acts never, except occasionally in a vaguely eschatological sense, envision a social setting in which Christians will hold political power and exercise governmental functions. The world of Christendom, variously defined, does not appear on these books' radar screens, for they typically imagine Christians in positions of relative powerlessness (although we have encountered some exceptions in this study in, e.g., Luke 23:50–51; Acts 17:4; 22:28) and the message of the gospel as a minority report that hardly convinces all who hear it. This does not mean that the Gospels and Acts prohibit Christians from wielding sociopolitical authority, only that they direct energy toward posing Jesus and his gospel as clashing with governing authority that expresses itself in defensiveness, violence, and ruthless self-preservation. While Christians in many parts of today's world enjoy access to sociopolitical power, they do well to remember that the New Testament's criticisms do not *limit* themselves to Rome, priestly aristocracies, or empires. Those who imagine that the values of the gospel hold out hope for government—not only civil government but ecclesial as well—that is totally immune to defensive abuses will not find the same optimism shared in the pages of the New Testament, nor in those of Western history.

Notes

Chapter 1: Introduction

1. Daniel J. Kornstein, *Kill All the Lawyers? Shakespeare's Legal Appeal* (Princeton, NJ: Princeton University Press, 1994), 12.

2. Except where otherwise indicated, all English translations of ancient texts are mine.

3. As I will discuss in chapter 2, it is difficult if not impossible to identify established procedural criteria for trials in the Roman provinces during the first century. Further complicating matters, some trial scenes may be the products of editorial attempts to correlate their legal details with Roman legal procedures from a later era. On this, see Erika Heusler, *Kapitalprozesse im lukanischen Doppelwerk: Die Verfahren gegen Jesus und Paulus in exegetischer und rechtshistorischer Analyse*, NTAbh: Neue Folge 38 (Münster: Aschendorff, 2000), 43–46, 179–82.

4. See a similar definition of trials in Saundra Schwartz, "The Trial Scene in the Greek Novels and in Acts," in *Contextualizing Acts: Lukan Narrative and Greco-Roman Discourse*, ed. Todd Penner and Caroline Vander Stichele SBLSymS 20 (Leiden: E. J. Brill, 2003), 111. Her list of the scenes in Acts that qualify as trials (136–37) diverges slightly from mine because of slight differences between our definitions. See also the list in Richard I. Pervo, *Profit with Delight: The Literary Genre of the Acts of the Apostles* (Philadelphia: Fortress Press, 1987), 43.

5. I treat the Gospel accounts according to the order in which those books were probably composed. Following the basic contours of the two-source hypothesis, I assume Markan priority and that Matthew and Luke were composed, each independently from the other, using Mark as a primary source. While John certainly incorporates traditions out of streams known also to the synoptic authors, I believe it was composed without access to the finished or near-finished forms of the other three Gospels.

6. The scholarly literature on these historical questions is immense. For representative examples of influential contributions, see S. G. F. Brandon, *The Trial of Jesus of Nazareth* (New York: Stein & Day, 1968); Raymond E. Brown, *The Death of the Messiah: From Gethsemane to the Grave; A Commentary on the Passion Narratives in the Four Gospels*, 2 vols., ABRL (New York: Doubleday, 1994), 1:237–877; Henry J. Cadbury, "Roman Law and the Trial of Paul," in *The Beginnings of Christianity*, part 1, *The Acts of the Apostles*, ed. F. J. Foakes-Jackson, Kirsopp Lake, and Henry J. Cadbury, 5 vols. (London: Macmillan, 1933), 5:297–338; Simon Légasse, *The Trial of Jesus*, trans. John Bowden

(London: SCM Press, 1997); Brian Rapske, *The Book of Acts and Paul in Roman Custody*, vol. 3 of *The Book of Acts in Its First Century Setting*, ed. Bruce W. Winter (Grand Rapids: Wm. B. Eerdmans Publishing Co., 1994); A. N. Sherwin-White, *Roman Society and Roman Law in the New Testament* (Oxford: Clarendon Press, 1963); Harry W. Tajra, *The Trial of St. Paul: A Juridical Exegesis of the Second Half of the Acts of the Apostles*, WUNT 2/35 (Tübingen: J. C. B. Mohr [Paul Siebeck], 1989); Paul Winter, *On the Trial of Jesus*, 2nd ed., SJ 1 (Berlin: De Gruyter, 1974).

7. Given the nature of Paul's extended trial in Acts 21–28, this angle of inquiry typically focuses on the rhetoric of trial speeches found there. For a representative range of studies, see H. Stephen Brown, "Paul's Hearing at Caesarea: A Preliminary Comparison with Legal Literature of the Roman Period," *SBL Seminar Papers, 1996*, SBLSP 35 (Atlanta: Scholars Press, 1996), 319–32; William Rudolf Long, "The Trial of Paul in the Book of Acts: Historical, Literary, and Theological Considerations" (PhD diss., Brown University, 1982), 159–257; Bruce J. Malina and Jerome H. Neyrey, *Portraits of Paul: An Archaeology of Ancient Personality* (Louisville, KY: Westminster John Knox Press, 1996), 64–99; Marion L. Soards, *The Speeches in Acts: Their Content, Context, and Concerns* (Louisville, KY: Westminster/John Knox Press, 1994); Fred Veltman, "The Defense Speeches of Paul in Acts," in *Perspectives on Luke-Acts*, ed. Charles H. Talbert (Danville, VA: Association of Baptist Professors of Religion, 1978), 243–56; Bruce W. Winter, "Official Proceedings and the Forensic Speeches in Acts 24–26," in *The Book of Acts in Its Ancient Literary Setting*, ed. Bruce W. Winter and Andrew D. Clarke, vol. 1 of *The Book of Acts in Its First Century Setting*, ed. Bruce W. Winter (Grand Rapids: Wm. B. Eerdmans Publishing Co., 1993), 305–36.

8. The literature on this topic, too, is vast. For representative examples of various methods and concerns, see Loveday Alexander, "The Acts of the Apostles as an Apologetic Text," in *Apologetics in the Roman Empire: Pagans, Jews, and Christians*, ed. Mark Edwards, Martin Goodman, and Simon Price (New York: Oxford University Press, 1999), 15–44; François Bovon, *The Last Days of Jesus*, trans. Kristin Hennessy (Louisville, KY: Westminster John Knox Press, 2006); Hans Conzelmann, *The Theology of St. Luke*, trans. Geoffrey Buswell (Philadelphia: Fortress Press, 1961), 137–49; Alexandru Neagoe, *The Trial of the Gospel: An Apologetic Reading of Luke's Trial Narratives*, SNTSMS 116 (Cambridge: Cambridge University Press, 2002), especially the survey of scholarship on 4–21; Todd C. Penner, *In Praise of Christian Origins: Stephen and the Hellenists in Lukan Apologetic Historiography* (New York: T&T Clark, 2004); Gerard S. Sloyan, *Jesus on Trial: A Study of the Gospels*, 2nd ed. (Minneapolis: Fortress Press, 2006); Paul W. Walaskay, *"And So We Came to Rome": The Political Perspective of St. Luke*, SNTSMS 49 (Cambridge: Cambridge University Press, 1983).

9. No two of these five books depict "the Christian gospel" in exactly the same way. The limited scope of this investigation requires me to speak of "the gospel" as a generalized abbreviation for both a message and a movement—in short, all that a New Testament writing has to say about Jesus, his message, and the enduring relevance of his life, death, and resurrection.

10. Schwartz, "Trial Scene," 109–17, 132–33. Schwartz describes courtroom scenes in ancient Greek novels as familiar sites for "the dramatization of ideology" (110). For more on the trials in these novels, see chapter 2 below.

11. On how the features and development of a narrative are vital pieces of interpreting its "theological contribution," see Beverly Roberts Gaventa, "Toward a Theology of Acts: Reading and Rereading," *Int* 42 (1988): 149–51, 157.
12. The ambiguity and multidimensionality of narrative only makes its ability to shape an audience more effective, even as it makes it difficult to pin down how a given narrative functions among an audience. Cf. the discussion of historiography, its narrative character, and its potential for aiding in self-definition in Daniel Marguerat, *The First Christian Historian: Writing the "Acts of the Apostles,"* SNTSMS 121 (Cambridge: Cambridge University Press, 2002), 5–13.
13. As chapter 9 will show, Paul's trial in Acts acknowledges both Jewish and Roman involvement in a way that reflects the complex and sometimes ambivalent political realities of the historical context. For example, Roman authorities both protect Paul from his Jewish opponents (as the tribune Lysias does twice in Acts 23:10–24) and conspire with those opponents against him (as the governor Festus does in Acts 25:1–12).

Chapter 2: Trials in Ancient Life and Literature

1. On the relevant ancient sources, see Sherwin-White, *Society,* 12–23; Heusler, *Kapitalprozesse,* 184–96.
2. For simplicity's sake, I consistently use the term "governor" in this book to refer to the top-ranking Roman official in an imperial province. In the first half of the first century CE, this person was called a "prefect" (in Latin, *praefectus*). By the end of the century, "procurator" (*procurator*) had become the recognized title. New Testament writings use the Greek word ἡγεμών (governor), a more general term for appointees to such an office. As chapter 8 mentions, arrangements were slightly different in Philippi (a Roman colony within the province of Macedonia) and Thessalonica (the Macedonian capital), although the imperial magistrates there likewise possessed considerable authority.
3. J. E. Lendon, *Empire of Honour: The Art of Government in the Roman World* (Oxford: Clarendon Press, 1997), 19. Lendon reports that in the second century this view of the governor as the conduit of the emperor's authority led to the practice of installing the emperor's portrait in courtroom venues to symbolize his presence in a governor's judicial duties.
4. Clifford Ando, *Imperial Ideology and Provincial Loyalty in the Roman Empire* (Berkeley: University of California Press, 2000).
5. Peter Garnsey and Richard Saller, *The Roman Empire: Economy, Society and Culture* (Berkeley: University of California Press, 1987), 20–26.
6. O. F. Robinson, *Penal Practice and Penal Policy in Ancient Rome* (New York: Routledge, 2007), 3.
7. For examples of various acts or confessions considered seditious in different times from the Roman Republic to the later Roman Empire, see Robinson, *Penal Practice.*
8. Sherwin-White, *Society,* 1–12, 22–23; Garnsey and Saller, *Empire,* 34–36; Peter Garnsey, "The Criminal Jurisdiction of Governors," *JRS* 58 (1968): 51–59.
9. Jean-Jacques Aubert, "A Double Standard in Roman Criminal Law? The Death Penalty and Social Structure in Late Republican and Early Imperial Rome," in *Speculum Iuris: Roman Law as a Reflection of Social and Economic Life in Antiquity,* ed. Jean-Jacques Aubert and Boudewijn Sirks (Ann Arbor: University of Michigan Press, 2002), 99.

10. K. Tuori, "Legal Pluralism and the Roman Empires," in *Beyond Dogmatics: Law and Society in the Roman World*, ed. J. W. Cairns and P. J. du Plessis, Edinburgh Studies in Law 3 (Edinburgh: Edinburgh University Press, 2007), 47–48; Brown, *Death*, 1:850–51; Saundra Charlene Schwartz, "Courtroom Scenes in the Ancient Greek Novels" (PhD diss., Columbia University, 1998), 13–14.

11. Lendon, *Empire*, 201–2.

12. Garnsey and Saller, *Empire*, 20, 111.

13. Ibid., 117.

14. Class and status are not precisely the same things, and any analysis of them and their distinctions depends on the sociological presuppositions brought to that analysis. I agree with Garnsey and Saller (ibid., 109) that debating the fine distinctions between these labels is often unfruitful, and so I use both interchangeably as a means of general reference to the social hierarchies that gave shape to Roman society.

15. Ramsay MacMullen, "Judicial Savagery in the Roman Empire," in *Changes in the Roman Empire: Essays in the Ordinary* (Princeton, NJ: Princeton University Press, 1990), 204–8; Lendon, *Empire*, 23.

16. Peter Garnsey, *Social Status and Legal Privilege in the Roman Empire* (Oxford: Oxford University Press, 1970), 65–152; Klaus Wengst, *Pax Romana and the Peace of Jesus Christ*, trans. John Bowden (Philadelphia: Fortress, 1987), 38–40; Robinson, *Penal Practice*, 195; Aubert, "Double Standard."

17. Garnsey, *Social Status*, 258. See the helpful discussion of honor in Roman society in Lendon, *Empire*, 30–106.

18. See examples in Gerhard E. Lenski, *Power and Privilege: A Theory of Social Stratification* (Chapel Hill: University of North Carolina Press, 1966), 222–24.

19. Lenski explains that birthrates and technological limitations keep agrarian societies from constituting themselves in ways that could alter gross inequities in wealth and privilege. Alternative social systems were probably unavailable to the ancients, unless they were somehow to opt for a much more dangerous existence in a much less durable society (ibid., 295–96). The Roman Empire's ability to maintain comparably impressive levels of material well-being for its people is perhaps the other side of the coin to the structures and practices that strike modern observers as oppressive and exploitative (see Ando, *Imperial Ideology*).

20. Quoted in Lendon, *Empire*, 7.

21. Garnsey, *Social Status*, 77–79.

22. For example, on evidence for both Jewish and Greek γερουσίαι in Alexandria during the first century, see Herbert A. Musurillo, *The Acts of the Pagan Martyrs: Acta Alexandrinorum* (London: Oxford University Press, 1954), 108–10.

23. See Hannah M. Cotton, "Jewish Jurisdiction under Roman Rule: Prolegomena," in *Zwischen den Reichen: Neues Testament und römische Herrschaft*, ed. Michael Labahn and Jürgen Zangenberg, Texte und Arbeiten zum neutestamentlichen Zeitalter 36 (Tübingen: Francke, 2002), 16–20, 24–25; Martin Goodman, *The Ruling Class of Judaea: The Origins of the Jewish Revolt against Rome, A.D. 66–70* (Cambridge: Cambridge University Press, 1987), 33–36.

24. Goodman, *Ruling Class*, 36–44, 110–13; Anthony J. Saldarini, *Pharisees, Scribes and Sadducees in Palestinian Society: A Sociological Approach* (Grand Rapids: Wm. B. Eerdmans Publishing Co., 2001), 302. On the problems historians face in determining the precise makeup and qualifications of this priestly aristocracy,

see Fergus Millar, *The Roman Near East, 31 BC–AD 337* (Cambridge, MA: Harvard University Press, 1993), 360–62.

25. Warren Carter, *Pontius Pilate: Portraits of a Roman Governor*, Interfaces (Collegeville, MN: Liturgical Press, 2003), 48.

26. Millar, *Near East*, 45–46. On this policy as a blatant expression of the high priests' status as Roman puppets, see Goodman, *Ruling Class*, 111–12.

27. Evidence indicates that Rome did not give the aristocracy authority over capital cases, with specific exceptions. On debates over the evidence, see ibid., 71–72. See also the discussion in chapter 6, on Jesus' trial in the Gospel according to John.

28. Ibid., 112–17.

29. Ibid., 46–49.

30. Regarding the dynamics imbedded in agrarian societies such as those that composed the Roman Empire, see, e.g., Lenski, *Power and Privilege*, 210–30.

31. For a recent overview that introduces some of the more familiar sociologists in these conversations (such as John H. Kautsky, Gerhard E. Lenski, and Gideon Sjoberg) and a number of scholars who have brought their theoretical models to New Testament studies (most notably, Warren Carter, Richard A. Horsley, and Richard L. Rohrbaugh), see Dennis C. Duling, "Empire: Theories, Methods, Models," in *The Gospel of Matthew in Its Roman Imperial Context*, ed. John Riches and David C. Sim, Early Christianity in Context, JSNTSup 276 (London: T&T Clark, 2005), 49–74.

32. Anthony Giddens, *The Constitution of Society: Outline of the Theory of Structuration* (Berkeley: University of California Press, 1984), 16. Giddens refers to this phenomenon as the "dialectic of control." Because, according to Giddens, power is intrinsically connected to the idea of human agency, to intervene in the world, to refrain from doing so, or somehow to make a difference to a state of affairs is to exercise power within a social system (14). See also his *Central Problems in Social Theory: Action, Structure and Contradiction in Social Analysis* (London: Macmillan, 1979), 149–50.

33. Goodman, *Ruling Class*, 15.

34. See Robinson, *Penal Practice*, 102–3.

35. On the emergence and evolution of differing perspectives, see Peter Oakes, "A State of Tension: Rome in the New Testament," in *The Gospel of Matthew in Its Roman Imperial Context*, ed. John Riches and David C. Sim, Early Christianity in Context, JSNTSup 276 (London: T&T Clark, 2005), 75–90.

36. Monika Fludernik and Greta Olson, "Introduction," in *In the Grip of the Law: Trials, Prisons and the Space Between*, ed. Monika Fludernik and Greta Olson (Frankfurt am Main: Peter Lang, 2004), xx.

37. Vincent Farenga, *Citizen and Self in Ancient Greece: Individuals Performing Justice and the Law* (Cambridge: Cambridge University Press, 2006); David Cohen, *Law, Violence, and Community in Classical Athens*, Key Themes in Ancient History (Cambridge: Cambridge University Press, 1995).

38. For other studies of ancient fiction as part of biblical narrative's literary milieu, see Ronald F. Hock, J. Bradley Chance, and Judith Perkins, eds., *Ancient Fiction and Early Christian Narrative*, SBLSymS 6 (Atlanta: Scholars Press, 1998); Jo-Ann A. Brant, Charles W. Hedrick, and Chris Shea, eds., *Ancient Fiction: The Matrix of Early Christian and Jewish Narrative*, SBLSymS 32 (Atlanta: Scholars Press, 2005).

39. Schwartz, "Courtroom Scenes." On her definition of a trial and the thirteen scenes that meet the criteria, see 25. On the dating of these novels, see 425–45.
40. On similar use of trial scenes in later literature, including apocryphal *Acts* and Philostratus's *Life of Apollonius of Tyana*, see Pervo, *Profit*, 47.
41. Schwartz, "Courtroom Scenes," 2.
42. For Schwartz's take on stylistic and ideological differences between the trials in the Greek novels and in Acts, see "Trial Scene," 117.
43. Schwartz, "Courtroom Scenes," 1–2.
44. Ibid., 383.
45. Ibid., 385–86; see also Pervo, *Profit*, 47–48. Dramatic turns and startling revelations also occur in the trial scenes in books 3 and 10 of the second-century Latin novel *Metamorphoses* (*The Golden Ass*), by Apuleius.
46. Schwartz, "Courtroom Scenes," 130–35.
47. Ibid., 386.
48. Ibid., 28; see also 385.
49. Carolyn J. Sharp, *Irony and Meaning in the Hebrew Bible*, Indiana Studies in Biblical Literature (Bloomington: Indiana University Press, 2009), 240.
50. Schwartz, "Courtroom Scenes," 387.
51. Ibid., 253–92.
52. Schwartz, "Trial Scene," 117. Schwartz attributes this to the elite Greek cultural context assumed by the novels and by their ancient readers. Elsewhere she argues that *Chaereas and Callirhoe* exhibits an ambivalence toward Roman imperial power that was typical for Greek culture under Roman rule ("Rome in the Greek Novel? Images and Ideas of Empire in Chariton's Persia," *Arethusa* 36 [2003]: 375–94).
53. See Susan Sered and Samuel Cooper, "Sexuality and Social Control: Anthropological Reflections on the Book of Susanna," in *The Judgment of Susanna: Authority and Witnesses*, ed. Ellen Spolsky, SBLEJL 11 (Atlanta: Scholars Press, 1996), 43–45. One rightly observes that the story does not allow Susanna herself to expose the abuses that led to her condemnation. Establishing Daniel's reputation comes across as just as important as the narrative's vindication of Susanna. See Amy-Jill Levine, "'Hemmed in on Every Side': Jews and Women in the Book of Susanna," in *A Feminist Companion to Esther, Judith and Susanna*, ed. Athalya Brenner, The Feminist Companion to the Bible 7 (Sheffield: Sheffield Academic Press, 1995), 303–23.
54. Other biblical writings employ judicial motifs to confirm the faithfulness of God and God's prophets. See, e.g., Jer. 26:1–19.
55. Musurillo, *Pagan Martyrs*.
56. Herbert A. Musurillo, "The Pagan Acts of the Martyrs," *TS* 10 (1949): 556–57. The most heated rhetoric appears in these three manuscripts: *Acta Isidori*, *Acta Hermaisci* (P.Oxy. 1242), and *Acta Appiani* (see Musurillo, *Pagan Martyrs*). The brash speech and caricatured portrayals of Roman officials seen in the most hostile passages of the *Acts of the Pagan Martyrs* are absent from the New Testament trial scenes and also differ from Christian accounts of martyrs' interrogations in later centuries.
57. For examples involving Seneca, Thrasea Paetus, Apollonius of Tyana, and others, see Ramsay MacMullen, *Enemies of the Roman Order: Treason, Unrest, and Alienation in the Empire* (Cambridge, MA: Harvard University Press, 1966), 75–77, 88–94, 312 n. 29.

Chapter 3: Jesus on Trial in the Gospel according to Mark

1. E.g., John R. Donahue, "Temple, Trial, and Royal Christology (Mark 14:53–65)," and Norman Perrin, "The High Priest's Question and Jesus' Answer (Mark 14:61–62)," in *The Passion in Mark: Studies on Mark 14–16*, ed. Werner H. Kelber (Philadelphia: Fortress, 1976), 61–79, 80–95. For Donald Juel, the trial introduces themes that become important in what follows (*Messiah and Temple: The Trial of Jesus in the Gospel of Mark*, SBLDS 31 [Missoula, MT: Scholars Press, 1977]).

2. Mark calls this assembly a συνέδριον (14:55; 15:1), which I translate as "council." A συνέδριον in Jesus' day was an ad hoc body called together by the high priest for a specific function, sometimes to convene hearings. It was not a permanent judicial body. See E. P. Sanders, *Judaism: Practice and Belief, 63 BCE–66 CE* (Philadelphia: Trinity Press International, 1992), 472–88; James S. McLaren, *Power and Politics in Palestine: The Jews and the Governing of Their Land, 100 BC–AD 70*, JSNTSup 63 (Sheffield: Sheffield Academic Press, 1991), 213–21; Goodman, *Ruling Class*, 112–17.

3. On the ironic connections between Peter's scene in Mark 14:66–72 and Jesus' trial, see Jerry Camery-Hoggatt, *Irony in Mark's Gospel: Text and Subtext*, SNTSMS 72 (Cambridge: Cambridge University Press, 1992), 171–74.

4. This is not to label the event as technically illegal. Doing so risks misconstruing the nature of first-century Roman provincial jurisprudence. See the discussion in the previous chapter and McLaren, *Power and Politics*, 97.

5. No Pharisees appear after Mark 12:13–17. The authorities who prosecute Jesus are the priestly aristocracy closely affiliated with the Jerusalem temple.

6. Ira Brent Driggers, "The Politics of Divine Presence: Temple as Locus of Conflict in the Gospel of Mark," *BibInt* 15 (2007): 240–41.

7. For Mark, written in light of the temple's destruction, the temple represents a failed institution and irretrievable theological vision whose passing requires a theological explanation. For a good overview of Jesus' comments about the temple and its failed leadership, see M. Eugene Boring, *Mark: A Commentary*, NTL (Louisville, KY: Westminster John Knox Press, 2006), 319–24.

8. These are Jesus' three most comprehensive "passion predictions" in Mark. Other passages that foretell aspects of his fate include 2:20; 9:9, 12; 10:45; 12:6–8; 14:8, 17–31. Although his language of παραδίδωμι, συνέδρια, ἡγεμών, and μαρτύριον in 13:9–11 addresses the legal jeopardy that his (and by extension, the Gospel of Mark's) audience will face, it also presages his own trial.

9. Cf. Ira Brent Driggers, *Following God through Mark: Theological Tension in the Second Gospel* (Louisville, KY: Westminster John Knox Press, 2007), 61–83.

10. Jesus encounters resistance from other people, as well (see Mark 5:17; 6:2–3), but that conflict is localized and apparently dissolved when he leaves the scene. Although he does not shy away from provocation (see, e.g., 3:1–5; 7:6–13; 11:15–17; 12:12), in Mark he does not consistently come across as polemical; even one outside his immediate circle can be an ally (9:38–40).

11. See, e.g., Mark 7:1–13; 8:15. The scribe of 12:28–34 suggests, however, that members of the religious elite are not beyond redemption, so to speak. Cf. Jairus in 5:21–43.

12. Questions and claims about the source of Jesus' authority are implicit even in passages that do not include explicit mention of "authority," such as Mark 1:9–12, 38; 2:1–12, 27–28; 3:22–30; 4:35–41; 6:2–3; 6:30–44; 8:1–10; 9:2–8, 37.

13. Working from the verb δεῖ in 8:31 and the dynamics of sociopolitical conflict in Mark, Brian K. Blount finds similar reasons for describing Jesus' suffering as inevitable (*Go Preach! Mark's Kingdom Message and the Black Church Today* [Maryknoll, NY: Orbis Books, 1998], 129–30). For Blount, inevitability lies in the fact that the kingdom Jesus inaugurates challenges and thus provokes those who hold power. Blount also argues that Jesus' suffering is necessary, in the sense that those who hold power have no choice but to crush him if they are to stop his preaching and its detrimental effects on their prerogatives.

14. Jesus' warning in Mark 8:15 about "the leaven of the Pharisees and the leaven of Herod" focuses on evil and corruption. A variant reading in Mark and alterations to the saying in Matt. 16:6–12 and Luke 12:1 may provide warrant for reading this less as a warning against Herod as a unique threat and more as a warning against the pervasive self-interest that Jesus sees in the ruling class of his day.

15. On Mark 10:42–45 as setting Jesus' life and death in complete opposition to humanity's notions of power and authority, see Sharyn Dowd and Elizabeth Struthers Malbon, "The Significance of Jesus' Death in Mark: Narrative Context and Authorial Audience," *JBL* 125 (2006): 271–97.

16. On the "tensions" this lends to Mark's theological portrait, see Driggers, *Following God*.

17. The present tense of παραδίδοται in Mark 9:31 does not mean that the "giving over" is already in process. Other usage of παραδίδωμι in Mark supports a future-tense translation.

18. Jesus' first passion prediction, in 8:31, does not include the word παραδίδωμι. The syntax of this prediction, with the verb δεῖ followed by four infinitives, might impute a different and perhaps more impersonally fated sense to the notion of Jesus' being "given over," if that verb appeared there.

19. Cf. Morna D. Hooker, *The Gospel according to Saint Mark*, BNTC (Peabody, MA: Hendrickson Publishers, 1991), 226; Boring, *Mark*, 277.

20. Judas's role as the first person whose actions land Jesus in custody (Mark 14:10–11, 18–21) does not rule out God's involvement. The entire process of "giving over" performed by Judas "the betrayer" (14:42, 44) and others becomes possible because God permits it.

21. At Gethsemane, Jesus acknowledges God's role, or deliberate lack thereof, in what is happening (Mark 14:36). This episode and its immediate aftermath indicate that God declines to grant Jesus' request for deliverance from the "hour" (14:35, 41) of his passion. The abandonment that Jesus experiences and laments in 15:34 can hardly be limited to his crucifixion; it begins in Gethsemane, when he is "given over."

22. See Sir. 4:19; Pss. 27:9–12 [26:9–12 LXX]; 140:8 [139:9 LXX]; Isa. 65:11–12; Ezek. 23:8–9 (cf. Origen, *Hom. Jer.* 4.5; 11.1 [PG 13.292.42–44; 13.368.4–6]; Chrysostom, *Hom. Jo.* 68.2 [PG 59.376.58–63]). Some of these passages employ the words in complementary or parallel fashion, treating them as corresponding actions or virtually synonymous.

23. If Mark understands Jesus as given over to demonic powers, readers receive only the subtlest indication of that. Some see Jesus' loud cries from the cross (15:34, 37) as a sign of demonic presence (e.g., Werner H. Kelber, "Conclusion: From Passion Narrative to Gospel," in Kelber, *The Passion in Mark*, 161–62). Even if Mark implies the presence of satanic power in the passion, still that power becomes manifest only through the authority structures of human society.

24. Cf. Perrin, "Question," 90–91. On the possibility that Jesus resists the injustice perpetuated upon him as he moves from Pilate to Golgotha, see William Sanger Campbell, "Engagement, Disengagement and Obstruction: Jesus' Defense Strategies in Mark's Trial and Execution Scenes (14.53–64; 15.1–39)," *JSNT* 26 (2004): 291–98.

25. The literature in question is the Mishnaic tractate *Sanhedrin* from the late second century. For a classic, concise summary of the apparent infractions on display in this scene, see Eduard Lohse, s.v. "συνέδριον," in *TDNT*, 7:868–70).

26. For overt statements on this, see John 2:19–22 and cf. Heb. 9:11–12. Mark appears to understand the community composed of the resurrected Jesus' followers as a replacement of the Jerusalem temple. They constitute a spiritual temple ("not made with hands"; Mark 14:58), which implies a criticism of that segment of the Jewish leadership that misused the temple and derived their own authority from it (see Mark 12:1–12 and cf. the discussion of Stephen's trial in chapter 7 of this book; cf. also Eph. 2:19–22; 1 Pet. 2:4–5). For arguments supporting this understanding of the temple at work in Mark, see Juel, *Messiah*; John R. Donahue, *Are You the Christ? The Trial Narrative in the Gospel of Mark*, SBLDS 10 (Missoula, MT: Society of Biblical Literature, 1973), 103–38. A promise to provide a new temple does not equal a promise to replace Judaism. Jesus' comments about the temple direct a polemic against its leadership and their practices. He does not oppose Judaism or declare temple rituals to be an inferior form of religious devotion. His parable about the vineyard in 12:1–9 rules out such readings, for there the fault and punishment belong to the tenants and not the vineyard itself.

27. Some elements of Judaism connected the proper functioning of the temple to the maintenance of cosmic order (Helen K. Bond, *Caiaphas: Friend of Rome and Judge of Jesus?* [Louisville, KY: Westminster John Knox Press, 2004], 37). Jesus thus appears dangerous on many levels.

28. On silence as a "legitimate defense tactic in antiquity," see Campbell, "Engagement," 286. On the potential hazards of remaining silent in other judicial contexts, see Ulrich Luz, *Matthew 21–28: A Commentary*, trans. James E. Crouch, Hermeneia (Minneapolis: Fortress, 2005), 495 n. 29.

29. Juel, *Messiah*, 169–209.

30. It is difficult and beyond the scope of this study to identify precisely how the council might understand Jesus' declaration in 14:62. Within the scope of Mark, the reference to being seated at the right hand of "the Power" (a reverent circumlocution for God) recalls 13:26 and the image of the Son of Man gathering his chosen ones. The contexts of Ps. 110 (see also Mark 12:36) and Dan. 7:13–14 both involve kingship and divinely authorized dominion. Jesus' claim brings to a boil the long-simmering conflict over his authority. See further Hooker, *Mark*, 362.

31. For figurative connections between sight and belief in Mark, see 4:11–12; 8:18, 22–26; 10:46–52; 15:32; 16:7.

32. For discussion of the debate, see, from a variety of perspectives, Darrell L. Bock, *Blasphemy and Exaltation in Judaism: The Charge against Jesus in Mark 14:53–65* (Grand Rapids: Baker Books, 2000); Adela Yarbro Collins, "The Charge of Blasphemy in Mark 14.64," *JSNT* 26 (2004): 379–401; Joel Marcus, "Mark 14:61: 'Are You the Messiah-Son-of-God?'" *NovT* 31 (1989): 125–41.

33. The result is not necessarily a narrative stereotype of all Jewish leaders who opposed Jesus and his followers' claims (contra Bond, *Caiaphas*, 107). Such

an interpretation downplays the particular sociopolitical prerogatives that the Jerusalem aristocracy held prior to 66 CE.

34. Ancient readers might have found such a depiction of Pilate consistent with his reputation for severe and overbearing governance. See Josephus, *Ant.* 18.55–62; Philo, *Embassy* 299–305; Luke 13:1.
35. Cf. Zech. 9:9; 1 Kgs. 1:38; 2 Kgs. 9:13.
36. Regarding the context and possible collaboration, see McLaren, *Power and Politics*, 98–101. Literary similarities between Mark 14:60–62 and 15:1–5 also connect the high priest and Pilate.
37. For examples, see the references supplied by Warren Carter, *Matthew and Empire: Initial Explorations* (Harrisburg, PA: Trinity Press International, 2001), 161.
38. On the ambiguity of Jesus' σὺ λέγεις (Mark 15:2) as a negation of the mockery that pervades the passion, see Joel Marcus, "Crucifixion as Parodic Exaltation," *JBL* 125 (2006): 87.
39. Many streams in Christian tradition, including Acts 8:32, have interpreted Jesus' silence in light of Isa. 53:7 and, by extension, the whole of Isa. 52:13–53:12. This leads some to read Jesus' trial demeanor as his obedient acceptance of injustice. However, Mark offers no explicit connection to that Isaianic theme at this point in the story, other than perhaps very indirectly through the word θαυμάζω in Mark 15:5 and Isa. 52:15 LXX. A major problem with interpreting Mark's (and Matthew's) passion narrative as a specific embodiment of Isa. 52–53 lies in the passion narrative's lack of key Isaianic vocabulary, such as ἁμαρτίαι, beyond παραδίδωμι (see Isa. 53:6, 12).
40. On historical evidence for releasing prisoners and the difficulty of confirming this as something Pilate actually practiced, see Adela Yarbro Collins, *Mark: A Commentary*, Hermeneia (Minneapolis: Fortress Press, 2007), 714–17; Brown, *Death*, 1:814–20.
41. On envy in Greco-Roman society, see Anselm C. Hagedorn and Jerome H. Neyrey, "'It Was Out of Envy that They Handed Jesus Over' (Mark 15.10): The Anatomy of Envy and the Gospel of Mark," *JSNT* 69 (1998): 15–38.
42. My reading of the forensic drama at this point in the scene is indebted to Helen K. Bond, *Pontius Pilate in History and Interpretation*, SNTSMS 100 (Cambridge: Cambridge University Press, 1998), 112–16; Carter, *Pilate*, 69–74.
43. If θέλετε and ὃν λέγετε in Mark 15:12 are original (cf. Matt. 27:17, 22), the point of Pilate's question is even sharper: it puts Jesus' royal identity into the crowd's own mouths as their title for him. Pilate's question does not deny Jesus' offense but has fun with the fact that the people are delivering up the one reputedly identified as their deliverer.
44. Aubert, "Double Standard," 116.
45. Cf. Giorgio Agamben's discussion of sovereignty, law, and abandonment in *Homo Sacer: Sovereign Power and Bare Life*, trans. Daniel Heller-Roazen (Stanford, CA: Stanford University Press, 1998), 25–29.
46. Brian K. Blount, *Cultural Interpretation: Reorienting New Testament Criticism* (Minneapolis: Fortress, 1995), 105–6.
47. Mark neither relieves Pilate of responsibility nor disperses it too widely. There is no indication that the crowd calling for Jesus' death is anything other than a group specially assembled by the high priest and his coconspirators and roused to action at a key moment.

48. The expression—τινι τὸ ἱκανὸν ποιέω—occurs infrequently in Greek literature. It does not necessarily connote acquiescence but can carry the sense of "gratify" or "give free rein to" (as in Herm. *Sim.* 65.5; see Michael W. Holmes, ed. and trans., *The Apostolic Fathers: Greek Texts and English Translations*, 3rd ed. [Grand Rapids: Baker Academic, 2007]). Cf. Diodorus Siculus, *Hist.* 31.30.1.

49. Martin Kähler, *The So-Called Historical Jesus and the Historic Biblical Christ*, trans. Carl E. Braaten (Philadelphia: Fortress Press, 1964), 80 n. 11.

50. Donald Juel, "The Function of the Trial of Jesus in Mark's Gospel," *SBL Seminar Papers, 1975*, 2 vols., SBLSP 14 (Missoula, MT: Scholars Press, 1975), 2:100.

51. William R. Herzog rightly notes a show trial's capacity to shame the accused (*Jesus, Justice, and the Reign of God: A Ministry of Liberation* [Louisville, KY: Westminster John Knox Press, 2000], 243). The ironic narration of this trial turns that dimension on its head, however, effectively shaming Pilate, the high priest, and his council for their inability to understand the things they themselves say.

52. On the christological tensions held together in the Markan trial and its aftermath, cf. Kelber, "Conclusion," 165–67, 170–71.

Chapter 4: Jesus on Trial in the Gospel according to Matthew

1. Compared to Mark, in Matthew's scenes of Jesus' arrest and trial, the elders play an increased role, while the scribes' involvement is lessened. Pharisees do not appear in connection with the Matthean passion narrative, but twice they act as the chief priests' allies (21:45–46; 27:62).

2. See Donald P. Senior, *The Passion Narrative according to Matthew: A Redactional Study*, BETL 39 (Leuven: Leuven University Press, 1975), 163–64.

3. The syntax of Matt. 27:1 makes a clearer transition than Mark 15:1a (mostly due to multiple appearances of συμβούλιον λαμβάνω, "confer," in Matt. 12:14; 22:15; 27:7; 28:12). This, as well as Matthew's technique of indicating the simultaneity of Peter's denial, suggests that 27:1 resumes Jesus' experience right where 26:68 left off. Therefore, Matthew's first trial scene, or at least Jesus' beating, lasts until sunrise, when Jesus is brought to Pilate. See W. D. Davies and Dale C. Allison, *A Critical and Exegetical Commentary on the Gospel according to Saint Matthew*, 3 vols., ICC (Edinburgh: T&T Clark, 1988–1997), 3:553; Senior, *Passion Narrative*, 210–17.

4. Davies and Allison, *Matthew*, 3:564.

5. David E. Garland, *Reading Matthew: A Literary and Theological Commentary on the First Gospel* (New York: Crossroad, 1993), 258.

6. See Amy-Jill Levine, "Anti-Judaism and the Gospel of Matthew," in *Anti-Judasm and the Gospels*, ed. William R. Farmer (Harrisburg, PA: Trinity Press International, 1999), 33. Levine's essay, along with those that respond to it in the same volume, cites many studies that can serve as an introduction to the nature, history, and ongoing theological relevance of Matthew's polemic.

7. Matthew's polemical edge against the Pharisees is well documented. For a concise catalog of conflict scenes in this Gospel, see Carter, *Pilate*, 79–80.

8. Given the magnitude of Herod's power and Roman loyalties, nothing suggests that his opposition to Jesus is petty. See Dorothy Jean Weaver, "Power and Powerlessness: Matthew's Use of Irony in the Portrayal of Political Leaders," in *Treasures New and Old: Recent Contributions to Matthean Studies*, ed. David

R. Bauer and Mark Allan Powell, SBLSymS 1 (Atlanta: Scholars Press, 1996), 182–87.

9. Davies and Allison, *Matthew*, 3:525.

10. Gerard S. Sloyan, "Recent Literature on the Trial Narratives of the Four Gospels," in *Critical History and Biblical Faith: New Testament Perspectives*, ed. Thomas J. Ryan (Villanova, PA: Villanova University, 1979), 163. Cf. D. R. Catchpole, "The Answer of Jesus to Caiaphas (Matt. 26.64)," *NTS* 17 (1971): 223–26.

11. The notion of calling someone to bear witness and be accountable in the presence of God connects to much of the Old Testament's use of ἐξορκίζω and its cognates, as well as ancient assumptions about oaths before a god. Further, if Lev. 5:1 can be admitted as evidence, see J. Duncan M. Derrett, "'I Adjure Thee' (Matthew 26,63)," *DRev* 115 (1997): 225–34.

12. Catchpole, "Answer."

13. Rowan Williams, *Christ on Trial: How the Gospel Unsettles Our Judgement* (Grand Rapids: Wm. B. Eerdmans Publishing Co., 2003), 31.

14. Jesus exposes Caiaphas's failure to perceive what a high priest presumably should, but it does not follow that Jesus has, as Bond argues, "usurped Caiaphas's high-priestly role" (*Caiaphas*, 126).

15. Catchpole, "Answer," 221–23.

16. Matthew's ἀπ' ἄρτι in 26:64 has spawned several interpretations about when they will see. Most likely the expression means "in the future" (NIV) instead of "from now on" (NRSV), although Matthew may be blurring the distinction between Jesus' future return (as in 24:30–31) and his ironic enthronement on the cross. See Davies and Allison, *Matthew*, 3:530–31.

17. If a standing Caiaphas recalls the unjust witnesses who stand in Ps. 35:11, then the dramatic moment becomes even more striking (see Davies and Allison, *Matthew*, 3:526–27). It also further discredits Caiaphas for the role of God's high priest.

18. Later developments remind readers that Pilate takes Jesus seriously. In Matt. 27:62–66 the chief priests and Pharisees easily persuade Pilate to take precautions to prevent rumors of a resurrected king. Later, in 28:11–15, the chief priests and elders bribe the governor's guards and promise to persuade (πείθω) Pilate if he learns that Jesus' tomb is empty. These passages assume Pilate's concern about Jesus and his followers. Even more, however, they show the Jewish leadership continuing to use every resource to shield themselves and the population from the truth about Jesus. They partner with Pilate and deceive him if necessary.

19. Senior, *Passion Narrative*, 236, 240–41.

20. Although ancient manuscripts differ over the content of 27:16–17, the arguments for considering "Jesus" as original are persuasive. See Davies and Allison, *Matthew*, 3:584 n. 20.

21. The switch to the plural ὄχλους in 27:20 (cf. singular forms in 27:15, 24) offers no statement about the size, composition, or disposition of the crowd. Matthew does not consistently distinguish between singular and plural forms of ὄχλος and sometimes uses them interchangeably (15:32–39; 21:8–11, 26, 46).

22. On the social and political relevance of dreams in antiquity, see Bart J. Koet, "Im Schatten des Aeneas: Paulus in Troas (Apg 16,8–10)," *Dreams and Scripture in Luke-Acts: Collected Essays*, CBET 42 (Leuven: Peeters, 2006), 157–60.

23. The context and the word δίκαιος (27:19) recall Jesus' mention of "righteous blood" in 23:35, part of a passage blaming religious leaders for murdering those whom God sends.
24. For the former translation, see Sir. 5:8; for the latter, John 12:19.
25. Garland, *Matthew*, 257, with emphasis added.
26. The extracanonical *Gospel of Peter* takes an entirely different view when Pilate's hand washing exonerates him and shifts control to Herod Antipas and the Jewish leadership (*Gos. Pet.* 1, 46).
27. Seen from the perspective of Matthew's original audiences, the crowd utters an ironic and tragic prophecy of the Jerusalem temple's destruction in 70 CE (Davies and Allison, *Matthew*, 3:591–92), not an invitation for divine punishment. As a prophecy, the verse allows Matthew to polemically identify the Jerusalem leadership's failure to embrace Jesus Christ as the cause of both the Judean people's sufferings in the Jewish-Roman War and the tribulations of the Christian communities in which this Gospel's author was situated. Understanding Matthew's theological explanation for the war's devastation does not remove the offense it causes, but it should contest interpretations that extend the theological significance of the crowd's statement in 27:25 far beyond what the narrative can bear and what the historical circumstances behind the narrative appear to warrant. See Anthony J. Saldarini, *Matthew's Christian-Jewish Community*, CSJH (Chicago: University of Chicago Press, 1994), 32–34.
28. Saldarini, *Community*, 28–34. Matthean usage and the logic of the narrative suggest that 27:25 refers to a subgroup of Jewish people, the crowd that is present and has been, to a member, misled by its leaders. On the wider debate over πᾶς ὁ λαός in this context, see Luz, *Matthew 21–28*, 501.
29. Although the grammar cannot clearly identify who flogs Jesus, it underscores Pilate's agency in the torture. This flogging also recalls the beating that Jesus received at the hands of the council members *themselves* in 26:67–68. On scourging as part of the Romans' crucifixion process, see Donald A. Hagner, *Matthew 14–28*, WBC 33B (Dallas: Word, 1995), 828.
30. Weaver, "Power," 195. Weaver's claims about Pilate's powerlessness in the trial stand at odds, however, with my analysis of the trial.
31. See additional ironies cataloged in Davies and Allison, *Matthew*, 3:593–94.
32. Carter contends that Pilate's hand washing "pretends that Jesus' crucifixion comes about because of their [the people's] demands, not because of the actions of the ruling elite" (*Matthew and Empire*, 166). Carter is likewise correct that Pilate thus "backgrounds" his involvement and "foregrounds the people's demand." However, Pilate does not carry the priestly aristocracy with him so far into the dramatic background, as if Matthew consistently groups all "the ruling elite" together. The whole of the trial keeps the high priest and his council much more prominent in the blame that Matthew levies upon them, mostly through their false dealings and influence over the crowd.
33. Luz observes that Pilate becomes a marginal character, and he correctly sees that this emphasizes the will of the crowd in 27:23 (*Matthew 21–28*, 499). This does not imply a marginalization of Pilate's judicial power, however, for Pilate marginalizes himself only when it becomes clear that the people, under the influence of their priestly leaders, will be able to bring the trial to Pilate's desired outcome and in doing so allow him to reinforce his political dominance.

Chapter 5: Jesus on Trial in the Gospel according to Luke

1. Unique features of the Lukan passion narrative have sparked many source-critical investigations. Most convincing are those concluding that no additional (non-Markan) accounts played a role in Luke's composition. See, e.g., Frank J. Matera, "Luke 22,66–71: Jesus before the ΠΡΕΣΒΥΤΕΡΙΟΝ," "Luke 23,1–25: Jesus before Pilate, Herod, and Israel," in *L'Évangile de Luc*, ed. F. Neirynck, 2nd ed., BETL 32 (Leuven: Leuven University Press, 1989), 517–33, 535–51; Donald Senior, *The Passion of Jesus in the Gospel of Luke*, The Passion Series 3 (Wilmington, DE: Michael Glazier, 1989); Marion L. Soards, *The Passion according to Luke: The Special Material of Luke 22*, JSNTSup 14 (Sheffield: Sheffield Academic Press, 1987).

2. Someone in antiquity tried to explain the narrative's introduction of Barabbas by adding the gloss found at 23:17.

3. Interpreters cannot agree, however, on just what this is. Neagoe reviews various studies that interpret Jesus' trial as putting God on trial, Israel on trial, Christianity's political innocence on trial, and other options (*Trial*, esp. 31–35). The possibility of a Lukan apologetic motive—political, theological, or both—behind the trial scenes relates to my approach but ultimately pursues other interpretive questions. See the discussion in chapter 7 and the representative sources named in n. 8 of chapter 1.

4. The chief priests and their Jerusalem-based associates also dominate the coordinated opposition to Jesus from 19:45 up to his arrest. No Pharisees appear after 19:39.

5. Jerome Neyrey notes that Satan demands "total dominance" to divide the group or assault their faith (*The Passion according to Luke: A Redaction Study of Luke's Soteriology*, Theological Inquiries [New York: Paulist Press, 1985], 32).

6. Luke identifies this group of chief priests and scribes as the πρεσβυτέριον (22:66). The word συνέδριον appears in a locative sense, referring to the presence of the council. In Acts the latter term indicates the council itself.

7. Senior, *Luke*, 21–39. In what follows, I add my perspective to Senior's categories to expand on their relevance for the trial.

8. For a detailed overview, see Joseph B. Tyson, *The Death of Jesus in Luke-Acts* (Columbia: University of South Carolina Press, 1986), 48–83.

9. Jon A. Weatherly, *Jewish Responsibility for the Death of Jesus in Luke-Acts*, JSNTSup 106 (Sheffield: Sheffield Academic Press, 1994), 70–73.

10. Robert C. Tannehill, *The Narrative Unity of Luke-Acts: A Literary Interpretation*, 2 vols. (Philadelphia, Minneapolis: Fortress Press, 1986–1990), 1:189.

11. As emphasized further below, Luke does not employ ὁ λαός in a universally representational sense, as if it indicates every Jew in Jerusalem or stands for the entire nation of Israel. See Weatherly, *Responsibility*, 50–175.

12. See also John T. Carroll, "Luke's Crucifixion Scene," in *Reimaging the Death of the Lukan Jesus*, ed. Dennis D. Sylva, BBB 73 (Frankfurt am Main: Anton Hain, 1990), 113–14.

13. If Jesus' prediction in Luke 9:44 implies, as do Mark 9:31 and Matt. 17:22, that God initiates the passion by giving Jesus to human authority and consequentially that the trial represents human authority having its way with Jesus, still Luke–Acts does not pursue this idea. Although Luke's passion narrative includes ample παραδίδωμι language, the crucified Jesus does not bemoan God's abandonment. Only once does Acts use παραδίδωμι when discussing Jesus' passion (3:13). Likewise, Luke's attention to the abuses of human power

has its own accent, for there is no Lukan parallel to Mark 9:13 and Matt. 17:12, and the criticism Jesus offers in Luke 22:25 is much less severe than that in its Synoptic parallels. Compared to Mark and Matthew, Luke is less interested in depicting the trial of Jesus as an arena that exposes and displays the abuses of human authority. As we will see, however, it does not follow that the Lukan trial is therefore inconsequential for questions about the gospel's relationship to the structures that maintain sociopolitical power.

14. On the political significance of this verse, see Joel B. Green, *The Gospel of Luke*, NICNT (Grand Rapids: Wm. B. Eerdmans Publishing Co., 1997), 775–76. Luke–Acts reiterates connections to Isa. 52:13–53:12 when the Ethiopian eunuch quotes Isa. 53:7–8 in Acts 8:32–35.

15. On God's "will" and Luke's understanding of a divine salvific plan, see Joseph A. Fitzmyer, *The Gospel according to Luke*, 2 vols., AB 28–28A (New York: Doubleday, 1981–85), 1:179–81.

16. Most assume that Luke 13:1 refers to an otherwise unattested event in which Pilate massacred a group of Galilean pilgrims in Jerusalem (Bond, *Pilate*, 194–96). On Pilate's reputation, see n. 34 of chapter 3.

17. Herod's authority over Galilee roughly paralleled Pilate's over Judea (Brown, *Death*, 1:763).

18. David L. Tiede, *Luke*, ACNT (Minneapolis: Augsburg Publishing House, 1988), 256.

19. Additional juridical aspects of Luke and Acts prompt readers to read the books as a connected narrative. For example, the trial scenes in Acts resemble Jesus' trial in Luke. Also, Luke 12:11–12 and 21:12–15 suggest that Jesus serves as an exemplar for his followers in jeopardy. I address these and other connections in chapters 7 and 9.

20. Eric Franklin, *Christ the Lord: A Study in the Purpose and Theology of Luke-Acts* (Philadelphia: Westminster Press, 1975), 92.

21. Heusler (in *Kapitalprozesse*) argues otherwise, that the evangelist composed a trial for Jesus (and one for Paul in Acts 21–26) that is conducted according to Roman juridical ideals. For her, this verisimilitude depicts a process that ultimately contends for Jesus' innocence in Roman eyes. More likely, any juridical verisimilitude here only makes the proceedings all the more galling, since the lack of serious inquiry mocks any shadow of a serious process.

22. See Green, *Luke*, 793–94.

23. Fitzmyer, *Luke*, 2:1462.

24. Brendan Byrne, "Jesus as Messiah in the Gospel of Luke: Discerning a Pattern of Correction," *CBQ* 65 (2003): 91; Green, *Luke*, 796.

25. They are exactly the same "crowd" mentioned in 22:47 and identified in 22:52 as elders and temple guards, along with the chief priests. See the convincing review of the narrative evidence by J. Bradley Chance, "The Jewish People and the Death of Jesus in Luke-Acts: Some Implications of an Inconsistent Narrative Role," *SBL Seminar Papers, 1991*, SBLSP 30 (Atlanta: Scholars Press, 1991), 51–54. Chance rightly observes that even if 23:4 refers to members of the Jewish people at large, still the people "are taking no active role to this point in the plot against Jesus. The distancing between the two groups (the leaders and the people) which has been prevalent to this point continues" (54).

26. For connections between διαστρέφω (23:2) and false prophets, see 1 Kgs. 18:17–18; Ezek. 13:22; Acts 13:8–10; 20:30. The Torah prescribes death for false prophets in Deut. 13.

27. The restatements of the charge and the grammar of 23:2 suggest that inciting unrest is the core accusation. The other two charges made in 23:2 explicate it. See Neagoe, *Trial*, 70; Green, *Luke*, 799–800.
28. On Luke 20:20–26 and the political significance of Roman tribute, see Green, *Luke*, 710–16.
29. Byrne, "Jesus," 89.
30. The enigmatic parable of the minas in Luke 19:11–27 also qualifies Luke's portrait of Jesus' kingship. It suggests that the kingdom of God is not about to appear immediately, and it offers the nobleman as a burlesque representation of the kind of ruler to which Jesus offers a stark contrast.
31. Carter characterizes Pilate as "arrogant," made politically careless by "the trappings of Roman power," and "capricious" (*Pilate*, 119). While I agree that there is a capricious element to Pilate's interest in exploiting (or dismissing) Jesus for the sake of political gain, I cannot detect arrogance, taken as a brash assumption of power. Pilate's lack of concern about Jesus and his potential to make trouble suggests either confusion or a clever tactic. The game he plays is an attempt to fortify and delineate his power vis-à-vis the Jerusalem elites, not cavalier political swashbuckling.
32. Tiede, *Luke*, 407.
33. John Nolland, *Luke 18:35–24:53*, WBC 35C (Dallas: Word, 1993), 1122.
34. The clothing may furnish an ironic representation of kingship, dignity, or heavenly glory. See Senior, *Luke*, 114.
35. Although Herod had some Jewish ancestry and as ruler of Galilee had knowledge of Jewish traditions and values, apparently most Palestinian Jews considered him an outsider. Luke presents him as Pilate's colleague, thereby emphasizing his role as the emperor's representative.
36. Pilate's comment in 23:15 suggests that Herod could have put Jesus to death, if he had judged that warranted.
37. Weatherly, *Responsibility*, 82–90; Green, *Luke*, 808 n. 61.
38. Chance, "People," 56.
39. Cf. Fitzmyer, *Luke*, 2:1488.
40. Byrne, "Jesus," 92. As discussed further below, from this it does not follow that Barabbas subverts Roman authority while Jesus does not. Their differences lie in the ways in which they might pose threats to the imperial order.
41. Contributing to the contrast, a criminal differentiates his own just execution (δικαίως) from Jesus' innocence (Luke 23:41), and a Roman centurion declares Jesus innocent (δίκαιος) after he dies (23:47). On the semantics of δίκαιος in 23:47, beyond simply "not guilty," see Brown, *Death*, 2:1163–67.
42. Senior, *Luke*, 118.
43. On the narrative's differentiation between Jewish leaders and people during the crucifixion, see Carroll, "Scene," 111–13. His examination of the narrative does not, however, establish his claim that ὁ λαός represents "all Israel."
44. See Weatherly, *Responsibility*, 56–76.
45. Cf. Tannehill, *Unity*, 1:198; Green, *Luke*, 792.
46. Especially by giving "the people" of Jerusalem such a critical place in the trial and in the focus of apostolic preaching (Acts 2–5, where the people's response is incredibly positive), Luke–Acts exhibits a polemical bent, although the history behind a possible Lukan polemic surely differs from the polemic in Matthew (see chap. 4). Interpreters vigorously debate both the possibility that Luke–Acts indicts the Jewish people of its time for rejecting Jesus Christ and

the significance of any such indictment. Chapters 7–9 of this book revisit the debates. In any case, we cannot neglect that fact that, no matter how critical a role the people of Jerusalem play in Jesus' trial, the narrative makes no suggestion of their perpetual guilt, and it pins blame in retrospect more squarely on Pilate, Herod, and the temple-based Jewish aristocracy.

47. Other parts of Luke anticipate worse political abuses to come. See 21:12–19; 23:27–31.
48. Tiede, *Luke*, 399.
49. A misguided tendency of some proposals poses false choices between two nearly *opposite* views. For example, Byrne (in "Jesus") argues as if either Jesus aims only to accomplish "peace (reconciliation) between human beings and God" in a way that has "no impact at all in an earthly, sociopolitical sense" (88; this is Byrne's view), or Jesus represents a way that is "fundamentally hostile to . . . the prevailing civic authority and order" (95). Byrne gives only lip service to the idea of Jesus' being "prophetically critical" of that authority and order (95). I contend that something like a prophetic criticism winds its way through the trial narratives of Luke–Acts, and that this criticism implies the gospel's subversive effects on "the prevailing civic authority and order" even as the gospel casts an indifferent glance toward the specific practices of the governing authorities. See also chapters 7–9, below.

Chapter 6: Jesus on Trial in the Gospel according to John

1. Witness language (μαρτυρέω, μαρτυρία) pervades John. See chapter 7 on its roots and its significance in Acts. For judgment language (κρίμα, κρίνω, κρίσις), see John 3:18–19; 5:22–30; 8:15–16, 26; 9:39; 12:31, 47–48; 16:11. Note also John's references to the Holy Spirit as an advocate (e.g., 15:26).
2. See, e.g., Andrew T. Lincoln, *Truth on Trial: The Lawsuit Motif in the Fourth Gospel* (Peabody, MA: Hendrickson Publishers, 2000), who argues that John tells the story of Jesus in a way that draws readers into a lawsuit between God (via Jesus) and Israel, making readers see themselves as jurors. On 4–6, Lincoln surveys several other scholars who have taken John as depicting Jesus' coming to the world as a great trial.
3. On the Roman soldiers and their number (perhaps up to 200 or 600 of them!), see Bond, *Pilate*, 166–67.
4. Literally, John 18:12 speaks of "the attendants of the Jews." This corresponds to "attendants from the high priests and the Pharisees" in 18:3.
5. John sometimes lumps the Pharisees with this group. See 3:1; 7:32; 9:13–18; 11:47, 57; 18:3. This likely reflects the Pharisees' authority in the evangelist's context, after the priesthood was wiped out by the war in 66–70 CE.
6. On the Johannine usage of οἱ Ἰουδαῖοι, see Sandra M. Schneiders, *Written That You May Believe: Encountering Jesus in the Fourth Gospel*, rev. ed. (New York: Crossroad, 2003), 45, 81–83. On the harmful ways in which John's polemical rhetoric has been construed in Christian interpretation, see 34–35, 75–76, and the works cited there.
7. Viewed across the whole narrative, John's portrayal of powerful Jewish figures is not entirely negative. See 4:46–54; 19:39–42.
8. Schneiders, *Written*, 155.
9. R. Alan Culpepper, *Anatomy of the Fourth Gospel: A Study in Literary Design* (Philadelphia: Fortress Press, 1983), 88–89.
10. Sloyan, "Literature," 165.

11. On its own this scene comes close to meeting the definition of a trial scene I gave in chapter 1. The defendant, however, remains not clearly defined. Although the healed man is interrogated and eventually "cast out," he and for a while his parents function as surrogate defendants as the Pharisees try to narrow their prosecutorial sights on Jesus, the true source of their concern. The inchoate nature of their investigation and the connections between this scene and Jesus' trial make this scene better understood as a thematic prelude to Jesus' trial. On thematic and structural connections between John 9 and the trial scenes involving Pilate, see Paul D. Duke, *Irony in the Fourth Gospel* (Atlanta: John Knox Press, 1985), 117–37.

12. Duke, *Irony*, 122.

13. Schneiders, *Written*, 160.

14. See Gail R. O'Day, "The Gospel of John," in *NIB* (Nashville: Abingdon Press, 1995), 9:806–7.

15. Brown, *Death*, 1:413–14.

16. O'Day, "John," 809–10.

17. Basic aspects of my reading of the drama in the seven scenes involving Pilate resonate with those offered in Bond, *Pilate*, 174–93; O'Day, "John," 811–27; David Rensberger, *Johannine Faith and Liberating Community* (Philadelphia: Westminster Press, 1988), 87–106.

18. O'Day, "John," 814.

19. For a clear statement of scholarly opinion and the relevant bibliography, see Luz, *Matthew 21–28*, 441. See also the extended discussion in Brown, *Death*, 1:363–72.

20. Marcus, "Crucifixion," 74 n. 7. Furthermore, this kingdom "manifests itself in this world wherever people listen to his voice" (Lincoln, *Truth*, 127).

21. "'Truth,' in John's Gospel, is what characterizes God. . . . Therefore, to know the truth is to know the God revealed in Jesus" (Craig R. Koester, *The Word of Life: A Theology of John's Gospel* [Grand Rapids: Wm. B. Eerdmans Publishing Co., 2008], 155).

22. Even if the Johannine Barabbas is a seditionist, then by calling for him "the Jews" would be pouring gasoline on a fire, seeking only to irritate Pilate with an impossible demand, just as he did to them when he suggested releasing Jesus.

23. O'Day, "John," 818. Although Josephus uses λῃστής in connection to rebellious social banditry, the term in the LXX suggests resonance with themes in Jesus' so-called shepherd discourse (see Hos. 7:1; Jer. 18:22; Ezek. 22:9).

24. Jennifer A. Glancy, "Torture: Flesh, Truth, and the Fourth Gospel," *BibInt* 13 (2005): 107–36. Glancy establishes "judicial torture" as a Roman practice through references to material roughly contemporaneous with Jesus and Pilate (123–24) and material from a later century (118–19). Most convincing is her appeal to 19:4 (121).

25. Stephen D. Moore's treatment of the scourging overstates its significance as the central and presumably specially emphasized point of a possible "seven-term chiasm" that structures the trial scenes involving Pilate (*Empire and Apocalypse: Postcolonialism and the New Testament* [Sheffield: Sheffield Phoenix, 2006], 62). His discussion of the grammatical ambiguity that suggests Pilate himself wields the whip against Jesus is, however, important to note (56–59).

26. In each of these verses, the reference to Jesus as ἄνθρωπος touches on the confusion about his authority and the question of whether he is indeed God's authorized agent. Pilate's statement unwittingly poses that question anew.

27. Glancy, "Torture," 125.

28. On 19:7 as the aristocracy's attempt to appeal to their political partnership with Pilate, see Warren Carter, *John and Empire: Initial Explorations* (New York: T&T Clark, 2008), 306–7; Raymond E. Brown, *The Gospel according to John*, 2 vols., AB 29–29A (Garden City, NY: Doubleday, 1966–70), 2:891. As for the specific "law" to which "the Jews" refer, see Lev. 24:16 and cf. John 5:18; 10:33.

29. On this translation of μᾶλλον ἐφοβήθη in 19:8, see Rensberger, *Johannine*, 94; O'Day, "John," 820.

30. Pilate's fear marks a critical development in Jesus' trial. Tom Thatcher does well to take Pilate's fear seriously, but he almost limits its import by equating "son of God" with Augustus and leaving subsequent emperors out of the equation (*Greater Than Caesar: Christology and Empire in the Fourth Gospel* [Minneapolis: Fortress Press, 2009], 85). I see John's trial making a less specific but no less potent connection between Jesus the Son and rhetoric about the authority of emperors also after Augustus.

31. Schneiders, *Written*, 162.

32. The neuter participle δεδομένον in 19:11 reveals that Jesus is not talking about political authority (ἐξουσία, a feminine noun) in a general sense.

33. Outside the trial scenes, John uses παραδίδωμι only in connection to Judas's betrayal (with a lone exception at 19:30). Within the trial scenes, it refers to people delivering Jesus over to various parties, to either Pilate or "the Jews."

34. On this translation of 19:12, reading the imperfect ἐζήτει as inceptive, see Rensberger, *Johannine*, 94.

35. Here ἀκούω takes a genitive object (τῶν λόγων τούτων; 19:13), in contrast to the accusative object in 19:8 (also 18:21). Such a construction indicates that Pilate understands and accepts what he hears (Brown, *John*, 2:854, 880).

36. Grammatical ambiguity in 19:13 leads some to wonder whether Pilate places Jesus upon the bench (cf. *Gos. Pet.* 7), but this pushes against the sense of the scene and Johannine usage. For reviews of evidence and proposals, see Brown, *Death*, 2:1388–93; Bond, *Pilate*, 190 n. 105. Even with Pilate sitting and delivering his judgment, irony persists in that he judges the one who has just issued a definitive judgment in 19:11 (see Duke, *Irony*, 134–35).

37. Additional irony springs from the detail that "the Jews" allege that Jesus "makes *himself* out to be a king" (19:12, with emphasis added).

38. John stamps this moment in specific place and time (19:13–14). Pilate presents Jesus as king and "the Jews" ratify it by calling for his crucifixion just as "regulations for the Passover feast go into effect" (O'Day, "John," 823).

39. Koester, *Word*, 71.

40. On the hymn and other traditions that name God as Israel's king, see Brown, *Death*, 1:849. See also John 8:33 and the people's rejection of God's kingship in 1 Sam. 8:7.

41. See Linda Hutcheon, *Irony's Edge: The Theory and Politics of Irony* (London: Routledge, 1994), 58–66. Irony can have a variety of effects, but it always suggests something new by bringing differing perspectives into relationship. This relationship fashions a new, ironic edge (see 44–56).

42. Cf. Rensberger's comment that John presents Christians in the late first century "with an alternative to both zealotry and collaboration," a positive invitation (*Johannine*, 100). Cf. Carter, *John and Empire*, 311, 341.

43. Some (e.g., Carter, *John and Empire*, 341) argue that John ultimately "mimics what it resists," because its dualistic language and outlook reproduce "the

grammar of empire." The historical context of the Johannine polemic may support this claim, and the triumphalistic rhythms of Johannine theology encourage such a perspective. At the same time, it is vital to note that John's Gospel operated within that historical context as resistance literature combating marginalization (see David Rensberger, "Anti-Judaism and the Gospel of John," in *Anti-Judasm and the Gospels*, ed. William R. Farmer [Harrisburg, PA: Trinity Press International, 1999]), 150–51). Indeed, the passing of that historical context alters John's rhetoric in the eyes of today's readers. However, although Johannine irony requires an "other" against which Jesus and his gospel define themselves, nevertheless the relational nature of irony subtly erodes a sense of absolute dualism at work in John's trial scenes. Irony inscribes a sense of alterity into John's message about God's dominion over human authority.

Chapter 7: Trials in Jerusalem in Acts 4–8

1. Tannehill describes the components of a "public accusation type scene" that recurs throughout Acts 16–19 as conflict erupts in various cities (*Unity*, 2:201–3). Not all of these scenes qualify as trials, since accusations are not always answered and judgments not always rendered.

2. On imprisonment and shame, see 2 Tim. 1:8, 12, 16; Brian Rapske, *The Book of Acts and Paul in Roman Custody*, vol. 3 of *The Book of Acts in Its First Century Setting*, ed. Bruce W. Winter (Grand Rapids: Wm. B. Eerdmans Publishing Co., 1994), 284–98; Craig S. Wansink, *Chained in Christ: The Experience and Rhetoric of Paul's Imprisonments*, JSNTSup 130 (Sheffield: Sheffield Academic Press, 1996), 59–61.

3. Note also the language of Christians who wrote within a generation of Acts: Ignatius calls the chains of his incarceration "spiritual pearls" (Ign. *Eph.* 11.2); Polycarp refers to those bonds as "appropriate for saints, crowns for those truly chosen by God and our Lord" (Pol. *Phil.* 1.1). On subsequent Christian writings' ability to redefine prisons as places of Christian identity and community formation, see Judith Perkins, *Roman Imperial Identities in the Early Christian Era* (New York: Routledge, 2009), 114–19.

4. Volker Stolle, *Der Zeuge als Angeklagter: Untersuchungen zum Paulusbild des Lukas*, BWANT 6/2 (Stuttgart: Kohlhammer, 1973), 218–19, 233–37, 276–77; cf. Neyrey, *Passion*, 89 (although I disagree with Neyrey's assertion that all the trials in Luke–Acts function as "trials of Israel").

5. Allison A. Trites, *The New Testament Concept of Witness*, SNTSMS 31 (Cambridge: Cambridge University Press, 1977). See also Marie-Eloise Rosenblatt, *Paul the Accused: His Portrait in the Acts of the Apostles*, Zacchaeus Studies: New Testament (Collegeville, MN: Liturgical Press, 1995), 3–7.

6. See Martin Dibelius, "The Speeches in Acts and Ancient Historiography," in *Studies in the Acts of the Apostles* (London: SCM Press, 1956), 138–85. On precursors to Dibelius's scholarship and his legacy, see Marion L. Soards, *The Speeches in Acts: Their Content, Context, and Concerns* (Louisville, KY: Westminster/John Knox Press, 1994), 1–11. Soards's book signals a corrective to Dibelius by giving attention to how the speeches function together within the whole of Acts.

7. For a landmark study of Stephen's speech that demonstrates its connection to the wider narrative, see Earl Richard, *Acts 6:1–8:4: The Author's Method of Composition*, SBLDS 41 (Missoula, MT: Scholars Press, 1978).

8. Douglas R. Edwards, "Surviving the Web of Roman Power: Religion and Politics in the Acts of the Apostles, Josephus, and Chariton's *Chaereas and Callirhoe*," in *Images of Empire*, ed. Loveday Alexander, JSOTSup 122 (Sheffield: Sheffield Academic Press, 1991), 187. There are more variations and nuances among the various perspectives on this topic than can be discussed here. For a concise survey, see Steve Walton, "The State They Were In: Luke's View of the Roman Empire," in *Rome in the Bible and the Early Church*, ed. Peter Oakes (Grand Rapids: Baker Academic, 2002), 2–12.

9. Richard J. Cassidy argues for the idea of a "nondeferential" church (*Society and Politics in the Acts of the Apostles* [Maryknoll, NY: Orbis Books, 1987], 143). See also Walter E. Pilgrim, *Uneasy Neighbors: Church and State in the New Testament*, OBT (Minneapolis: Fortress, 1999), 125–43.

10. See, e.g., Todd Penner, "Civilizing Discourse: Acts, Declamation, and the Rhetoric of the *Polis*," and Gary Gilbert, "Roman Propaganda and Christian Identity in the Worldview of Luke-Acts," in *Contextualizing Acts: Lukan Narrative and Greco-Roman Discourse*, ed. Todd Penner and Caroline Vander Stichele, SBLSymS 20 (Leiden: E. J. Brill, 2003), 65–104, 233–56; Alexander, "Apologetic Text"; Vernon K. Robbins, "Luke-Acts: A Mixed Population Seeks a Home in the Roman Empire," in *Images of Empire*, ed. Loveday Alexander, JSOTSup 122 (Sheffield: Sheffield Academic Press, 1991), 202–21.

11. See, in particular, these dissertations (some revised for publication): Heusler, *Kapitalprozesse;* William Rudolf Long, "The Trial of Paul in the Book of Acts: Historical, Literary, and Theological Considerations" (PhD diss., Brown University, 1982); Neagoe, *Trial;* Heiki Omerzu, *Der Prozess des Paulus: Eine exegetische und rechtshistorische Untersuchung der Apostelgeschichte*, BZNW 115 (Berlin: Walter de Gruyter, 2002); Pervo, *Profit;* Rapske, *Roman Custody;* Rosenblatt, *Paul the Accused;* Stolle, *Zeuge;* and Harry W. Tajra, *The Trial of St. Paul: A Juridical Exegesis of the Second Half of the Acts of the Apostles*, WUNT 2/35 (Tübingen: J. C. B. Mohr [Paul Siebeck], 1989). Another important contribution is Schwartz, "Trial Scene."

12. Caiaphas was high priest at this point in history, although Annas had previously been so. This is not the only instance where Luke–Acts speaks of them together (see Luke 3:2).

13. Goodman, *Ruling Class*, 79. Although some historians are wary of too neatly associating the Sadducees with the high-priestly families and other members of the Judean Jewish aristocracy, Acts does not suppose otherwise. For the ancient sources on the Sadducees and a cautious appraisal, see Gary G. Porton, "Sadducees," *ABD* 5:892–95.

14. Other ancient writings confirm the claim that the Sadducees did not believe in a coming resurrection. See Josephus, *J.W.* 2.164–166; *Ant.* 18.16–17.

15. Neagoe, *Trial*, 149.

16. Peter and John's favor among the λαός protects them from the leadership, according to 4:21. This resembles Jesus' passion, in which the λαός preserve Jesus for a time (Luke 19:47–48; 20:6, 19; 22:2). On ways in which Acts 4 resonates with Jesus' passion in Luke, see Tannehill, *Unity*, 2:68–69.

17. S. C. Winter, "ΠΑΡΡΗΣΙΑ in Acts," in *Friendship, Flattery, and Frankness of Speech: Studies on Friendship in the New Testament World*, ed. John T. Fitzgerald, NovTSup 82 (Leiden: E. J. Brill, 1996), 192.

18. On the conflict's escalation, see Schwartz, "Trial Scene," 120–21; Tannehill, *Unity*, 2:63–65.

19. F. Scott Spencer, *Journeying through Acts: A Literary-Cultural Reading* (Peabody, MA: Hendrickson Publishers, 2004), 69.
20. Tannehill, *Unity*, 2:66.
21. Peter's statement here recalls his Pentecost sermon, which, in Acts 2:22–36, connects crucifixion, resurrection, exaltation, and the giving of the Spirit.
22. On God's βουλή, see John T. Squires, *The Plan of God in Luke-Acts*, SNTSMS 76 (Cambridge: Cambridge University Press, 1993).
23. The narrative treats Gamaliel as a mediator, a member of the council yet differentiated from it. He speaks to the council as "you" and falls silent when the council nevertheless orders the apostles flogged. See Richard I. Pervo, *Acts: A Commentary*, Hermeneia (Minneapolis: Fortress Press, 2009), 148.
24. Cf. John A. Darr, "Irenic or Ironic? Another Look at Gamaliel before the Sanhedrin (Acts 5:33–42)," in *Literary Studies in Luke-Acts: Essays in Honor of Joseph B. Tyson*, ed. Richard P. Thompson and Thomas E. Phillips (Macon, GA: Mercer University Press, 1998), 121–39.
25. Some interpreters suggest that the violence and absence of a formal judgment make it inappropriate to call this scene a trial (see the brief discussion in Neagoe, *Trial*, 152). However, the narrator certainly initiates the scene in ways that recall the conflicts of Acts 4–5 (see Tannehill, *Unity*, 2:65) and Jesus' trial in Luke. The accusers and judges finally abandon debate to impose their will on Stephen. Historical inquiries into the legality of Stephen's stoning steer into a dead end, because a small amount of relevant data cannot yield a clear answer (Sherwin-White, *Society*, 35–43). When the people abandon the pursuit of a formal judgment and act violently out of sheer rage, they abandon the trial only in a formal sense. The narrative nevertheless uses this development to convey judgments of its own.
26. On Acts 6:1–8:3 and the interpretive debates created by this text, see Penner, *Praise*, 1–103, 262–330.
27. Richard, *Acts 6:1–8:4*.
28. Beverly Roberts Gaventa, *The Acts of the Apostles*, ANTC (Nashville: Abingdon Press, 2003), 129; Neagoe, *Trial*, 166–68.
29. On Moses as a prophet, see Deut. 18:15–19; 34:10; Acts 3:22.
30. Penner, *Praise*, 293.
31. Contra George A. Kennedy, *New Testament Interpretation through Rhetorical Criticism*, SR (Chapel Hill: University of North Carolina Press, 1984), 121–22.
32. The speech may also demonstrate that Stephen and the Christian movement embody values greatly esteemed in the Greco-Roman world (Penner, *Praise*, 262–330).
33. Note the expression "this land in which *you* now live" in 7:4 and the switch from "our ancestors" to "your ancestors" in 7:51–52 (Soards, *Speeches*, 68).
34. Other scenes between Stephen's death and Paul's trial further the depiction of violence perpetrated in Jerusalem (e.g., 9:26–30; 12:1–4).
35. Trials without Roman officials do not suggest a sociopolitical or religious context in which those officials are immaterial. The words of Acts 4:27 keep the reality and alliances of Roman authority present in readers' eyes.

Chapter 8: Trials in Philippi and Thessalonica in Acts 16–17

1. The syntax of Acts 16:20–21 gives no strong reason to suppose that Paul and Silas's Philippian accusers are Jewish. If the narrator means for readers to

identify them as Jews, then it is astounding that this is not made clear as a means of further incriminating a group of characters who deal in divination. In other settings, Jews who engage in magic are clearly identified as such either explicitly (13:6) or by the context (8:9–24).

2. Ivoni Richter Reimer, *Women in the Acts of the Apostles: A Feminist Liberation Perspective*, trans. Linda M. Maloney (Minneapolis: Fortress Press, 1995), 171–80.

3. See John B. Weaver, *Plots of Epiphany: Prison-Escape in Acts of the Apostles*, BZNW 131 (Berlin: Walter de Gruyter, 2004), 256–58; Richter Reimer, *Women*, 154–56.

4. Apollo remained a prominent deity across the Roman world, and his importance in the history of imperial Rome grew as Octavian increasingly cultivated a strong personal (and public) identification between himself and this god. Luke may regard connections between Apollo (represented by the divinatory spirit) and Roman power as particularly significant for the story's setting, Philippi, given the city's history and legacy. It was the site of Octavian and Antony's victory over Cassius and Brutus in 42 BCE and was made a Roman colony after that battle. As Octavian settled many of his soldiers there, Philippi's size and Roman identity began to increase. This intensified after the battle of Actium in 30 BCE, when Octavian sent more colonists to Philippi and renamed the colony after himself as *Colonia Iulia Augusta Philippensis*. Perhaps, then, in the Acts account it is not a stretch for the slave girl's owners to interpret Paul's display of power over the Python spirit in a more far-reaching sense, as on par with a challenge to Roman identity and values, insofar as these things remained active in the Augustan legacy present in Philippi into the first century CE. On Philippi's Roman character and the enduring importance of Augustus there, see Joseph H. Hellerman, *Reconstructing Honor in Roman Philippi: Carmen Christi as Cursus Pudorum*, SNTSMS 132 (Cambridge: Cambridge University Press, 2005), 64–87; Peter Oakes, *Philippians: From People to Letter*, SNTSMS 110 (Cambridge: Cambridge University Press, 2001), 74–75.

5. On the legal powers of στρατηγοί, see Tajra, *Trial*, 10–11.

6. On stock imagery and formulas from scenes of divinely aided escapes from prison in other Hellenistic literature, see Weaver, *Plots*, 1–91.

7. Paul and Silas's choice to remain where they are, and not merely the awesome spectacle of the earthquake, prompts the jailer's desire "to be saved." His suicidal intentions in the earthquake's immediate aftermath suggest that more than wonder or fear prompts him to consider seeking assistance from the prisoners or embracing their god.

8. The question of Roman citizenship and the rights it might confer upon someone who is "uncondemned" (ἀκατάκριτος; 16:37) is taken up in chapter 9.

9. As implied by ἐξάγω (v. 39), the magistrates' apology occurs within the ruined prison structure. Paul and Silas's restoration, then, is not necessarily an open-air spectacle in full view of the entire city. Nevertheless, the magistrates' public entrance into and exit from the building does possess a public quality.

10. Weaver, *Plots*, 284–88.

11. Spencer, *Journeying*, 180.

12. On the legal powers of the politarchate, see Tajra, *Trial*, 34–35.

13. On translating οἰκουμένη in 17:6 as "empire," see Luke Timothy Johnson, *The Gospel of Luke*, SP 3 (Collegeville, MN: Liturgical Press, 1991), 74.

14. On the political logic that connects the charges in 17:6–7, see Cassidy, *Society*, 90.
15. Sherwin-White, *Society*, 95.
16. In Luke–Acts, ταράσσω conveys the sense of "agitate" or "shake up." See Luke 1:12; 24:38; Acts 15:24; 17:13.
17. Tannehill, *Unity*, 2:216–17; Spencer, *Journeying*, 183.
18. The Ephesus scene reveals that Paul has friends in high places there: the Asiarchs ("officials of the province of Asia" in the NRSV). It is difficult to say much concerning their political power, given the lack of clarity about their office. See C. K. Barrett, *A Critical and Exegetical Commentary on The Acts of the Apostles*, 2 vols., ICC (Edinburgh: T&T Clark, 1994–98), 2:930.
19. Schwartz ("Trial Scene," 125–27) and Neagoe (*Trial*, 192–95) are willing to grant these three scenes status as trials, even though both appear aware of the ways in which each scene only approximates or falls short of a more complete trial.
20. Cf. Spencer, *Journeying*, 169–71.
21. Pervo recognizes the political and symbolic significance of Roman colonies by describing them as "pieces of Rome, as it were, bulbs planted at strategic sites" (*Acts*, 402).
22. Weaver, *Plots*, 278.

Chapter 9: Paul on Trial in Acts 21–28

1. See Beverly Roberts Gaventa, "The Overthrown Enemy: Luke's Portrait of Paul," in *SBL Seminar Papers, 1985*, SBLSP 24 (Atlanta: Scholars Press, 1985), 439–49.
2. See further Penner, *Praise*, 297.
3. For a more thorough treatment of these three texts, see Matthew L. Skinner, *Locating Paul: Places of Custody as Narrative Settings in Acts 21–28*, SBLAB 13 (Atlanta: Society of Biblical Literature, 2003), 94–103.
4. Spencer, *Journeying*, 104–6.
5. On ways in which Luke–Acts connects Jesus' and Paul's charges and trials, see A. J. Mattill Jr., "The Jesus-Paul Parallels and the Purpose of Luke-Acts: H. H. Evans Reconsidered," *NovT* 17 (1975): 32–36; Robert F. O'Toole, *The Unity of Luke's Theology: An Analysis of Luke-Acts*, GNS 9 (Wilmington, DE: Michael Glazier, 1984), 68–72. The numerous differences between Jesus' trial in Luke and Paul's trial in Acts require us to think of their trials as connected or associated, not parallel.
6. See an extensive list of terminological connections between Luke 21:12–15 and the book of Acts in Neyrey, *Passion*, 87–88.
7. In Acts, only Paul succeeds in offering an explicit *defense*. Alexander tries to make a defense (ἀπολογέομαι) to the mob in Ephesus in 19:33, but they shout him down. In Luke, ἀπολογ- terminology appears only in two closely related passages (12:13; 21:14).
8. Some interpreters dispute, on formal criteria, which speeches in Acts 22–26 should be technically designated as "defense speeches" (see Heusler, *Kapitalprozesse*, 43–46, 179–82). The constellation of ἀπολογ-language surrounding Paul's custody provides sufficient narrative-critical justification for characterizing Paul's entire trial as a defense of himself and his gospel.
9. The term in Acts 20:19 that the NRSV and RSV render as "trials" (πειρασμός) refers not to legal contexts but to general hardships that test moral stamina and persistence.

10. "Imprisonment" translates δεσμά, "chains," a metonym signifying incarceration and its humiliation. Joseph A. Fitzmyer's translation of Acts 20:23 accurately renders the sense of ongoing warnings: "The Holy Spirit has been warning me from city to city that chains and hardships await me" (*The Acts of the Apostles*, AB 31 [New York: Doubleday, 1998], 673).

11. See Gaventa, *Acts*, 286–90.

12. The prophecy of Agabus resembles Luke 18:32 more than it does the events that actually befall Paul in Acts 21:27–33, where Roman soldiers—not Jews—are the ones who seize and bind him. This minor inexactitude actually draws even more attention to the similarities between Acts 21:11 and Luke 18:32 (cf. also Acts 28:17).

13. Jacob Jervell, "Paul: The Teacher of Israel: The Apologetic Speeches of Paul in Acts," in *Luke and the People of God: A New Look at Luke-Acts* (Minneapolis: Augsburg Publishing House, 1972), 170–71. Jervell's analysis of the trial speeches unfortunately does not take into account the significance of the trial setting and other dimensions of the narrative.

14. Contra Alexander, "Apologetic Text," 43.

15. Schwartz, "Trial Scene," 127–28. Schwartz offers a series of scenes from *Chaereas and Callirhoe* as an example.

16. Robert C. Tannehill, "The Narrator's Strategy in the Scenes of Paul's Defense: Acts 21:27–26:32," *Forum* 8 (1992): 257.

17. The cry of those who incite the mob in 21:28 resembles the false witnesses' testimony against Stephen in 6:13.

18. Similar to Acts 16:37, again in 22:25 the issue is the torture of an "uncondemned" (ἀκατάκριτος) citizen, one with no formal judgment against him. Many commentators mention citizens' protections from binding and torture; see Luke Timothy Johnson, *The Acts of the Apostles*, SP 5 (Collegeville, MN: Liturgical Press, 1992), 301–2; Fitzmyer, *Acts*, 589, 712; Sherwin-White, *Society*, 71–76; Robinson, *Penal Practice*, 107. See also exceptions cited by Glancy, "Torture," 123–24. Whether the historical Paul was really a Roman citizen is not immediately germane to this study. For an overview of that question and bibliography, see Pervo, *Acts*, 554–56.

19. Paul's comment in 23:5 is sarcasm. He certainly knows who Ananias is, but he does not think the current political circumstances and the actions of the council make it possible for Ananias to presume the authority and fulfill the functions of a true high priest. On Paul's reaction to Ananias's objectionable behavior in this scene, see Johnson, *Acts*, 397.

20. On the connections between resurrection and the eternal rule of God's Anointed in Luke–Acts, see Tannehill, "Strategy," 265–66.

21. It warrants remembering that Luke's Gospel mentions no Pharisees on the high priest's council, let alone none participating in action against Jesus in Jerusalem. On the limits of the Pharisees' political power during the first century, see Saldarini, *Pharisees*, 281–87.

22. Pervo, *Profit*, 46. The distinction made in 24:9 between Tertullus and "the Jews" suggests that Tertullus is not one of Paul's Jewish opponents but someone they have hired.

23. Bruce Winter, "The Importance of the *Captatio Benevolentiae* in the Speeches of Tertullus and Paul in Acts 24:1–21," *JTS* 42 (1991): 505–31.

24. See Walaskay, *"And So,"* 54–55.

25. The conversations appear to be frequent, in light of the adverb πυκνότερον and the imperfect verb ὡμίλει in 24:26.

26. Tannehill, *Unity*, 2:301.
27. The Roman historian Tacitus famously skewered Felix's reputation, saying that he "practiced every kind of cruelty and lust, wielding the power of king with all the instincts of a slave" (*Hist.* 5.9; [Moore, LCL]).
28. Scholars in Roman law, limited by lack of relevant sources about the period and location in question, cannot agree about whether such a right to appeal was guaranteed or whether it was a unique benefit of Roman citizenship. For bibliography, see Pervo, *Acts*, 611–12 n. 34. In any case, Festus does not hesitate to grant what Paul demands. Paul's appeal becomes effective and apparently, in light of 26:31–32, nonrescindable except by Paul himself.
29. When in Rome, meeting with leaders of the local Jews, Paul explains the basis of his appeal differently (Acts 28:18–19). He does not apologize for his decision to face Roman authority; he only assures the Roman Jews that his doing so does not imply an intent to prosecute Judaism.
30. The narrative gives no indication that whole crowds of Jews (τὸ πλῆθος τῶν Ἰουδαίων; 25:24) in Caesarea oppose Paul. Readers have seen only the πλῆθος in Jerusalem (21:36) and the divided πλῆθος of the high priest's council (23:7).
31. On Agrippa's blended identity and role in the trial, see Skinner, *Locating Paul*, 146–47.
32. See Marguerat, *Historian*, 202.
33. On the speech's theological themes and their relationship to its structure, see Gaventa, *Acts*, 338–48. On the speech as the trial's climactic theological statement, see Robert F. O'Toole, *Acts 26: The Christological Climax of Paul's Defense (Ac 22:1–26:32)*, AnBib 78 (Rome: Biblical Institute Press, 1978); Neagoe, *Trial*, 201–5.
34. Tannehill, "Strategy," 266.
35. On Castor and Pollux, the "Twin Brothers" mentioned in 28:11, see Marguerat, *Historian*, 73.
36. On connections between the terminology of 28:17, 23 and expressions referring to Roman law and civil society, see Winter, "ΠΑΡΡΗΣΙΑ," 198.
37. It is difficult to understand why Schwartz excludes Acts 28:17–28 from her survey of trial scenes in Acts, for this passage reasonably fits her own definition of a trial. Even if there are no accusers or judges present, accusations and judgments are conveyed. This is not unique, for Festus conveys accusations into the sixth trial scene, which does not seem to include Paul's actual accusers from Jerusalem (25:13–27). Schwartz contends that Paul's trial ends with Agrippa's statement in 26:32, which exonerates Paul and "brings closure to the trials." Schwartz claims, curiously, that this frees Luke from the dangerous business of including a scene that shows Paul in a legal contest in the heart of imperial power, in Rome itself ("Trial Scene," 131–32).
38. Gaventa, *Acts*, 364.
39. Barrett, *Acts*, 2:1241–42. Even if the Roman Jews are not entirely forthright about their knowledge of Paul's reputation, it is clear that they do not intend to assist in prosecuting him.
40. See Conrad Gempf, "Luke's Story of Paul's Reception in Rome," in *Rome in the Bible and the Early Church*, ed. Peter Oakes (Grand Rapids: Baker Academic, 2002), 54–58.
41. Marguerat, *Historian*, 219.
42. The narrative sends mixed messages with Paul's severe and denunciatory statement to his Roman guests and with the subsequent two verses that sum-

marize his two years in Rome. His judgment does not close a door on those who do not accept his message; it does not declare them guilty of apostasy or exclude them from membership in Israel. Readers must not run too quickly over the facts that some of the Roman Jews are persuaded by Paul and that Paul continues to welcome and preach to "all" who come to him after this (28:30). Acts stops short of pronouncing or endorsing any definitive split or permanent alienation between the people of Israel and the message of the gospel, although it appears to acknowledge historical contexts in which similar divisions have already become entrenched.

43. Marguerat, *Historian*, 147.
44. Jerome Neyrey, "The Forensic Defense Speech and Paul's Trial Speeches in Acts 22–26: Form and Function," in *Luke-Acts: New Perspectives from the Society of Biblical Literature Seminar*, ed. Charles H. Talbert (New York: Crossroad, 1984), 210–24. For similar analyses of Paul's defense speeches, see Fred Veltman, "The Defense Speeches of Paul in Acts," in *Perspectives on Luke-Acts*, ed. Charles H. Talbert (Danville, VA: Association of Baptist Professors of Religion, 1978), 243–56; William R. Long, "The Paulusbild in the Trial of Paul in Acts," *SBL Seminar Papers, 1983*, SBLSP 22 (Chico, CA: Scholars Press, 1983), 87–105.
45. The potential for the forces of nature to visit Paul with judgment or malice appears to be an element of these scenes. Through what look like trials by nature, God defends Paul and thereby declares his innocence. On this topic, see C. H. Talbert and J. H. Hayes, "A Theology of Sea Storms in Luke-Acts," *SBL Seminar Papers, 1995*, SBLSP 34 (Atlanta: Scholars Press, 1995), 321–28; Marguerat, *Historian*, 218–20.
46. Marguerat, *Historian*, 220.
47. Skinner, *Locating Paul*, 151–64.
48. For more discussion of the "ironic relationships" created by Paul's exercising authority over his custodial circumstances in Acts 21–28, see Matthew L. Skinner, "Unchained Ministry: Paul's Roman Custody (Acts 21–28) and the Sociopolitical Outlook of the Book of Acts," in *Acts and Ethics*, ed. Thomas E. Phillips, New Testament Monographs 9 (Sheffield: Sheffield Phoenix, 2005), 90–93.
49. God's guidance does not obliterate Paul's agency in Acts. See Charles H. Cosgrove, "The Divine ΔΕΙ in Luke-Acts: Investigations into the Lukan Understanding of God's Providence," *NovT* 26 (1984): 168–90.
50. George Kennedy notes, "Of the rhetorical features of Acts the most important historically is the way the apostles utilize occasions to preach the gospel. Whenever given an occasion to speak, even in defense of specific charges against them personally, they try to convert the situation into an opportunity to proclaim the message of Jesus and convert others. That is what really matters to them, not their personal danger, or the needs of the moment" (*Interpretation*, 140). See also, in addition to the analysis above, Tannehill, *Unity*, 2:290–91, 314–17, 327–29. Cf. Neagoe, *Trial*, 195–206; Stolle, *Zeuge*, 147.
51. D. L. Mealand, "The Close of Acts and Its Hellenistic Greek Vocabulary," *NTS* 36 (1990): 589–95; Gerhard Delling, "Das letzte Wort der Apostelgeschichte," *NovT* 15 (1973): 201–2.
52. On the state's use of physical locations to intersect and control a social world, see Barbara Harlow, "Sites of Struggle: Immigration, Deportation, Prison, and Exile," in *Reconfigured Spheres: Feminist Explorations of Literary Space*, ed.

Margaret R. Higonnet and Joan Templeton (Amherst: University of Massachusetts Press, 1994), 109.

53. Jacob Jervell, *The Theology of the Acts of the Apostles*, New Testament Theology (Cambridge: Cambridge University Press, 1996), 134; Walaskay, *"And So,"* 63.

54. See, e.g., Jervell, *Theology*, 105–6, 134. Likewise, Seyoon Kim's analysis of Acts is heavily indebted to Jervell, and it seems hampered by the peculiar assumption that Acts cannot be considered "anti-imperial" since its characters do not actively set out to materialize the political realities of God's reign in the here and now (*Christ and Caesar: The Gospel and the Roman Empire in the Writings of Paul and Luke* [Grand Rapids: Wm. B. Eerdmans Publishing Co., 2008], 151–90).

55. Franklin, *Christ*, 138.

56. Gilbert, "Roman Propaganda," 255.

57. James C. Scott, *Domination and the Arts of Resistance: Hidden Transcripts* (New Haven, CT: Yale University Press, 1990), 136.

58. Ibid., 136–82. Scott notes that authorities usually find it prudent to tolerate such thinly veiled expression of nonconformity, as long as it does not threaten their ability to manage the wider public sphere (204).

Bibliography

Agamben, Giorgio. *Homo Sacer: Sovereign Power and Bare Life*. Translated by Daniel Heller-Roazen. Stanford, CA: Stanford University Press, 1998.

Alexander, Loveday. "The Acts of the Apostles as an Apologetic Text." Pages 15–44 in *Apologetics in the Roman Empire: Pagans, Jews, and Christians*. Edited by Mark Edwards, Martin Goodman, and Simon Price. New York: Oxford University Press, 1999.

Ando, Clifford. *Imperial Ideology and Provincial Loyalty in the Roman Empire*. Berkeley: University of California Press, 2000.

Aubert, Jean-Jacques. "A Double Standard in Roman Criminal Law? The Death Penalty and Social Structure in Late Republican and Early Imperial Rome." Pages 94–133 in *Speculum Iuris: Roman Law as a Reflection of Social and Economic Life in Antiquity*. Edited by Jean-Jacques Aubert and Boudewijn Sirks. Ann Arbor: University of Michigan Press, 2002.

Barrett, C. K. *A Critical and Exegetical Commentary on the Acts of The Apostles*. 2 vols. International Critical Commentary. Edinburgh: T&T Clark, 1994–1998.

Blount, Brian K. *Cultural Interpretation: Reorienting New Testament Criticism*. Minneapolis: Fortress Press, 1995.

———. *Go Preach! Mark's Kingdom Message and the Black Church Today*. Maryknoll, NY: Orbis Books, 1998.

Bock, Darrell L. *Blasphemy and Exaltation in Judaism: The Charge against Jesus in Mark 14:53–65*. Grand Rapids: Baker Books, 2000.

Bond, Helen K. *Caiaphas: Friend of Rome and Judge of Jesus?* Louisville, KY: Westminster John Knox Press, 2004.

———. *Pontius Pilate in History and Interpretation*. Society for New Testament Studies Monograph Series 100. Cambridge: Cambridge University Press, 1998.

Boring, M. Eugene. *Mark: A Commentary*. New Testament Library. Louisville, KY: Westminster John Knox Press, 2006.

Bovon, François. *The Last Days of Jesus*. Translated by Kristin Hennessy. Louisville, KY: Westminster John Knox Press, 2006.

Brandon, S. G. F. *The Trial of Jesus of Nazareth*. New York: Stein & Day, 1968.

Brant, Jo-Ann A., Charles W. Hedrick, and Chris Shea, eds. *Ancient Fiction: The Matrix of Early Christian and Jewish Narrative*. Society of Biblical Literature Symposium Series 32. Atlanta: Scholars Press, 2005.

Brown, H. Stephen. "Paul's Hearing at Caesarea: A Preliminary Comparison with Legal Literature of the Roman Period." Pages 319–32 in *SBL Seminar Papers*,

1996. Society of Biblical Literature Seminar Papers 35. Atlanta: Scholars Press, 1996.

Brown, Raymond E. *The Death of the Messiah: From Gethsemane to the Grave; A Commentary on the Passion Narratives in the Four Gospels.* 2 vols. Anchor Bible Reference Library. New York: Doubleday, 1994.

———. *The Gospel according to John.* 2 vols. Anchor Bible 29–29A. Garden City, NY: Doubleday, 1966–70.

Byrne, Brendan. "Jesus as Messiah in the Gospel of Luke: Discerning a Pattern of Correction." *Catholic Biblical Quarterly* 65 (2003): 80–95.

Cadbury, Henry J. "Roman Law and the Trial of Paul." Pages 297–338 in vol. 5 of *The Beginnings of Christianity.* Part 1, *The Acts of the Apostles.* Edited by F. J. Foakes-Jackson, Kirsopp Lake, and Henry J. Cadbury. 5 vols. London: Macmillan, 1933.

Camery-Hoggatt, Jerry. *Irony in Mark's Gospel: Text and Subtext.* Society for New Testament Studies Monograph Series 72. Cambridge: Cambridge University Press, 1992.

Campbell, William Sanger. "Engagement, Disengagement and Obstruction: Jesus' Defense Strategies in Mark's Trial and Execution Scenes (14.53–64; 15.1–39)." *Journal for the Study of the New Testament* 26 (2004): 283–300.

Carroll, John T. "Luke's Crucifixion Scene." Pages 108–24 in *Reimaging the Death of the Lukan Jesus.* Edited by Dennis D. Sylva. Bonner biblische Beiträge 73. Frankfurt am Main: Anton Hain, 1990.

Carter, Warren. *John and Empire: Initial Explorations.* New York: T&T Clark, 2008.

———. *Matthew and Empire: Initial Explorations.* Harrisburg, PA: Trinity Press International, 2001.

———. *Pontius Pilate: Portraits of a Roman Governor.* Interfaces. Collegeville, MN: Liturgical Press, 2003.

Cassidy, Richard J. *Society and Politics in the Acts of the Apostles.* Maryknoll, NY: Orbis Books, 1987.

Catchpole, D. R. "The Answer of Jesus to Caiaphas (Matt. 26.64)." *New Testament Studies* 17 (1971): 213–26.

Chance, J. Bradley. "The Jewish People and the Death of Jesus in Luke-Acts: Some Implications of an Inconsistent Narrative Role." Pages 50–81 in *SBL Seminar Papers, 1991.* Society of Biblical Literature Seminar Papers 30. Atlanta: Scholars Press, 1991.

Cohen, David. *Law, Violence, and Community in Classical Athens.* Key Themes in Ancient History. Cambridge: Cambridge University Press, 1995.

Collins, Adela Yarbro. "The Charge of Blasphemy in Mark 14.64." *Journal for the Study of the New Testament* 26 (2004): 379–401.

———. *Mark: A Commentary.* Hermeneia. Minneapolis: Fortress Press, 2007.

Conzelmann, Hans. *The Theology of St. Luke.* Translated by Geoffrey Buswell. Philadelphia: Fortress Press, 1961.

Cosgrove, Charles H. "The Divine ΔEI in Luke-Acts: Investigations into the Lukan Understanding of God's Providence." *Novum Testamentum* 26 (1984): 168–90.

Cotton, Hannah M. "Jewish Jurisdiction under Roman Rule: Prolegomena." Pages 13–28 in *Zwischen den Reichen: Neues Testament und römische Herrschaft.* Edited by Michael Labahn and Jürgen Zangenberg. Texte und Arbeiten zum neutestamentlichen Zeitalter 36. Tübingen: Francke, 2002.

Culpepper, R. Alan. *Anatomy of the Fourth Gospel: A Study in Literary Design.* Philadelphia: Fortress Press, 1983.

Darr, John A. "Irenic or Ironic? Another Look at Gamaliel before the Sanhedrin (Acts 5:33–42)." Pages 121–39 in *Literary Studies in Luke-Acts: Essays in Honor of Joseph B. Tyson*. Edited by Richard P. Thompson and Thomas E. Phillips. Macon, GA: Mercer University Press, 1998.

Davies, W. D., and Dale C. Allison. *A Critical and Exegetical Commentary on the Gospel according to Saint Matthew*. 3 vols. International Critical Commentary. Edinburgh: T&T Clark, 1988–1997.

Delling, Gerhard. "Das letzte Wort der Apostelgeschichte." *Novum Testamentum* 15 (1973): 193–204.

Derrett, J. Duncan M. "'I Adjure Thee' (Matthew 26,63)." *Downside Review* 115 (1997): 225–34.

Dibelius, Martin. "The Speeches in Acts and Ancient Historiography." Pages 138–85 in *Studies in the Acts of the Apostles*. London: SCM Press, 1956.

Dowd, Sharyn, and Elizabeth Struthers Malbon. "The Significance of Jesus' Death in Mark: Narrative Context and Authorial Audience." *Journal of Biblical Literature* 125 (2006): 271–97.

Driggers, Ira Brent. *Following God through Mark: Theological Tension in the Second Gospel*. Louisville, KY: Westminster John Knox Press, 2007.

———. "The Politics of Divine Presence: Temple as Locus of Conflict in the Gospel of Mark." *Biblical Interpretation* 15 (2007): 227–47.

Duke, Paul D. *Irony in the Fourth Gospel*. Atlanta: John Knox Press, 1985.

Duling, Dennis C. "Empire: Theories, Methods, Models." Pages 49–74 in *The Gospel of Matthew in Its Roman Imperial Context*. Edited by John Riches and David C. Sim. Early Christianity in Context. Journal for the Study of the New Testament: Supplement Series 276. London: T&T Clark, 2005.

Edwards, Douglas R. "Surviving the Web of Roman Power: Religion and Politics in the Acts of the Apostles, Josephus, and Chariton's *Chaereas and Callirhoe*." Pages 179–201 in *Images of Empire*. Edited by Loveday Alexander. Journal for the Study of the Old Testament: Supplement Series 122. Sheffield: Sheffield Academic Press, 1991.

Farenga, Vincent. *Citizen and Self in Ancient Greece: Individuals Performing Justice and the Law*. Cambridge: Cambridge University Press, 2006.

Fitzmyer, Joseph A. *The Acts of the Apostles*. Anchor Bible 31. New York: Doubleday, 1998.

———. *The Gospel according to Luke*. 2 vols. Anchor Bible 28–28A. New York: Doubleday, 1981–85.

Fludernik, Monika, and Greta Olson, "Introduction." Pages xiii–liv in *In the Grip of the Law: Trials, Prisons and the Space Between*. Edited by Monika Fludernik and Greta Olson. Frankfurt am Main: Peter Lang, 2004.

Franklin, Eric. *Christ the Lord: A Study in the Purpose and Theology of Luke-Acts*. Philadelphia: Westminster Press, 1975.

Garland, David E. *Reading Matthew: A Literary and Theological Commentary on the First Gospel*. New York: Crossroad, 1993.

Garnsey, Peter. "The Criminal Jurisdiction of Governors." *Journal of Roman Studies* 58 (1968): 51–59.

———. *Social Status and Legal Privilege in the Roman Empire*. Oxford: Oxford University Press, 1970.

Garnsey, Peter, and Richard Saller. *The Roman Empire: Economy, Society and Culture*. Berkeley: University of California Press, 1987.

Gaventa, Beverly Roberts. *The Acts of the Apostles*. Abingdon New Testament Commentaries. Nashville: Abingdon, 2003.

———. "The Overthrown Enemy: Luke's Portrait of Paul." Pages 439–49 in *SBL Seminar Papers, 1985*. Society of Biblical Literature Seminar Papers 24. Atlanta: Scholars Press, 1985.

———. "Toward a Theology of Acts: Reading and Rereading." *Interpretation* 42 (1988): 146–57.

Gempf, Conrad. "Luke's Story of Paul's Reception in Rome." Pages 42–66 in *Rome in the Bible and the Early Church*. Edited by Peter Oakes. Grand Rapids: Baker Academic, 2002.

Giddens, Anthony. *Central Problems in Social Theory: Action, Structure and Contradiction in Social Analysis*. London: Macmillan, 1979.

———. *The Constitution of Society: Outline of the Theory of Structuration*. Berkeley: University of California Press, 1984.

Gilbert, Gary. "Roman Propaganda and Christian Identity in the Worldview of Luke-Acts." Pages 233–56 in *Contextualizing Acts: Lukan Narrative and Greco-Roman Discourse*. Edited by Todd Penner and Caroline Vander Stichele. Society of Biblical Literature Symposium Series 20. Leiden: E. J. Brill, 2003.

Glancy, Jennifer A. "Torture: Flesh, Truth, and the Fourth Gospel." *Biblical Interpretation* 13 (2005): 107–36.

Goodman, Martin. *The Ruling Class of Judaea: The Origins of the Jewish Revolt against Rome, A.D. 66–70*. Cambridge: Cambridge University Press, 1987.

Green, Joel B. *The Gospel of Luke*. New International Commentary on the New Testament. Grand Rapids: Wm. B. Eerdmans Publishing Co., 1997.

Hagedorn, Anselm C., and Jerome H. Neyrey. "'It Was Out of Envy that They Handed Jesus Over' (Mark 15.10): The Anatomy of Envy and the Gospel of Mark." *Journal for the Study of the New Testament* 69 (1998): 15–56.

Hagner, Donald A. *Matthew 14–28*. Word Biblical Commentary 33B. Dallas: Word, 1995.

Harlow, Barbara. "Sites of Struggle: Immigration, Deportation, Prison, and Exile." Pages 108–24 in *Reconfigured Spheres: Feminist Explorations of Literary Space*. Edited by Margaret R. Higonnet and Joan Templeton. Amherst: University of Massachusetts Press, 1994.

Hellerman, Joseph H. *Reconstructing Honor in Roman Philippi: Carmen Christi as Cursus Pudorum*. Society for New Testament Studies Monograph Series 132. Cambridge: Cambridge University Press, 2005.

Heusler, Erika. *Kapitalprozesse im lukanischen Doppelwerk: Die Verfahren gegen Jesus und Paulus in exegetischer und rechtshistorischer Analyse*. Neutestamentliche Abhandlungen: Neue Folge 38. Münster: Aschendorff, 2000.

Hock, Ronald F., J. Bradley Chance, and Judith Perkins, eds. *Ancient Fiction and Early Christian Narrative*. Society of Biblical Literature Symposium Series 6. Atlanta: Scholars Press, 1998.

Holmes, Michael W., ed. and trans. *The Apostolic Fathers: Greek Texts and English Translations*. 3rd ed. Grand Rapids: Baker Academic, 2007.

Hooker, Morna D. *The Gospel according to Saint Mark*. Black's New Testament Commentaries. Peabody, MA: Hendrickson Publishers, 1991.

Hutcheon, Linda. *Irony's Edge: The Theory and Politics of Irony*. London: Routledge, 1994.

Jervell, Jacob. "Paul: The Teacher of Israel: The Apologetic Speeches of Paul in Acts." Pages 153–83 in *Luke and the People of God: A New Look at Luke-Acts*. Minneapolis: Augsburg Publishing House, 1972.

———. *The Theology of the Acts of the Apostles*. New Testament Theology. Cambridge: Cambridge University Press, 1996.

Johnson, Luke Timothy. *The Acts of the Apostles.* Sacra pagina 5. Collegeville, MN: Liturgical Press, 1992.

———. *The Gospel of Luke.* Sacra pagina 3. Collegeville, MN: Liturgical Press, 1991.

Juel, Donald. "The Function of the Trial of Jesus in Mark's Gospel." Pages 83–104 in vol. 2 of *SBL Seminar Papers, 1975.* 2 vols. Society of Biblical Literature Seminar Papers 14. Missoula. MT: Scholars Press, 1975.

———. *Messiah and Temple: The Trial of Jesus in the Gospel of Mark.* Society of Biblical Literature Dissertation Series 31. Missoula, MT: Scholars Press, 1977.

Kelber, Werner H. "Conclusion: From Passion Narrative to Gospel." Pages 153–80 in *The Passion in Mark: Studies on Mark 14–16.* Edited by Werner H. Kelber. Philadelphia: Fortress Press, 1976.

Kennedy, George A. *New Testament Interpretation through Rhetorical Criticism.* Studies in Religion. Chapel Hill: University of North Carolina Press, 1984.

Kim, Seyoon. *Christ and Caesar: The Gospel and the Roman Empire in the Writings of Paul and Luke.* Grand Rapids: Wm. B. Eerdmans Publishing Co., 2008.

Koester, Craig R. *The Word of Life: A Theology of John's Gospel.* Grand Rapids: Wm. B. Eerdmans Publishing Co., 2008.

Koet, Bart J. "Im Schatten des Aeneas: Paulus in Troas (Apg 16,8–10)." Pages 147–71 in *Dreams and Scripture in Luke-Acts: Collected Essays.* Contributions to Biblical Exegesis and Theology 42. Leuven: Peeters, 2006.

Kornstein, Daniel J. *Kill All the Lawyers? Shakespeare's Legal Appeal.* Princeton, NJ: Princeton University Press, 1994.

Légasse, Simon. *The Trial of Jesus.* Translated by John Bowden. London: SCM Press, 1997.

Lendon, J. E. *Empire of Honour: The Art of Government in the Roman World.* Oxford: Clarendon Press, 1997.

Lenski, Gerhard E. *Power and Privilege: A Theory of Social Stratification.* Chapel Hill: University of North Carolina Press, 1966.

Levine, Amy-Jill. "Anti-Judaism and the Gospel of Matthew." Pages 9–36 in *Anti-Judasm and the Gospels.* Edited by William R. Farmer. Harrisburg, PA: Trinity Press International, 1999.

———. "'Hemmed in on Every Side': Jews and Women in the Book of Susanna." Pages 303–23 in *A Feminist Companion to Esther, Judith and Susanna.* Edited by Athalya Brenner. The Feminist Companion to the Bible 7. Sheffield: Sheffield Academic Press, 1995.

Lincoln, Andrew T. *Truth on Trial: The Lawsuit Motif in the Fourth Gospel.* Peabody, MA: Hendrickson Publishers, 2000.

Long, William R. "The Paulusbild in the Trial of Paul in Acts." Pages 87–105 in *SBL Seminar Papers, 1983.* Society of Biblical Literature Seminar Papers 22. Chico, CA: Scholars Press, 1983.

———. "The Trial of Paul in the Book of Acts: Historical, Literary, and Theological Considerations." PhD diss., Brown University, 1982.

Luz, Ulrich. *Matthew 21–28: A Commentary.* Translated by James E. Crouch. Hermeneia. Minneapolis: Fortress Press, 2005.

MacMullen, Ramsay. *Enemies of the Roman Order: Treason, Unrest, and Alienation in the Empire.* Cambridge, MA: Harvard University Press, 1966.

———. "Judicial Savagery in the Roman Empire." Pages 204–17 in *Changes in the Roman Empire: Essays in the Ordinary.* Princeton, NJ: Princeton University Press, 1990.

Malina, Bruce J., and Jerome H. Neyrey. *Portraits of Paul: An Archaeology of Ancient Personality.* Louisville, KY: Westminster John Knox Press, 1996.

Marcus, Joel. "Crucifixion as Parodic Exaltation." *Journal of Biblical Literature* 125 (2006): 73–87.

———. "Mark 14:61: 'Are You the Messiah-Son-of-God?'" *Novum Testamentum* 31 (1989): 125–41.

Marguerat, Daniel. *The First Christian Historian: Writing the "Acts of the Apostles."* Society for New Testament Studies Monograph Series 121. Cambridge: Cambridge University Press, 2002.

Matera, Frank J. "Luke 22,66–71: Jesus before the ΠΡΕΣΒΥΤΕΡΙΟΝ." Pages 517–33 in *L'Évangile de Luc.* Edited by F. Neirynck. 2nd ed. Bibliotheca ephemeridum theologicarum lovaniensium 32. Leuven: Leuven University Press, 1989.

———. "Luke 23,1–25: Jesus before Pilate, Herod, and Israel." Pages 535–51 in *L'Évangile de Luc.* Edited by F. Neirynck. 2nd ed. Bibliotheca ephemeridum theologicarum lovaniensium 32. Leuven: Leuven University Press, 1989.

Mattill, A. J., Jr. "The Jesus-Paul Parallels and the Purpose of Luke-Acts: H. H. Evans Reconsidered." *Novum Testamentum* 17 (1975): 15–46.

McLaren, James S. *Power and Politics in Palestine: The Jews and the Governing of Their Land, 100 BC–AD 70.* Journal for the Study of the New Testament: Supplement Series 63. Sheffield: Sheffield Academic Press, 1991.

Mealand, D. L. "The Close of Acts and Its Hellenistic Greek Vocabulary." *New Testament Studies* 36 (1990): 583–97.

Millar, Fergus. *The Roman Near East, 31 BC–AD 337.* Cambridge, MA: Harvard University Press, 1993.

Moore, Stephen D. *Empire and Apocalypse: Postcolonialism and the New Testament.* Sheffield: Sheffield Phoenix, 2006.

Musurillo, Herbert A. *The Acts of the Pagan Martyrs: Acta Alexandrinorum.* London: Oxford University Press, 1954.

———. "The Pagan Acts of the Martyrs." *Theological Studies* 10 (1949): 555–64.

Neagoe, Alexandru. *The Trial of the Gospel: An Apologetic Reading of Luke's Trial Narratives.* Society for New Testament Studies Monograph Series 116. Cambridge: Cambridge University Press, 2002.

Neyrey, Jerome. "The Forensic Defense Speech and Paul's Trial Speeches in Acts 22–26: Form and Function." Pages 210–24 in *Luke-Acts: New Perspectives from the Society of Biblical Literature Seminar.* Edited by Charles H. Talbert. New York: Crossroad, 1984.

———. *The Passion according to Luke: A Redaction Study of Luke's Soteriology.* Theological Inquiries. New York: Paulist Press, 1985.

Nolland, John. *Luke 18:35–24:53.* Word Biblical Commentary 35C. Dallas: Word, 1993.

O'Day, Gail R. "The Gospel of John." Pages 491–865 in vol. 9 of *The New Interpreter's Bible.* 12 vols. Nashville: Abingdon Press, 1995.

O'Toole, Robert F. *Acts 26: The Christological Climax of Paul's Defense (Ac 22:1–26:32).* Analecta biblica 78. Rome: Biblical Institute Press, 1978.

———. *The Unity of Luke's Theology: An Analysis of Luke-Acts.* Good News Studies 9. Wilmington, DE: Michael Glazier, 1984.

Oakes, Peter. *Philippians: From People to Letter.* Society for New Testament Studies Monograph Series 110. Cambridge: Cambridge University Press, 2001.

———. "A State of Tension: Rome in the New Testament." Pages 75–90 in *The Gospel of Matthew in Its Roman Imperial Context.* Edited by John Riches and David C. Sim. Early Christianity in Context. Journal for the Study of the New Testament: Supplement Series 276. London: T&T Clark, 2005.

Omerzu, Heiki. *Der Prozess des Paulus: Eine exegetische und rechtshistorische Untersuchung der Apostelgeschichte.* Beihefte zur Zeitschrift für die neutestamentliche Wissenschaft 115. Berlin: Walter de Gruyter, 2002.

Penner, Todd. "Civilizing Discourse: Acts, Declamation, and the Rhetoric of the *Polis.*" Pages 65–104 in *Contextualizing Acts: Lukan Narrative and Greco-Roman Discourse.* Edited by Todd Penner and Caroline Vander Stichele. Society of Biblical Literature Symposium Series 20. Leiden: E. J. Brill, 2003.

———. *In Praise of Christian Origins: Stephen and the Hellenists in Lukan Apologetic Historiography.* New York: T&T Clark, 2004.

Perkins, Judith. *Roman Imperial Identities in the Early Christian Era.* New York: Routledge, 2009.

Pervo, Richard I. *Acts: A Commentary.* Hermeneia. Minneapolis: Fortress, 2009.

———. *Profit with Delight: The Literary Genre of the Acts of the Apostles.* Philadelphia: Fortress Press, 1987.

Pilgrim, Walter E. *Uneasy Neighbors: Church and State in the New Testament.* Overtures to Biblical Theology. Minneapolis: Fortress Press, 1999.

Rapske, Brian. *The Book of Acts and Paul in Roman Custody.* Vol. 3 of *The Book of Acts in Its First Century Setting.* Edited by Bruce W. Winter. Grand Rapids: Wm. B. Eerdmans Publishing Co., 1994.

Rensberger, David. "Anti-Judaism and the Gospel of John." Pages 120–57 in *Anti-Judasm and the Gospels.* Edited by William R. Farmer. Harrisburg, PA: Trinity Press International, 1999.

———. *Johannine Faith and Liberating Community.* Philadelphia: Westminster Press, 1988.

Richard, Earl. *Acts 6:1–8:4: The Author's Method of Composition.* Society of Biblical Literature Dissertation Series 41. Missoula, MT: Scholars Press, 1978.

Richter Reimer, Ivoni. *Women in the Acts of the Apostles: A Feminist Liberation Perspective.* Translated by Linda M. Maloney. Minneapolis: Fortress Press, 1995.

Robbins, Vernon K. "Luke-Acts: A Mixed Population Seeks a Home in the Roman Empire." Pages 202–21 in *Images of Empire.* Edited by Loveday Alexander. Journal for the Study of the Old Testament: Supplement Series 122. Sheffield: Sheffield Academic Press, 1991.

Robinson, O. F. *Penal Practice and Penal Policy in Ancient Rome.* New York: Routledge, 2007.

Rosenblatt, Marie-Eloise. *Paul the Accused: His Portrait in the Acts of the Apostles.* Zacchaeus Studies: New Testament. Collegeville, MN: Liturgical Press, 1995.

Saldarini, Anthony J. *Matthew's Christian-Jewish Community.* Chicago Studies in the History of Judaism. Chicago: University of Chicago Press, 1994.

———. *Pharisees, Scribes and Sadducees in Palestinian Society: A Sociological Approach.* Grand Rapids: Wm. B. Eerdmans Publishing Co., 2001.

Sanders, E. P. *Judaism: Practice and Belief, 63 BCE–66 CE.* Philadelphia: Trinity Press International, 1992.

Schneiders, Sandra M. *Written That You May Believe: Encountering Jesus in the Fourth Gospel.* Rev. ed. New York: Crossroad, 2003.

Schwartz, Saundra Charlene. "Courtroom Scenes in the Ancient Greek Novels." PhD diss., Columbia University, 1998.

———. "Rome in the Greek Novel? Images and Ideas of Empire in Chariton's Persia." *Arethusa* 36 (2003): 375–94.

———. "The Trial Scene in the Greek Novels and in Acts." Pages 105–37 in *Contextualizing Acts: Lukan Narrative and Greco-Roman Discourse.* Edited by Todd

Penner and Caroline Vander Stichele. Society of Biblical Literature Symposium Series 20. Leiden: E. J. Brill, 2003.

Scott, James C. *Domination and the Arts of Resistance: Hidden Transcripts.* New Haven, CT: Yale University Press, 1990.

Senior, Donald P. *The Passion Narrative according to Matthew: A Redactional Study.* Bibliotheca ephemeridum theologicarum lovaniensium 39. Leuven: Leuven University Press, 1975.

———. *The Passion of Jesus in the Gospel of Luke.* The Passion Series 3; Wilmington, DE: Michael Glazier, 1989.

Sered, Susan, and Samuel Cooper. "Sexuality and Social Control: Anthropological Reflections on the Book of Susanna." Pages 43–55 in *The Judgment of Susanna: Authority and Witnesses.* Edited by Ellen Spolsky. Society of Biblical Literature Early Judaism and Its Literature 11. Atlanta: Scholars Press, 1996.

Sharp, Carolyn J. *Irony and Meaning in the Hebrew Bible.* Indiana Studies in Biblical Literature. Bloomington: Indiana University Press, 2009.

Sherwin-White, A. N. *Roman Society and Roman Law in the New Testament.* Oxford: Clarendon Press, 1963.

Skinner, Matthew L. *Locating Paul: Places of Custody as Narrative Settings in Acts 21–28.* Society of Biblical Literature Academica Biblica 13. Atlanta: Society of Biblical Literature, 2003.

———. "Unchained Ministry: Paul's Roman Custody (Acts 21–28) and the Sociopolitical Outlook of the Book of Acts." Pages 79–95 in *Acts and Ethics.* Edited by Thomas E. Phillips. New Testament Monographs 9. Sheffield: Sheffield Phoenix, 2005.

Sloyan, Gerard S. *Jesus on Trial: A Study of the Gospels.* 2nd ed. Minneapolis: Fortress, 2006.

———. "Recent Literature on the Trial Narratives of the Four Gospels." Pages 136–76 in *Critical History and Biblical Faith: New Testament Perspectives.* Edited by Thomas J. Ryan. Villanova, PA: Villanova University, 1979.

Soards, Marion L. *The Passion according to Luke: The Special Material of Luke 22.* Journal for the Study of the New Testament: Supplement Series 14. Sheffield: Sheffield Academic Press, 1987.

———. *The Speeches in Acts: Their Content, Context, and Concerns.* Louisville, KY: Westminster/John Knox Press, 1994.

Spencer, F. Scott. *Journeying through Acts: A Literary-Cultural Reading.* Peabody, MA: Hendrickson Publishers, 2004.

Squires, John T. *The Plan of God in Luke-Acts.* Society for New Testament Studies Monograph Series 76. Cambridge: Cambridge University Press, 1993.

Stolle, Volker. *Der Zeuge als Angeklagter: Untersuchungen zum Paulusbild des Lukas.* Beiträge zur Wissenschaft vom Alten und Neuen Testament: 6th Folge, 2. Stuttgart: Kohlhammer, 1973.

Tajra, Harry W. *The Trial of St. Paul: A Juridical Exegesis of the Second Half of the Acts of the Apostles.* Wissenschaftliche Untersuchungen zum Neuen Testament: 2nd Reihe, 35. Tübingen: J. C. B. Mohr (Paul Siebeck), 1989.

Talbert, C. H., and J. H. Hayes. "A Theology of Sea Storms in Luke-Acts." Pages 321–36 in *SBL Seminar Papers, 1995.* Society of Biblical Literature Seminar Papers 34. Atlanta: Scholars Press, 1995.

Tannehill, Robert C. *The Narrative Unity of Luke-Acts: A Literary Interpretation.* 2 vols. Philadelphia, Minneapolis: Fortress Press, 1986–1990.

———. "The Narrator's Strategy in the Scenes of Paul's Defense: Acts 21:27–26:32." *Forum* 8 (1992): 255–69.

Thatcher, Tom. *Greater Than Caesar: Christology and Empire in the Fourth Gospel*. Minneapolis: Fortress Press, 2009.

Tiede, David L. *Luke*. Augsburg Commentary on the New Testament. Minneapolis: Augsburg Publishing House, 1988.

Trites, Allison A. *The New Testament Concept of Witness*. Society for New Testament Studies Monograph Series 31. Cambridge: Cambridge University Press, 1977.

Tuori, K. "Legal Pluralism and the Roman Empires." Pages 39–52 in *Beyond Dogmatics: Law and Society in the Roman World*. Edited by J. W. Cairns and P. J. du Plessis. Edinburgh Studies in Law 3. Edinburgh: Edinburgh University Press, 2007.

Tyson, Joseph B. *The Death of Jesus in Luke-Acts*. Columbia: University of South Carolina Press, 1986.

Veltman, Fred. "The Defense Speeches of Paul in Acts." Pages 243–56 in *Perspectives on Luke-Acts*. Edited by Charles H. Talbert. Danville, VA: Association of Baptist Professors of Religion, 1978.

Walaskay, Paul W. *"And So We Came to Rome": The Political Perspective of St. Luke*. Society for New Testament Studies Monograph Series 49. Cambridge: Cambridge University Press, 1983.

Walton, Steve. "The State They Were In: Luke's View of the Roman Empire." Pages 1–41 in *Rome in the Bible and the Early Church*. Edited by Peter Oakes. Grand Rapids: Baker Academic, 2002.

Wansink, Craig S. *Chained in Christ: The Experience and Rhetoric of Paul's Imprisonments*. Journal for the Study of the New Testament: Supplement Series 130. Sheffield: Sheffield Academic Press, 1996.

Weatherly, Jon A. *Jewish Responsibility for the Death of Jesus in Luke-Acts*. Journal for the Study of the New Testament: Supplement Series 106. Sheffield: Sheffield Academic Press, 1994.

Weaver, Dorothy Jean. "Power and Powerlessness: Matthew's Use of Irony in the Portrayal of Political Leaders." Pages 179–96 in *Treasures New and Old: Recent Contributions to Matthean Studies*. Edited by David R. Bauer and Mark Allan Powell. Society of Biblical Literature Symposium Series 1. Atlanta: Scholars Press, 1996.

Weaver, John B. *Plots of Epiphany: Prison-Escape in Acts of the Apostles*. Beihefte zur Zeitschrift für die neutestamentliche Wissenschaft 131. Berlin: Walter de Gruyter, 2004.

Wengst, Klaus. *Pax Romana and the Peace of Jesus Christ*. Translated by John Bowden. Philadelphia: Fortress Press, 1987.

Williams, Rowan. *Christ on Trial: How the Gospel Unsettles Our Judgement*. Grand Rapids: Wm. B. Eerdmans Publishing Co., 2003.

Winter, Bruce. "The Importance of the *Captatio Benevolentiae* in the Speeches of Tertullus and Paul in Acts 24:1–21." *Journal of Theological Studies* 42 (1991): 505–31.

———. "Official Proceedings and the Forensic Speeches in Acts 24–26." Pages 305–36 in *The Book of Acts in Its Ancient Literary Setting*. Edited by Bruce W. Winter and Andrew D. Clarke. Vol. 1 of *The Book of Acts in Its First Century Setting*. Edited by Bruce W. Winter. Grand Rapids: Wm. B. Eerdmans Publishing Co., 1993.

Winter, Paul. *On the Trial of Jesus.* 2nd ed. Studia judaica 1. Berlin: De Gruyter,
    1974.
Winter, S. C. "ΠΑΡΡΗΣΙΑ in Acts." Pages 185–202 in *Friendship, Flattery, and Frank-
    ness of Speech: Studies on Friendship in the New Testament World.* Edited by John T.
    Fitzgerald. Supplements to Novum Testamentum 82. Leiden: E. J. Brill, 1996.
Zanker, Paul. *The Power of Images in the Age of Augustus.* Translated by Alan Shapiro.
    Ann Arbor: University of Michigan Press, 1988.

Scripture Index

Name and Subject Index